D1516615

THE ROMAN CONQUEST OF ITALY

The Ancient World

General editor: **T. J. Cornell**
Professor of Ancient History, University of Manchester

The Ancient World series exists to publish works combining scholarship with accessibility on central aspects of the political, cultural and social history of Europe, the countries of the Mediterranean, and the Near and Middle East from the origins of human society to the period of Late Antiquity. The books are designed to appeal both to students and to a wide range of readers with a serious interest in the field.

Titles in print

The Cults of the Roman Empire
Robert Turcan
Translated by Antonia Nevill

The Roman Conquest of Italy
Jean-Michel David
Translated by Antonia Nevill

Greek Religion*
Walter Burkert
Translated by John Raffan

The Athenian Democracy
Mogens Herman Hansen
Translated by J. A. Crook

* Published in the USA by Harvard University Press

THE ROMAN CONQUEST
OF ITALY

Jean-Michel David

Translated by Antonia Nevill

BLACKWELL
Publishers

DG
250
.5
D3813
1996

138566

Copyright © Edition Aubier, 1994
Translation copyright © Antonia Nevill 1996

The right of J. M. David to be identified as author of this work has been asserted in accordance with the Copyright, Designs and Patents Act 1988.

First published in French by Aubier as *La Romanisation de l'Italie*, 1994.
First published in English, 1996, with the help of the French Ministry of Culture and Communication.

2 4 6 8 10 9 7 5 3 1

Blackwell Publishers Ltd
108 Cowley Road
Oxford OX4 1JF
UK

Blackwell Publishers Inc.
238 Main Street
Cambridge, Massachusetts 02142
USA

All rights reserved. Except for the quotation of short passages for the purposes of criticism and review, no part of this publication may be reproduced, stored in a retrieval system, or transmitted, in any form or by any means, electronic, mechanical, photocopying, recording or otherwise, without the prior permission of the publisher.

Except in the United States of America, this book is sold subject to the condition that it shall not, by way of trade or otherwise, be lent, resold, hired out, or otherwise circulated without the publisher's prior consent in any form of binding or cover other than that in which it is published and without a similar condition including this condition being imposed on the subsequent purchaser.

British Library Cataloguing in Publication Data

A CIP catalogue record for this book is available from the British Library.

Library of Congress Cataloging-in-Publication Data

David, Jean-Michel.
   [Romanisation de l'Italie. English]
   The Roman conquest of Italy / Jean-Michel David ; translated by Antonia Nevill.
      p.   cm.
   Includes bibliographical references and index.
   ISBN 0–631–20321–4. — ISBN 0–631–20325–7 (pbk.)
   1. Rome—History—Republic, 265–30 B.C.   2. Italic peoples—History.
3. Rome—Ethnic relations.   4. Italic peoples—Cultural assimilation.   I. Title
DG250.5.D3813   1996
937'.02—dc20
                                                                     96–17076
                                                                        CIP

Printed in Great Britain by Hartnolls Limited, Bodmin, Cornwall

This book is printed on acid-free paper

CONTENTS

INTRODUCTION

At the end of the third century BC what did Etruscans, Samnites, Carthaginians in Sardinia, Gauls in the Po Valley and Greeks in southern Italy or Sicily have in common? All kinds of things still distinguished them from one another: language, culture, religion, and social and political organization. They simply shared the fact that they were subject to the sole domination of Rome which, during this same century, had completed the expansion of its power throughout the peninsula and neighbouring islands. Two centuries later, however, differences had become blurred and, from some aspects, even completely effaced: all these peoples had become Romanized.

The concept of Romanization had the merit of being ambiguous. What do we actually mean by the term? The process of acculturation that transformed all those peoples into Romans wearing a toga and speaking Latin? Or the one that might be termed political, which turned the inhabitants of Italy into citizens of Rome, taking part in the decisions that were made there, voting on laws, choosing magistrates, even getting themselves elected when they attained the requisite level of wealth and respectability? The two aspects – cultural and political – certainly deserve to be differentiated for they are related to different happenings in the evolution of societies. But neither can they be completely separated, for they are the product of the history of those societies itself. How can we compare them, then, keeping the distinction that allows us to identify and analyse them while taking account of the deep-seated relationship that links them to one another? The use of such a convenient term will not do. We must use another method, a rather deeper analysis of the actual sociological conditions which, from the Second Punic War to the end of Augustus's reign, led the peoples of Italy to lose their former multitude of identities to become an essentially unified community of Roman citizens.

In fact, the problem is one of scale. The events which affected the peninsula during those two and a half centuries were among the most important in the entire history of antiquity: Hannibal's campaign, his victories and ultimate defeat; the Roman conquest of the eastern Mediterranean regions; the consequent influx of wealth and slaves; the changes in Italian agriculture; the slave rebellions and the agrarian demands that led the Gracchi to propose their reforms; the Social War that followed the Romans' refusal to grant Roman citizenship to the Italians; the civil wars that decimated the aristocracy before a new equilibrium was finally created with the return of peace and the institution of the Augustan monarchy. We can understand how traumatic it must have been for a populace who experienced severe demographic losses, large-scale immigration and movements of people and profound upheavals in the composition of society. We can also imagine the culture shock suffered by individuals living through the transition from the diversity of political organizations to domination by one single city over the rest, then the invasion of minds and attitudes by those Hellenistic values which made commonly accepted traditions and standards waver.

By becoming Romanized, Italy was unified – culturally, politically and also according to the concept people had of the geographical area that must be understood by that name.

At the start of the second century, it was obvious to the early writers that the peninsula's real frontier was created by the Alps, which formed its northern boundary. The references made by Polybius and Cato leave no doubt about this point.[1] Until the middle of the first century, however, the Po Valley was not treated like the other regions. After the Social War, in fact, when Roman citizenship was granted to the peoples of Italy who demanded it, an exception was made of those Cisalpine peoples who did not belong to colonies that had been founded by Rome: they were only truly incorporated into the Roman community by Caesar in 49. As for the islands, Sicily, Sardinia and Corsica had never been regarded as part of Italy and, until the Empire, they were administered by magistrates dispatched there specially.

How far must the geographical limits of this study be taken? Obviously to the point where we can best understand the mechanisms of unification and integration. These are concerned not only with political and cultural history, but also with the profound movements that affected these societies. The entire peninsula and its neighbouring islands were caught up in the same process of economic and demographic transformation, which had profound consequences for the overall equilibrium. Indeed, we have only to think of the importance of events such as the colonization in the Cisalpine territories, the slave wars in Sicily or the role played by that island and Sardinia in keeping Rome supplied with grain, to understand that we must take account of them in the following analysis.

For all that, the real problem posed by defining Italy is not one of geography, but has to do with the fact that it was created by the very process of unification. There was a time when Italy represented the area over which Rome had extended its domination: in the middle of the third century, when the conquest had been completed, a map of it was placed on a wall of the temple of Tellus.[2] Then it became the framework for a sense of belonging to a totality which went beyond specific civic or ethnic identities. It thus became one of the very forms of 'being Roman', in so far as submission to and integration into a single political and cultural whole were the factors that allowed it to take on substance. Yet it was also different, even in opposition to it: this unity could on occasion either legitimize a challenge to Roman authority – as in the case of the Social War – or provide the basis for the exercise of government – one thinks of Augustus – which went beyond the framework of the city-state and began to aspire to universality. The issue of the Romanization of Italy, and of its unification into a single political and cultural ensemble, posed the question of extending values conceived in the framework of the city-state over a vast territory. They already foreshadowed those of the homogeneity of the Roman Empire in the unity of methods of representation and self-awareness.

The question we must ask is about those who played a part in this process, to be precise, those who became Romanized and were integrated into the new ensemble formed by the territory governed by Rome. Who else could they be except those who entered into all the other aspects of political and social life in Italy, the aristocrats who, locally, had the upper hand of their compatriots and ruled society as a whole?

Each city-state or each ethnic group in fact preserved its own elite which controlled its destiny. The role of these diverse dominant classes remained fundamental to the functioning of human groups. They were the rich, most often landowners, and powerful, dictating the life of their community. To some extent they were the local equivalent of the Roman senatorial aristocracy, which is not at all surprising, as ancient societies were absolutely inegalitarian and political structures took note of the domination of this handful of families over the rest of the population.

It was these individuals who, faced with the events mentioned earlier, by dint of making difficult decisions had to find the means of preserving *in situ* the power and authority they had inherited: for instance, making the right choice between Hannibal and Rome, ensuring that they had access to the riches coming from the Orient, adapting to the changes affecting Italian agriculture and not finding themselves in the camp of the vanquished in all the conflicts, peaceable or violent, that shook the Roman world. As far as the instruments of controlling the social life of the Mediterranean world were becoming concentrated in the hands of the magistrates and senators of Rome, it became increasingly necessary for these powerful men to possess the means of promoting their own interests among those who effectively made the decisions, to become integrated, by hook or by crook, into the sphere of Roman political power.

The general organization of civic structures certainly presented ways of intervening. The representatives of a state dominated by Rome could always embark on an embassy, emphasize their rights or present their demands. But the growing inequality between the two sides made such approaches increasingly risky. What sense could they make any longer when one party had become a Mediterranean power and the other had remained a small town in Italy? It is true that the relationships of patronage provided other means of recourse. A Roman aristocrat in fact needed to respond effectively to the demands addressed to him by his 'clients' if he was to safeguard his authority and the image people had of his power. And the city-states in Italy did not miss the opportunity of belonging to these *cliente-lae*. But as a means of intervention it was unreliable, always at the mercy of the choices of others or constraints that weighed upon it.

Some other way was necessary, and it is understandable that the matter of Roman citizenship, direct participation in Rome's affairs, even access to its magistracies, swiftly became essential. So we can envisage that, at times which varied accordingly to milieux and regions, a dynamic was created that led Italians to become intergrated into a civic ensemble broadened to embrace the entire peninsula.

Such a desire, however, ran up against profound problems. Let us leave aside the fact that the original Romans, populace and aristocrats combined, had little wish to share the advantages of a domination which they alone had exercised, and that a war was necessary to make up their minds to it. Rather, let us note that, in order to seek to adopt Roman identity and have it acknowledged, one had first to renounce one's own. In antiquity, belonging to a community was a fundamental feature, constituting the very definition of an individual. The city-state, or the tribe for those who lived in a more flexible and loose-knit fashion in villages and districts, was the normal structure for the functioning of social relations, the one in which all feelings of solidarity were contained, and where the personality of its members was formed and expressed. Giving it up meant that a process of personal and collective devaluation had taken place, that in some way the natural framework of social life had lost part of its necessity and legitimacy.

Looked at from this viewpoint, the phenomenon of Romanization assumes a quite different importance. The transformation of Italy into a homogeneous ensemble of citizens belonging to the same political structure and sharing the same cultural traits meant also that the many and varied societies which had formerly composed it experienced a profound crisis in which they became lost. The social fabric was seriously affected by wars and population movements. Traditional structures were thrown off balance by new forms of creating wealth which stemmed mainly from the fact that Italy as a whole opened out widely on to the rest of the Mediterranean world. Former powers were shifted towards the new centre of authority. Traditional systems of reference that determined behaviour and self-image disappeared: society's crisis was also an identity crisis.

The new question posed was about what processes could be

used to construct a new social consciousness, this time based on belonging to a unified community, composed of Roman citizens and enlarged to embrace the whole of Italy. In other words, what were the new models which inspired people to imitation and encouraged them to identification?

In the main, they were provided by the Hellenistic world. Over there, those in power were kings who ruled over empires. Civic life there was enriched and enhanced by rhetoric and philosophy. In thinking and ways of artistic expression, everything revealed the demand for superior quality. Of course, the first people to have been fascinated and to have adopted the new values were the Roman aristocrats themselves, who rapidly became Hellenized. But those in other regions of Italy were not necessarily left out. Sometimes they were even in the lead. All, therefore, began to share the same language formed from commonly held cultural values and social standards.

This change, however, by no means did away with the relationship of domination that had been established during the preceding centuries. It was in the heart of the old structure that changes were effected, leading to the transformation of the Italian aristocracies of former times, so different from one another, into a new one composed of Roman citizens, the most ambitious of whom were even prepared to take part in the political management of Rome's affairs. Of course, Roman aristocrats played a growing role in their integration. In fact – as far as they could – they controlled the processes of incorporation into Roman citizenship and advancement in the civic hierarchy. Taking up Hellenistic models, mainly for their own purposes, Roman aristocrats copied them and turned them into the instruments of their own influence. By their example, and by the standards they sometimes imposed, they took over and unified the system of values and attitudes. The framework of political references and matters at stake was no longer confined to the limited area of Rome's territory, but henceforth extended to encompass all Italy, which had become the new community of Roman citizens; until such time as the entire Empire was won over, in its turn, under the unremitting influence of the same necessities.

When all these historical happenings have to be taken into account, the ambitions of this book may seem disproportionate. Nothing of the kind. All the episodes just mentioned, most of the factors that occurred in the various phases of the process of Romanization have already been examined and studied meticulously by historians of the end of the Roman Republic. Mainly in the last twenty or so years, the number of publications has grown, notably in Italy, and they have made some fundamental contributions. The reader will soon understand that what he or she is being offered is a synthesis, or perhaps a perspective, of the principal results of the rich, substantial and often exciting researches which, in a short time, have refreshed the idea one might have had of Italian society in the last two centuries BC.[3]

Map 1 The peoples of Italy

Map 2 The regions of Italy instituted by Augustus

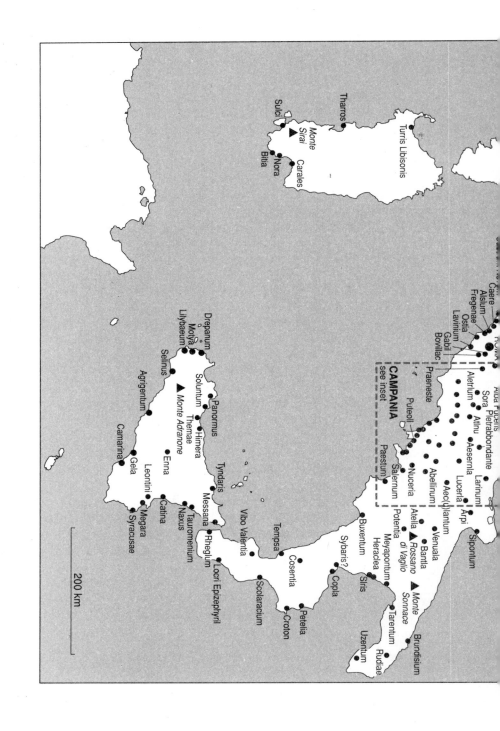

200 km

Tharros
Turris Libisonis
Sulci
Monte
Sirai
Nora
Bitia
Carales

Drepanum
Motya
Lilybaeum
Selinus
Soluntum
Panormus
Agrigentum
Monte Adranone
Themae
Himera
Camarina
Enna
Gela
Leontini
Catina
Megara
Syracusae
Tyndaris
Messana
Naxus
Tauromenium
Vibo Valentia
Rhegium
Locri Epizephyrii
Tempsa
Cosentia
Scolaracium
Croton
Petelia
Copia
Sybaris?
Siris
Buxentum
Heraclea
Meyapontum
Monte
Sonnace
Tarentum
Uzentum
Rudiae
Brundisium
Siponturm
Arpi
Venusia
Bantia
Rossano
di Vaglio
Potentia
Atella
Aec(u)lantum
Luceria
Larinum
Abellinum
Nuceria
Aesernia
Attnu
Aletrium
Sora Pietrabbondante
Salernum
Paestum
Puteoli
Praeneste
Bovillae
Gabii
Lavinium
Ostia
Fregenae
Alsium
Caere
Alba Fucens
ROMA
CAMPANIA
see inset

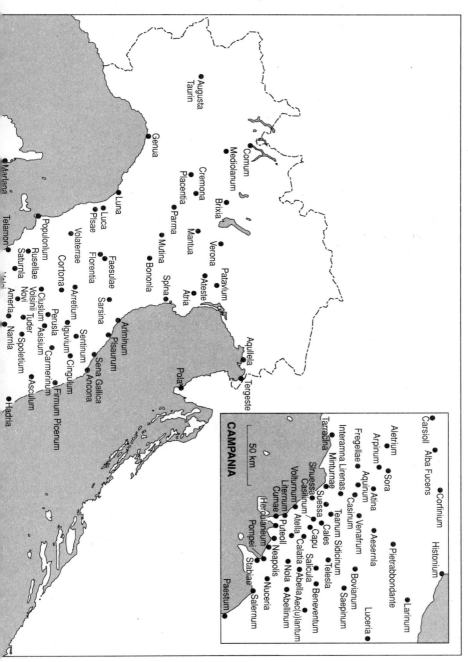

Map 3 The towns of Italy

The Towns of Italy

Aec(u)lanum	Aeclanum	Mediolanum	Milan
Agrigentum	Agrigento	Messana	Messina
Aletrium	Aletri	Metapontum	Metapontum
Aquileia	Aquileia	Minturnae	Minturno
Ariminium	Rimini	Mutina	Modena
Arretium	Arezzo	Naxus	Naxos
Asisium	Assisi	Neapolis	Naples
Ateste	Este	Ostia	Ostia
Atria	Adria	Panormus	Palermo
Augusta Taurinorum	Turin	Parma	Parma
Barium	Bari	Patavinum	Padua
Beneventum	Benevento	Perusia	Perugia
Bononia	Bologna	Pisae	Pisa
Brixia	Brescia	Pisaurum	Pesaro
Brundisium	Brindisi	Placentia	Piacenza
Cannae	Cannae	Pompei	Pompeii
Canusium	Canosa	Populonium	Populonia
Capua	Capua	Praeneste	Praeneste
Carales	Cagliari	Puteoli	Pozzuoli
Carseoli	Carseoli	Reate	Rieti
Catina	Catania	Rhegium	Reggio
Clusium	Chiusi	Salernum	Salerno
Comum	Como	Selinus	Selinunte
Cortona	Cortona	Soluntum	Solunte
Cremona	Cremona	Spoletium	Spoleto
Croton	Crotone	Tarentum	Taranto
Cumae	Cumae	Tarquinii	Tarquinia
Faesulae	Fiesole	Tarracina	Terracina
Florentia	Florence	Tauromenium	Taormina
Genua	Genoa	Tergeste	Trieste
Herculaneum	Herculaneum	Tuder	Todi
Iguvium	Gubbio	Turris Libisonis	Porto Torres
Lilybaeum	Lilybaeum	Verona	Verona
Locri	Locri	Volaterrae	Volterra
Luca	Lucca	Volci	Vulci
Mantua	Mantua		

1

THE PEOPLES OF ITALY

At the end of the third century BC Roman domination extended over all Italy. The third Samnite War up till 290, then the war against Pyrrhus, followed by the capture of Tarentum in 272, had enabled Rome to subjugate the entire southern part. The operations accompanying the first Punic War from 264 to 241, then the conquest of Sardinia and Corsica, starting in 237, had brought in their wake the submission of Italy's neighbouring islands. In the north, Etruria and Umbria had been in complete subjection since the middle of the sixties. In contrast, the conquest of Cisalpine Gaul was much more recent, having followed the victory at Telamon in 225 when the Romans pushed as far as the foot of the Alps.

The hold that Rome henceforth exerted over Italy had not yet caused the disappearance of the differences dividing the various peoples of the peninsula. They were numerous and had as much to do with the specifically ethnic characteristics of language and culture as with the differing forms of social organization. Certain groups, in fact, had been organized in city-states for a long time, whereas others still remained faithful to the ancient structures of village and tribe.

But as always, when it comes to ancient societies, our knowledge of both kinds remains extraordinarily uneven and fragmentary. Some of these peoples belonged to history in the sense that they made sufficient use of inscriptions or numbered among themselves authors of literary texts explicit enough for us to be relatively well informed about their social structures and way of life. Such was the case, of course, for Rome and the Greek cities in Sicily and southern Italy; it would probably also apply to the Etruscans if only we were able to interpret correctly the few documents that have managed to come down to us. By contrast, the others are known to us only through two main sources of information: the references to them left to us by their more wordy neighbours, and the finds that archaeologists have brought to light. Some very rare inscriptions might be added, all the more precious because they are our sole means of assessing the nature, and sometimes the origin, of the languages they used.

The description which follows will suffer to some extent from these uncertainties. Certainly, archaeological data often provide useful indications concerning social organization and trade movements, but they allow us to identify a group only when it offers very specific cultural features. The other most frequently used criteria are only slightly pertinent: the names which Greek and Latin authors used to designate a people, the particular linguistic features of which some vestige has been preserved. They are no true guarantee of either the origins or the homogeneity of a group. Consequently, we must make the best of what we *do* have.

The Po Valley

Indubitably, the peoples of the Po Valley stood out from the rest. The region had undergone large-scale upheavals at the beginning of the fourth century, when a great wave of Celtic immigrants had strengthened the tribes that were already there and had eventually swamped the indigenous inhabitants. The Gauls were thus the dominant group, but they had not caused the complete disappearance of earlier populations – Ligures, Veneti and Etruscans, to name only the chief ones.

The Ligures occupied the north-west corner of the peninsula in very early times. Their settlements extended on either side of the Alps and the so-called Ligurian arc of the Apennines. They were composed of villages (*vici*) and fortified hilltop sites (*oppida*) which together formed the basic political units (*pagi*). Sometimes the latter federated into larger units which communally managed certain areas of livestock breeding.[1] They were largely Celticized at the end of the third century, so that all the questions that were asked even in antiquity regarding their identity and origins remain mostly unresolved.[2]

The situation of the Veneti was not very different. They were ensconced in the north-east corner of Cisalpine Gaul. They spoke an Indo-European language very close to Latin and, during the course of preceding periods, they had developed a very original culture, known as Atestine. But in its final phase, which corresponds to the period of the fourth to second centuries, it had been subjected to numerous influences, chiefly Etruscan and Celtic. There again, early authors hardly made any distinction between them and the Gauls who surrounded them.[3] The only difference was that the aristocracy who governed them had always been Rome's ally and, so its seems, their social organization remained stable even into the period of Romanization.[4]

In the region that they had largely dominated in the sixth and fifth centuries, the Etruscans no longer enjoyed the importance that had once been theirs. The main sites that archaeologists have been able to identify and study – Marzabotto, the ancient Felsina (Bologna) and the port of Spina – had been abandoned or had declined, starting from the middle of the fourth century. Centres of population remained despite all, notably in urban surroundings, as at Felsina or Adria.[5]

The groups who lived there certainly preserved their cultural features and probably also something of their former dominant position. Indeed, Etruscan models retained a certain capacity for spreading their influence.[6] Anyway, that is what we are led to suppose by some cemeteries in the Bologna region, dating to the end of the fourth century or the beginning of the third, where the association of Gaulish and Etruscan tombs suggests a process of cohabitation, reciprocal acculturation and then the fusion of the old dominant group and the new.[7]

However, the Gaulish populations formed the main body of the inhabitants of Cisalpine Gaul. They were already present there, but the invasions of the early fourth century were probably decisive and allowed them to dominate the region completely. It was an important event. Gaulish bands spread throughout the peninsula, and one took Rome in 386. Conflicts and insecurity lasted for about thirty years, then these populations became almost entirely settled.[8] They nevertheless remained largely in touch with the other Gaulish tribes who lived beyond the Alps. Trade was constant within the Celtic ensemble, with new waves of immigrants arriving from time to time to strengthen the presence of these people in Italy by adding fresh contingents. Until the end of the third century, the Cisalpine Gauls thus broadly preserved their own ethnic characteristics.

The importance of the warrior aristocracy in social organization was one of its dominant features. 'In such societies, nothing mattered as much as ties of vassalage, for the man who was most feared and who had the greatest authority was the one around whom gathered the largest number of companions, in order to place themselves at his command,' wrote Polybius.[9] And there is little reason to suppose that on this point the Cisalpine Gauls differed fundamentally from their cousins in Transalpine Gaul, as Caesar described them two centuries later. Chiefs appeared here and there in documentation, sometimes referred to as kings, but it would be extremely difficult to define their powers and methods of appointment as there are so many lacunae in our information on the subject. But there is absolutely no doubt that one of the dominant traits of this society was the importance given to warrior qualities.[10] Those third-century Gauls were still fearsome fighters; they continued to enlist as mercenaries, and to be held in high regard, in every conflict that affected the Mediterranean world.

Nevertheless, this society did not have the civic organization which was predominant at that time in the whole of the Roman and Hellenistic world. Political units as mentioned by the early writers were first and foremost tribal in nature.[11] The names borne by the Gauls, which were obviously those that they had given themselves, referred to ethnic groups which had sometimes become split up during migrations. For instance, the Boii, who gave their name to Bohemia, and their neighbours the Lingones had homonyms who lived in Transalpine Gaul. For most of these groups, therefore, collective identity was probably of the kind that manages to cement bonds of unity by the affirmation of a mythical consanguinity.

Nevertheless, the actual units of social organization were smaller. The populations of the Po Valley lived mostly in townships or villages, but in periods of insecurity, or quite simply to preserve part of their possessions, they used fortified settlements that are equally well attested in the Celtic world and among the

Ligures or Veneti. Real political powers were watered down in these rural areas.[12] But certain towns known as *oppida*, fortified or not, began to acquire importance and to become political centres around which these Celtic or Celticized communities would be organized when they had been Romanized. The origin of these kinds of proto-cities could vary greatly. Some had been there before Gaulish domination: Mantua, for example, Padua or Como. Others, like Milan or Brescia, were in the act of being constituted, thus following a process of urbanization which affected the whole of the Celtic world.[13]

In general, the Cisalpine populations of the late third century were involved in an overall trading activity, with the Transalpine peoples on the one hand and the rest of Italy on the other, which tended to make a distinction between them according to whether they were on the north or south side of the Po. I mentioned before the assimilation of the Gaulish and Etruscan aristocracies as revealed through the Boian cemeteries in the Bologna region. The process of acculturation was even more advanced among the Senones who, installed on the Adriatic coast on the foothills of the Apennines, found themselves in direct contact with Italic populations. In fact, among the objects discovered in tombs it is very difficult to pick out those of specifically Latin make. Many influences are noticeable: Etruscan games, Umbrian weapons, Tarentine or Campanian jewels and tableware, which lead one to suppose that those Gauls were already merging into a far larger Italian whole.[14] In contrast, north of the Po, Transalpine influences were much stronger, and the Cenomani and Insubres preserved their own cultural traditions to a far greater extent.[15] The difference between the north and south of the Po Valley was not without significance. It also matched the positions occupied by either side in their relations with central Italy, and especially with the Roman world.

The conquest had been made in two main stages. Apart from the Gaulish incursions in the interior of the peninsula, the first clash took place in 295, when the Romans carried off a hard-won victory near Sentinum over a coalition of Etruscans, Umbrians, Samnites and Gauls. Ten years later it was followed by a series of operations waged against the Senones and Boii, allied with the Etruscans, details of which are hard to reconstruct. In essence, they led the Romans to react after an initial defeat suffered at Arezzo in 283, crush the Senones, seize their territory on which they founded the town of Sena Gallica, then, some years later in 268, the Latin colony of Rimini, finally imposing their rule over the Boii by treaty.

Hostilities resumed after the Punic War, in 238, probably because the Romans stepped up their pressure on the western part of Cisalpine Gaul. An early failure of the Transalpine and Cisalpine Gaulish peoples at Rimini in 236 was followed in 232 by the proposal of the tribune of the plebs C. Flaminius to divide up and share out the part of the conquered territory of the *ager gallicus* that had not yet been used. The Boii, Insubres and Ligures felt threatened, and engaged in an offensive that resulted in the defeat at Telamon in 225. The Romans then set about systematically subduing the Po Valley. They completed its conquest in 222, and in 218 founded the Latin colonies of Cremona and Piacenza.

It would be unwise to exaggerate the differences that made all these peoples distinct from one another, but it should be noted that neither the chronology nor the conditions of their submission to Roman domination were the same everywhere. Some were conquered early on and brutally, for example, the Senones; others, like the Veneti, belatedly and maintaining a relationship of alliance. Between the two, circumstances obviously varied widely, but they foreshadowed the situation that prevailed in the second and first centuries when, after the second Punic War, the Cisalpine region south of the Po was again very largely colonized and Romanized, whereas the north side remained peopled by allies of Rome, broadly autonomous, so that the integration of these two parts of the Po Valley into the Roman ensemble did not take place with the same timing or according to the same methods.

Central and Southern Italy

In contrast, most of the peoples of the centre of the peninsula were generally embraced in a partly ethnic *koine*, as the greater number of them, Latin or Italic, spoke languages or lived according to broadly common or similar rules, but also in a culture under the influence of a Hellenization that was at work to varying degrees in the whole of Italy.

The Etruscans, however, were the first exception to this general definition. As much by their own characteristics as by the vigour of their historical traditions, they in fact occupied a place apart in the Italian world, though the era of their greatest splendour was over. They no longer held dominion, as they had at the end of the sixth century, over an area that stretched from the Po Valley to Campania and at that time included Rome, which was subject to them. The situation had been reversed. Campania had become Samnite at the end of the fifth century. The Gauls had taken over Cisalpine at the beginning of the fourth. And now it was Rome which imposed its will on an Etruria that had been reduced to its earliest size. Of course, during the fifth century, all these events could not help having a serious effect on the whole of society. But starting in the fourth century, a certain agricultural and commercial prosperity had returned, to the benefit of the aristocracy in the first place.[16]

From its origins, the whole of Etruscan society had been organized around the aristocrats. They owned the land and ran political life. Culturally, they imposed their values and methods of representation. It was they who built those gigantic tombs where they reproduced the arrangement of their domestic living space. They were the ones who enjoyed the way of life made up of games and banquets that we see represented there. In other words, it was they who produced what is called Etruscan civilization. They were not the only ones, but they broadly and strongly dominated the rest of the population. In fact, the early authors stress the size of the slave classes or those verging on slavery. It was an original feature of the Etruscan world that there existed a category of dependants who occupied a sort of intermediate position betwen liberty and slavery, and there is no other example of this in Italy.[17] Perhaps, however, a middle class was beginning to emerge, thanks to the emancipation of some of them,[18] but this certainly did not go as far as fundamentally altering the overall social organization.

The main development had been something different. Each city had its own institutions and, among the names of the magistrates, we can pick out *zilath (praetores)*, *camthi (aediles)*, *sarvenas*, *zelarvenas (decemviri, vigintiviri)*, and among them priests, *cepen*, *netsvis*, *haruspex* and *maru*. To these local institutions was added a sort of federal league council which periodically assembled the delegates of the twelve principal cities of Etruria.[19] Now, this civic organization had probably been structured at the expense of royal and gentilitial forms. The importance accorded by the aristocrats to holding magistracies was thus greater, and their symbols were more often represented.[20]

The sense of prestige and family legitimacy remained extraordinarily powerful. At Tarquinia, in the first century AD, families still preserved and celebrated the memory of magistracies held by certain great ancestors as early as the fifth century BC, taking care to have them mentioned in inscriptions in their honour.[21] And it is possible that, among all the exploits evoked with such pride, those accomplished against the Romans may have been in the forefront. At all events, the paintings of the 'Francis' tomb at Vulci would suggest so, even if, since they are datable to the second half of the fourth century, they were earlier than the completion of the conquest. Indeed, they recall a victory that had been won in past times against the Romans and, by symbolically identifying the latter with the Trojans, for the victorious Vulcians they reawakened the glorious image of the heroes of the *Iliad*.[22]

Etruscan originality was therefore not an empty expression. Many other features could be mentioned to reveal it. It lay chiefly in the continuity of religious and cultural traditions; architectural ones too, about which we are slightly better informed – the temples, and especially the tombs, which remained monumental in form.[23] For the Etruscan aristocrats, who were manifestly attached to them, they constituted the signs of their identity.

Nevertheless, they had to obey the Romans. After many much earlier episodes, the conquest was achieved during the last decades of the fourth century and first decades of the third. The defeat suffered by the Etruscans in 295 at the battle of Sentinum, together with the Gauls, Umbrians and Samnites they had mobilized with them, had probably been decisive. One after the other, the various cities were definitively subdued: Rusella in 294, then, after a final defeat in 283 at Lake Vadimonis, Tarquinia in 281, Volsinii and Vulci in 280, Caere in 273. Henceforth treaties guaranteed obedience, but if the cities in the north had had to pay a tribute, the more southerly ones had lost part of their territory. On Vulci's, the Latin colony of Cosa was founded in 273. On that of Caere, Roman colonies were created: Pyrgi and Castrum Novum in 264 (?), Alsium in 247 and Fregenae in 245.[24] Roads were constructed, the Clodian perhaps in 287 or 285 inland, and the Aurelian in 241 along the coast.

Here again, the difference in the treatment of the two parts of Etruria matched varying degrees of integration. In 390, the Caerites had received the right of *hospitium publicum*, and in 353, the concession of citizenship without suffrage [25] which probably justified their complete incorporation into the Roman community. Thus the population of the two cities – and of course the aristocrats of the two communities were the first to be concerned – had the possibility of contracting marriages and entering into a system of reciprocal kinship. Alliances between aristocratic Roman families and those of southern Etruria were in any case of long standing. Without going back as far as the period of the Etruscan kings who had ruled Rome, it may be noted for example that the consul of 276 and 271, C. Genucius Clepsina, was descended from a Roman family, the Genucii, who had allied themselves with a Tarquinian family, the Cleusina.[26]

It is understandable that the Roman rulers should have paid such attention to defending the interests of Etruscan aristocrats when the latter were threatened by the rebellion of the lower classes. For instance, it was a Roman army that put down the rising of 302 against the Cilnii of Arezzo.[27] Furthermore, when the plebeians of Volsinii seized power in 265, the Romans occupied the town, destroyed it and resettled it a few kilometres away.[28] At the same time they pillaged the sanctuary of Voltumna and took to Rome some 2,000 bronze statues that were there. This site was also the meeting-place of the old federal league of the Etruscans. The latter was now dissolved, if it had not already been, and its seat probably symbolically transferred to Rome by the evocation of the god. Twenty years later, a similar kind of event occurred. In 241 the city of Falerii, which had rebelled, was destroyed in its turn and, a few years later, rebuilt on the plain.

In this regard, Roman domination was no longer the exercise of an external power assuring itself from a distance of a community's loyalty. The degree of intervention shown in the case of Volsinii signified at best a sharing of responsibilities in the exercise of civic power, at worst a direct management of the city's affairs. All these forms of annexation, symbolic or actual, partial or total as in the case of Caere, certainly struck at a *de facto* unity that had already been created, but they obviously emphasized and complemented it. For if Roman aristocracy became integrated, it probably did so in order to gain greater control, and if it meted out punishment it was in order to strike within the civic body only those who had truly declared themselves its enemies, while preserving for the rest the advantage of alliance.

Farther east and south, the entire chain of the Apennines, which might be regarded as the heart of the Italian peninsula, was occupied by peoples who were given the overall title of Italic and who, in the main, shared the same ethnic traits. They revered the same gods, and spoke dialects that were comparatively close, grouped in two subsets: Oscan in the southern part of Italy and Umbrian in the northern. There was relatively little to distinguish them from the Latin populations with whom they shared the same Indo-European origin. Although their destinies had been difficult, they were none the less slightly behindhand, compared with the other populations, chiefly Etruscans, Greeks and Latins, in their adoption of civic models of social organization.[29]

As they appear to us through the sparse traces of them preserved in their language, the instituions in fact gave more importance to the people (*tota* or *touto*) whom they distinguished from the town (*ocri*) as two opposite poles in the life of the group.[30] Many factors can explain this situation, for instance, the natural conditions which, allied with historical circumstances, had led these peoples frequently to preserve a social organization based on the association of living in villages and the consciousness of an ethnic unity, or which had led them to base a large part of their economy on pastoral activities linked with transhumance, which are less compatible than others with the classic model of the city-state. So for them social organization was most often contained within the political framework of *pagi* assembling villages (*vici*) and *oppida* which had served as fortified sites before the Roman conquest. Meeting places in rural zones, communal sanctuaries like, for example, among the Vestini, that of Jupiter Victor of the ten *pagi*, or among the Pentrian Samnites, that of Pietrabbondante, permitted the practice of communal life and ensured the cohesion of ethnic ensembles in the heart of which one could really experience the feeling of a common identity, of belonging to the same *nomen*.[31] Magistrates, the *meddices*, governed all these groups, observing a hierarchy which insisted that some played only a local role while others, who bore the title *meddix tuticus*, had authority over the whole of the people.

The Italics were also poor and demographic pressure on them was hard. There was a well-attested tradition of the *ver sacrum*, which consisted of consecrating to the god Mars all the children born in one year and, when they had reached maturity, sending them off to settle in another region under a leader with a totemic animal.[32] For many of the more settled populations, all these people were therefore restless and dangerous neighbours, mercenaries too, who easily found employment. In any case, they held warrior values in the highest regard. This is borne out by the abundance of weapons found in the burial sites and, perhaps even more explicitly, by the tomb paintings in which those who had settled in Campania and become Hellenized had themselves represented as fighters. Nevertheless, differences appear between one group and another. The Umbrians, who lived near the Etruscans and had been subject to them,[33] had borrowed from them a large part of their cultural features, notably the alphabet, which they had used since at least the beginning of the fourth century. During the third century they had gradually organized themselves into states; magistrates, *uthur* and *marones*, had made an appearance.[34] Two cities were of principal importance, Todi and Gubbio for which, above all, we have invaluable information provided by the Eugubine tables, inscriptions on bronze which preserved the rules for certain religious ceremonies. As for their Etruscan neighbours, the defeat they had suffered with them at Sentinum in 295 had probably marked the end of their independence. A little later, in 266, the capture of Sarsina, at the edge of the Cisalpine region, completed the process of sumbission to Roman authority. Latin colonies were founded on their territory, Narni in 299 and Spoleto in 241.[35] In 220, the Via Flaminia which led to Rimini finally attached them to Rome. Then the silence of our sources leads us to suppose that the situation remained as it was without any major upsets.

The traditions of the Picentes, who lived farther east on the Adriatic slopes of the Apennines, connected them with the more southerly Sabini, from whom they apper to have been separated by one of those migrations linked with the *ver sacrum*. At all events that was how they explained their name, *picus* (green woodpecker), as that was the totemic animal which had led them.[36] They spoke a dialect similar to that of the Umbrians. There were probably still some Illyrian elements among them, but the proportion is unknown. It is also very difficult to know to what extent their social organization was of the civic type. The groups in which they were to be recognized in the fifth century bore the name *toutas* and their chiefs were known as *nerf* or *pupur*.[37] Their principal town Asculum (Ascoli Piceno) probably became the centre of a city-state, but it is impossible to ascertain exactly when. Perhaps it had even been so as early as the third century when, after the Roman conquest, it had remained the sole autonomous part of the region. Indeed in 268, the same year in which Rimini was founded on the territory of the Senones, the consuls P. Sempronius Sophus and Ap. Claudius Russus won a victory over the Picentes which earned them a triumph. At the time a large part of the territory was confiscated, part of the population deported, and in 264 a Latin colony was set up at Firmum Picenum. At their expense the Romans thus made sure of domination over the entire northern part of the Adriatic coast.

In the centre of the peninsula lived a whole series of peoples – Sabini, Vestini, Marrucini, Aequi, Hernici, Marsi, Volsci and Paeligni, to name only the principal ones, who are sometimes referred to as Sabelli and belonged to the same overall category of Italic peoples. Their various dialects were sometimes similar to the Oscan grouping, and sometimes the Umbrian. Those in the more mountainous parts had probably preserved the pre-civic form of social organization of the *pagi* and *vici*.[38] But the more southern dwellers, chiefly the Marsi, Aequi and Volsci, living in areas that were more open and neighbouring on Latium and Campania, were organized in states and had adopted a civic type of identity.[39]

In essence, these regions had been subdued during the second half of the fourth century, the last Sabini to remain independent having been conquered in the first decades of the third century.[40] Certain territories had been incorporated with that of Rome, and their inhabitants had received citizenship without suffrage, then in 268 full citizenship. Elsewhere colonies with Latin rights had been founded: Alba Fucens (303) and Carseoli (302 or 298) for the Aequi; Fregellae (328) and Sora (303) for the Hernici, Hadria (290–286) for the Praetuttii. Roads had been built connecting them with Rome: the Via Valeria in 307 to the heart of the Apennines, and possibly the Via Caecilia in 283, to the north, as far as the Adriatic. In fact, at the end of the third century, all these peoples had been integrated, some for several generations, with the most Romanized part of Italy.

Of all the Italic peoples, the Samnites were probably the most important. They occupied the central part of the Apennine chain. At the beginning of the third century they had not yet become organized into states, and the principal unit remained the people (*touto*), subdivided into *pagi*. Sources show four main groups: the Pentri, Caudini, Hirpini and Carricini, to whom we should probably add the Frentani, structured like all these peoples around their communal sanctuaries. A dawning Hellenization had already shown itself among them, as evidenced by the presence between the third and second centuries of totally Greek deities, such as Ceres, Hercules, Flora and Proserpine, or the adoption of Greek-type architectural models in the construction of the temple in the great regional sanctuary of Pietrabbondante. The *meddices* who ruled them probably represented a well-established aristocracy. Indeed, the names of the same families – the Betitii, Decitii, Herii, Papii, Satrii, Staii or Statii – are regularly mentioned by our sources when speaking of the region's history.[41]

They were perfectly capable of mobilizing themselves and federating into a league when they needed to fight. Then they made formidable adversaries. The Romans knew something of this, as they had faced them in long, hard wars (sometimes accompanied by setbacks), including the battle of the Caudine Forks, which remained notorious. This war, which they had waged against King Pyrrhus, was virtually over in 272. Whole sections of Samnite territory had been confiscated. Latin colonies had been founded there throughout the war years: Luceria in 314, Saticula in 313, Venusia in 291, Beneventum in 268 and Aesernia in 263. The Samnite league was dissolved. Communities which remained autonomous were weakened and separated from one another. The southernmost, such as those of the Caudini, in any case started to change: they had been fragmented and the new units that appeared thus became true city-states.[42]

The farther south one goes, the stronger Greek influence tended to become. The entire southern coast of Italy, apart of course from the eastern part of Sicily, had been occupied by Greek colonies which had been implanted there from the eighth century BC. It is not surprising, therefore, that all the populations inhabiting that area of the peninsula bore strong marks of this presence. In parallel, however, the Italic peoples, particularly the Samnites, had also tended to spread southwards and occupy all the regions extending towards the south-west, towards the toe of the boot as it were. So the human landscape was extremely diversified, combining the differences and mingling the influences – Greek, Oscan and henceforth Latin.

The regions that were historically most marked by this process were of course southern Latium and Campania. The oldest known populations there were the Ausones, who belonged to the same linguistic group as the Latins, and of whom certain elements remained under the name Aurunci. The Greek cities there had been among the first to be founded: Cumae in the eighth century, then Naples and Dikaiarcheia, the future Pozzuoli. Later, between the seventh and fifth centuries, the region had been dominated by the Etruscans, who were credited with the founding of Capua. During the last decades of the fifth century, the whole region had passed under the domination of Italic populations. Capua became an Oscan town associated at the end of the fifth century with a few other cities in a federal league. Cumae had undergone the same fate. Naples alone preserved its Greek identity. Its institutions had persisted, and demarchs and archons were still numbered among its magistrates.[43] All these towns, to which many more may be added, though of lesser importance, such as Atella, Calatia and Casilinum in the north, or Herculaneum, Pompeii, Stabiae and Sorrento in the south, were thus governed by Hellenized Italic aristocrats who had adapted their language and institutions to the framework of the city. The cities of Capua, Pompeii, Herculaneum and Nola had a senate and people's assemblies and were goverend by *meddices* who were recruited from the few aristocratic families for whom the dominant figure was that of a warrior, especially a horseman; so, at least, he appeared at the end of the fourth century in the rich tombs in Capua, Cumae or Poseidonia (Paestum).[44]

At the end of the fourth century Roman dominion had been established. The Samnite Wars provided the opportunity. Tradition recorded notably in 343 that Capua, threatened by new Italic incursions, surrendered to Roman protection (a *deditio*). This was the occasion of the first Samnite War. There is no need to refer here to many other episodes that ensured, as in any case they are much debated. Whatever may have happened, the outcome of these campaigns was that all the cities in Campania came under Rome's authority. Some, notably Capua and Cumae, received the benefit of citizenship without suffrage. In contrast, others such as Naples remained as allies. Latin colonies had been founded on confiscated territories, for instance, Cales in 334, Suessa Aurunca in 313, Interamna Lirenas in 312, and others with Roman citizens at Minturnae and Sinuessa in 295. In 312 the Via Appia had linked all these regions to Rome. At the end of the third century Campania in its entirety was broadly integrated into the strictly Roman political ensemble, to the extent that, although exaggeratedly, it was sometimes spoken of as a Romano-Capuan state.[45]

Farther south, Lucanians and Bruttians inhabited present-day Basilicata and Calabria. They were Italic peoples, but their presence in these regions was somewhat more recent than that of their neighbours, and by their differences they revealed the diversity of the influences they had experienced. Both had been Hellenized over the centuries. Then Lucania had been Samnitized during the fourth century under the influence of migrations from the north. The language of inscriptions and the titles of their leaders as they appear there were most frequently of the Oscan type. In contrast, the Bruttians were more imbued with Greek cultural traits.

Nevertheless, they all knew the same social organization as the Italic peoples. In these mountainous regions, the economy was chiefly based on livestock breeding and use of the forests. Their communities were organized on a tribal basis (*touto* or *demos*, depending on the language) and were led by *meddices* or *basileis*, especially when war made it necessary to form associations and choose a chief to lead them in combat. As in the rest of the Italic world, fortified centres served as their refuge, and sanctuaries determined the places for meetings and probably for federal gatherings as, for example, in Lucania, that of the goddess Mefite Utiana at Rossano di Vaglio, which from the fourth to the second century yielded some forty inscriptions, at first Oscan written in the Greek alphabet, then Latin, bearing witness simultaneously to the continuity of a social organization and processes of acculturation.[46]

Like their northern neighbours, the Lucanians and Bruttians had played an important role in the history of the Greek cities in the region in the fourth and the beginning of the third century. In fact the Lucanians had captured several of them, in particular Poseidonia (Paestum) which remained under their rule. They also intervened, alongside or against them, either collectively or individually as the renowned mercenaries that they were, during the various wars that set them in opposition to one another or to Rome. The final episode which resulted in their subjection was of course the war with Pyrrhus, king of Epirus, whose allies they were until his defeat in 275. In 272 they were definitively crushed, part of their territory being confiscated and a Latin colony, Paestum, founded at Poseidonia (in 273).

In the south-east of the peninsula, the ethnic data changed perceptibly. Italic peoples had not penetrated to that point. The populations inhabiting present-day Puglia were probably Illyrian. This name is applied rather conventionally to populations of Balkan origin who spoke an Indo-European language, but one that differed from Greek, Latin or Oscan. Historians and geographers of antiquity often varied in their way of designating them, which leads one to assume both internal modifications and a certain ignorance on the part of their Greek, then Roman, neighbours. In the archaic period they were collectively known as Iapyges, then they were called Apulians, and a distinction was made between the Daunians north of the Aufidus, the Peucetians in the centre, and the Messapians (or Calabri) and the Sallentini at the tip of the peninsula. In every case they were peoples who during the fifth and fourth centuries had become Hellenized on contact with the Greek world, Italiot cities and especially Tarentum, which made its presence felt throughout the whole of southern Italy, but also under the influence of northern Greece. As far as we can know them through the archaeological data that have been preserved, they were rural populations organized around proto-urban centres defined by imposing defence walls that were erected during the fourth century, and dominated by aristocracies whose traces remain either in houses, sometimes with a peristyle, found on the sites of Monte Sannace and Arpi,[47] or more generally, especially at Canosa and again in Arpi, in the monumental tombs they had built.[48]

The difference between the two populations, however, lay in the fact that the Daunians, who were more to the north, came under a Samnite and Campanian influence which did not reach the Peucetians and Messapians, and were also subjected more rapidly than they were to Roman domination. Indeed, at the end of the fourth century they found themselves Rome's allies in the second Samnite War. We thus learn that on occasion some points of their territory were in the hands of their foes and that some of their towns, like Canosa or Arpi, were real city-states in that they could hold talks with Rome. If there were any further need, the Latin colonies founded after the two Samnite Wars, Luceria in 314 and Venusia in 291, helped to emphasize still further the growing urbanization.[49] In contrast, farther south the conquest of the Peucetians and Messapians occurred only a little later in 267 and 266, after the defeat of Tarentum, whose allies they had been in the war with Pyrrhus. And in 244 the Latin colony of Brindisi was founded, perhaps connected with Rome in 225 by the Via Minucia.[50]

The Coasts of Southern Italy and the Islands

Like the islands, the south coast of the peninsula was dominated by the last two great ethnic groups who contributed to the diversity of the Italian inhabitants, the Punicized populations of Sicily and Sardinia and, above all, the Greeks, who had founded some of their largest and most important cities there.

As in Campania, the process of colonization had started in the eighth century BC. The first cities to be founded were Naxos, Leontini, Catana, Megara Hyblaea, Syracuse and Gela in Sicily; Sybaris, Croton, Tarentum, Locris, Metapontum and Siris on the mainland coast. The first had been founded by Chalcis, Megara and Corinth, the others by the Achaeans or Lacedaemonians. Thurii was a fifth-century pan-Hellenic foundation carried out under the aegis of Athens. Then these cities in their turn had flourished and founded others: for instance, Selinus founded by Megara Hyblaea at the end of the seventh century and Agrigentum by Gela at the beginning of the sixth century; Poseidonia founded by Sybaris in the seventh century, and Heraclea founded by Tarentum in the fifth century in place of Siris, which had been destroyed.

All these cities were profoundly Greek. The populations they embraced had preserved their customs and language very disinctly. In the texts that have come down to us, especially the inscriptions, it is possible to pick out idiomatic features that match the dialects used in the founding cities. Similarly, the gods worshipped or civic institutions were most often borrowed directly from them. For example, in Tarentum, which had been founded by Sparta, the cults observed corresponded to those known in the sanctuaries of Laconia and, when it came to political bodies, a king was to be found among the magistrates; probably also *ephors*, a *strategos* for exceptional circumstances, a *boule* and *heliaea* matching those of Sparta and other Dorian cities, Argos or Epidaurus.[51] In any case there was a fundamental reason for this. The colonies reproduced their mother-city both in the composition of the population which had emerged from them and in the social structures and methods of political organization which had been redefined in identical fashion at the time of the foundation.

Consequently, these cities in Sicily or what was known as 'Magna Graecia' or 'Greater Greece' participated fully in the life of the rest of the Hellenic world. This was true for trade, of course, but just as much so for cultural exchanges and political life. To quote only a few examples, it may be recalled that Plato had come to Syracuse and met Archytas, the Pythagorean who governed Tarentum; that Lysippus had probably worked in the same town, where he had created two colossal statues, and that Syracuse had been totally involved in the Peloponnesian War, since it was there that Greek ambitions foundered. Hardly any differences separated these cities of the West from the other cities of the Balkan peninsula and Asia Minor. Within the Italian world, however, their place was very special. In the third century the liveliest were still the principal source of the spread of cultural influences which encouraged the Hellenization of Italy. Their political weight, too, was such that they were truly the active agents in the region's history.

It is unnecessary to lay much emphasis on events prior to the third century. To keep matters simple, let us pick out the two principal stress lines. On the one hand, those that set the various ethnic groups against one another: Greeks and Carthaginians in rivalry for possession of Sicily, Greeks and Italics because the latter put constant pressure on the cities of Greater Greece and, to mention only the final episode, Mamertine mercenaries from Campania had seized Messina in the 280s and had massacred part of the population. On the other hand, there were stresses that divided the Greeks. In fact, conflicts set cities fighting among themselves or, within those very cities, aristocrats against the lower classes. If we are to believe our sources, the struggles between the two latter categories were even one of the recurring features of life in these cities.[52] The result was a constant political instability: pretexts for wars multiplied, for the vanquished from one city would take refuge in another and spend their time trying to obtain the means of revenge from their hosts.

In the third century the majority of these cities had thus lost their autonomy, either because they had been conquered by the Italics or Carthaginians, or because they found themselves subjected to the domination of the two powers that had ultimately eclipsed the rest – Tarentum and Syracuse.

The former was a very large city which, at the beginning of the century, must have numbered over 200,000 inhabitants. Its economy was well developed: Tarentine craftsmen produced fabrics, pottery articles, and gold and silverware which were spread and imitated throughout mainland Italy. Its political role was no less great since it had ended by dominating all the Greek world in Italy. Moreover, it enjoyed a considerable cultural influence which derived from the importance of the artistic and intellectual activity carried on there, and notably from the Pythagorean school, of which it was the centre. Its influence spread over the whole of southern Italy, and this necessarily brought it into conflict with Rome; indeed, Tarentum was one of those rare cities which were capable of rivalling it.[53]

The first clashes occurred at the end of the fourth century, but open conflict took place only when the Romans allied themselves with the other cities of Greater Greece against the Lucanians. At that point they intervened directly in the region. In 280 the Tarentines appealed to Pyrrhus, king of Epirus, who at first defeated the Roman armies but, after various episodes, was beaten by them in 275 and had to leave Italy. From then on an isolated Tarentum could not avoid the conquest that took place in 272 and was followed by a treaty which turned it into its victor's ally. All the other Greek cities in the peninsula then found themselves reduced to sharing the same situation.

The place occupied by Syracuse was probably even more considerable. Since the fifth century it had most frequently been governed by tyrants who had succeeded in achieving its hegemony over the cities of Sicily. It had thus become the chief adversary of the Carthaginians in the numerous battles that had ranged them against the Greeks for possession of the island. Agathocles, who ruled at the beginning of the third century, had even attempted a landing in Africa. Then Pyrrhus in his turn had come to fight the Carthaginians. Finally, from about 275, it had been governed by Hieron II, who had resumed the combat. With all these personages, and especially the last-named, who remained in power until the end of the century, Sicily began to experience the same monarchic-type political organization as that of the kingdoms in the Orient. Hieron, in fact, had assumed all the attributes of the Hellenistic sovereigns and had surrounded himself with a court. He had reorganized the administration, notably the system of collecting tithes on the harvests, which he had borrowed from a Lagid example and which would later be of use to the Romans.[54]

The first Punic War was the chance for Roman conquest. The pretext used was the surrender (*deditio*) by the Mamertines of Messina to the Romans. The latter, by accepting in 264 that these Italians should put themselves in their hands, were infringing earlier treaties which prohibited them from intervening in the island. The Carthaginians began a campaign. In the early stages Hieron sided with them, but later he became the ally of Rome, which basically meant he was adopting the Greek cause of fighting the Punic enemy, and he remained on Rome's side until the final victory of 241. At that time Syracuse's importance was even greater than before. Most of the other cities had in fact suffered a good deal from these successive wars: Gela had disappeared in 282, Camarina had been destroyed in 258, Selinus around 252 and Agrigentum must have been very much weakened, since it had to accept colonists in 207. At the same time Sicily came under Roman rule and became a province, formally administered by praetors from 227.

With Sicily, and then the conquest of Sardinia and Corisca which occurred between 240 and 225, Punic or very strongly Punicized populations were integrated into the Roman Empire. Certainly, none of these islands had been part of ancient Italy, but they were so close to it that it is fair to give a rapid description of their state of civic and cultural development.

Phoenician colonization was earlier than Greek. Occupation of certain sites had in fact commenced before the founding of Carthage. Then the latter had taken over and set up trading posts and colonies as early as the ninth century, but it had not been on the scale of the Greek undertaking. The regions that had been occupied were confined to the south of Sardinia and the western tip of Sicily. So we may cite, in the first case, the towns of Nora, Sulcis, Tharros, Cagliari and Bithia and, in the second island,

Motya, Palermo, Solus and Lilybaeum, which was founded after the destruction of Motya in the fourth century, and Selinus, taken from the Greeks at the end of the fifth century. All these cities were conquered by the Romans during the first Punic War for Sicily then, from 237 to 231, for Sardinia and Corsica. These two islands were subsequently transformed into a province, but their pacification was not immediate and further campaigns proved necessary to quell revolts.

Until then the Punic nature of these cities had remained un-altered. Their language, religion and the little we know of their political institutions makes this plain. Indeed, suffetes appear in inscriptions from Bithia, and mention of Phoenician gods occurs almost everywhere: Baal Hammon, Tanit and Astarte, of course, but also Melqart, Eshmoun and the god Sid in Sardinia. In a world where henceforth all architecture was similarly deter-mined by Hellenistic rules, sanctuaries preserved a particular layout: small rooms, as at Solus, arranged according to an irreg-ular plan, but housing the statue of a god which all the modelling seemed to make into a Greek Zeus.[55]

Of course, this Punic civilization tended to extend beyond the confines of the cities, to the interior of the islands where in-digenous populations lived. In Sicily the latter comprised three ethnic groups: the Siculi in the east, who belonged to the same linguistic ensemble as the Latins and Ausones, the Sicani in the west and the Elymi in the north-west, who had perhaps been pushed back there by the first group. All had suffered greatly from the incessant wars of the fourth and third centuries, and those groups that had survived were mostly Hellenized. Some sites, such as Mount Adranonus, were also affected by Punic influence.[56]

In contrast, conditions in Sardinia were much more favourable to the development of the Phoenician influence. In the interior of the island, Sardinian gods had been affected by the occurrences of *interpretatio punica*. The god Babay, who was revered in numerous votive inscriptions between the fourth century BC and the first AD, had been assimilated with the god Sid. In the valley of Antas, a god was worshipped who later took the name Sardus Pater, and who at that time was regarded as the son of Melqart and Tanit. Near San Salvatore de Cabras, a protohistoric subter-ranean tomb which preserved the monumental architecture of the Sardinian nuraghi had been adapted to Punic rituals by the addition of basins for purificatory water. Other instances could be cited, but I will mention only one, Monte Sirai, a site near Sulcis. At the end of the third century, when the Carthaginians abandoned the acropolis, the Punicized populations settled there without altering the model of the rectilinear streets and orthogonal crossroads: just as they were at the time of the Roman conquest, the Sardinian populations had never known any civilizing influence other than that of Carthage.[57]

The differences from one region of Italy to another were thus still extremely noticeable, even at the end of the third century, when the peninsula and its neighbouring islands had passed completely under Roman domination. Ethnic and linguistic diversity was strong, even though a distinction must be made between central Italy, peopled with Latins, Etruscans and Italics who were relatively close to one another, and the more peripheral zones of Sicily and, chiefly, Sardinia and Cisalpine Gaul, which really belonged to other cultural categories. But more than this diversity, it was the unevenness in the development of civic organization that marked the disparities between the various societies. It was not that they were disorganized, but the aristocracies which dominated them had not always found that establishing municipal institutions fitted in with their methods of government. However, two strong historical currents were already at work, and leading to unity: the dominance of Rome, which was being established throughout the third century, and a process of Hellenization which had been going on even longer and was gradually leading all these peoples, including the Romans, to share the same religious and cultural values.

ROME, ITALY AND HELLENISM

Despite its diversity, Italy tended to become unified under the influence of Roman rule. The state of Rome itself was transformed, first because the authority it exerted led it to modify the structures of its administration, and chiefly because, like the rest of the Italian world, it was swept into a process of economic and cultural opening-up, and thence integration into the larger ensemble of the Hellenized world.

The Organization of Roman Rule

At the end of the third century, Rome had become a great Mediterranean power. The organization of its political system was still that of a city-state, but it would be a closer approach to historical reality if one were to regard it as a territorial state broadly embracing more than a tenth of peninsular Italy and dominating the rest. At first sight, these two definitions may seem hard to reconcile. The political functioning of a state normally demanded the direct participation of citizens in decision-making, which was scarcely compatible with the expanse of the area henceforth under Rome's control. Therein lay a contradiction for which solutions were beginning to be found, and on these depended the future constitution of a Roman empire.

As with every city in antiquity, Rome's territory comprised the town and the surrounding countryside, and was known as the *ager romanus*. It was divided into tribes in which Roman citizens were registered and which served as the framework for the levying of taxes and the recruitment of soldiers. In the fifth century BC, it embraced Rome and its immediate surroundings, shared between four urban and seventeen rustic tribes. At the end of the third century BC, it was widely extended since it swept across the entire centre of the peninsula from the Tyrrhenian Sea to the Adriatic, following a pattern reminiscent of that of the papal states in the nineteenth century. It occupied a surface area of about 27,000 square kilometres and was peopled by nearly a million inhabitants[1] – which represented a large population; for those who had the right of full citizenship, fourteen new rustic tribes had been created, to reach the figure of thirty-five tribes, which never varied thereafter.

One of the characteristics of this territory was that it had been formed by the annexation of some of the peoples and cities subdued in earlier periods. The situation which, for the Romans, defined the connection between a city they had defeated and themselves was in fact determined by the relationship termed *deditio in fidem*. The conquered people yielded to the victors and authorized them to make use of their possessions and men. Sometimes, as in the instance of Capua or the Mamertines, this act of yielding power could be made by a state which was in no way at war with Rome but simply wished to place itself under Roman protection. Theoretically, power thus conceded knew no limits. One might even imagine it could go as far as the total destruction of the city if the victor thought it a good thing. That was not the case, however. Most often the *deditio* was met by a *receptio in fidem*. The Senate or magistrate who happened to be dealing with the vanquished, depending on whether or not they had fought savagely, whether or not they constituted a threat, or depending on the value of their territory, adopted different attitudes ranging from complete incorporation to keeping the city in its former state, but henceforth bound by a treaty (*foedus*).

In all cases, the city that remained found itself subject to both Roman authority and Roman protection: authority, because it was indebted to Rome's generosity for its continued existence and therefore owed obedience, and protection, because in receiving the vanquished city as a dependant Rome had committed itself to keeping it alive. The connection between the two partners thus borrowed its fundamental features from the relationship of *fides* that linked the patron and his client or the master and his freedman. Often, once the booty and slaves were sold, part of the lands confiscated to the profit of the *ager publicus*, i.e. the public domain of the Roman people, the conquered city was maintained in its general framework, but depopulated and impoverished.

When they were annexed, city-states nevertheless retained a certain autonomy. They kept their magistrates and institutions, but lost the attributes of independece, and chiefly the possibility of entering into relations with other peoples when important issues were to be tackled. Their inhabitants of course received Roman citizenship but, with a few exceptions, not the right to vote; this meant that they were burdened with all the fiscal and military charges while at the same time losing any chance of having some say in possible decision-making. They were designated by the term *municipium*, which in the strict sense meant that the members of the community (*municipes*) took their share of the collective expenses (*munus*).[2]

The lands that had been confiscated obviously did not stay unused. Frequently, though not systematically, they were granted individually (*viritim*) to citizens of properly Roman origin who had settled in the territory of the defeated peoples. In this way groups of Roman citizens with full rights appeared in Italy (*conventus civium romanorum*). Sometimes, too, small settlements (*fora*) were created by the Roman authority, particularly when roads were being built. These small townships were added to the civic frameworks already in existence, without in any way forming city-states in the fullest sense.[3] Other citizens were mingled with the rest of the population. For this heterogeneous population it was necessary to increase the number of rustic tribes and, above all, to create special administrative and legal arrangements, since people were too distant from Rome to be able to turn to the capital city's magistrates. The praetor would then appoint prefects who came to ensure that judicial functions were put into operation on the spot.

Needless to say, this kind of duality could not last very long. A blending process took place between the Italian and Roman groups, bringing in its wake occurrences of acculturation, and legal and political integration: Romanization in both senses of the word. Eventually, by being registered in the tribes and by individual or collective concession of the right to vote, the citizens of the *municipia* who had no right of suffrage became true Roman citizens. They kept their civic background, however, their own city with its specific religious and institutional features, so that while they now participated fully in the community of Roman citizens, they preserved in part their old identity.[4]

The town of Capua was a fine example of this type of Italian city. In 343 it had given itself up to the Romans by *deditio* then, several years later, it became a *municipium* whose inhabitants held Roman citizenship *sine suffragio*. It thus preserved its own magistrates, the *meddices*, and to some extent its identity. It therefore had its own political life, and it would seem right that its inhabitants could not take part in Roman elections. As its soldiers were Roman citizens, they were mobilized in Rome's service, but probably remained in autonomous units, like the *legio Campana* which was posted to the garrison at Reggio in 282. Roman authority prevailed, however, as is shown in an allusion made by Livy to an intervention in the city's legislation[5] by the praetor in 318, or above all the same episode of the *legio Campana*. The crime commited by the soldiers when they massacred the inhabitants of Reggio was in fact suppressed by Roman magistrates. But their execution drew a protest from a tribune of the plebs who saw it as an attack on the right of *provocatio*, which authorized any citizen threatened with capital punishment to make an appeal to the people.[6] In the end links were gradually created between the populations of the two cities, as is suggested by those matrimonial alliances attested by our sources, between the family of the Pacuvii Calavii of Capua and those of the Claudii Purchri and Livii Salinatores in Rome.[7]

This policy of incorporation was followed as long as the process of conquest affected regions near to Rome. But it ceased to be suitable when Rome's domination extended beyond central Italy. It was in fact abandoned in the third century, and from then on, if Roman supremacy was to be ensured reliance had to be placed, on one hand, on colonies founded in conquered territories, and on the other, on the obedience and loyalty of allied city-states.

The colonies were purely the creation of Roman authority. The settling of colonists (*deductio*) was carried out in accordance with a precise procedure: a commission of three Roman magistrates dealt with the division of the territory intended for the new city, which was taken from land confiscated from some conquered people. Plots of land were then demarcated and allocated to the new inhabitants.[8] The first colonies had been founded in the fourth century. A distinction was made between those which were composed of Roman citizens and those of citizens with Latin rights.

In the first instance, as their name implies, the inhabitants were citizens who enjoyed their full rights, civic and political, but formed a new community outside Rome's territory. These colonies were few in number and not highly populated. The number of colonists remained very low, generally about 300, plus the members of their families. The plots of land were meagre (between half and one hectare), but the income they produced was probably complemented by the possibility of access to communal funds. It is also true that the colonists preserved all their possessions and rights in Rome[9] and that, when these foundations were originally conceived, it was probably not considered that they should have their own magistrates.[10]

The policy guiding the settlement of these colonies was not, in fact, to turn them into centres of population. Until the end of the third century they had all been set up along the coasts and were called maritime colonies. Ostia was a good example. It had been created early in the fourth century.[11] The plan of the original foundation may still be seen in the urban layout: it was hardly more than a rectangular *castrum*, about 200 by 125 metres, divided into four quarters by the intersection of the two main roads, with very modest buildings, since extremely little has survived. These colonies were, in fact, merely tiny settlements, without proper municipal organization, whose function was essentially military, guarding Roman territory on the coast.

In contrast, the colonies known as Latin were much more important foundations. Unlike the colonies of citizens, their inhabitants did not enjoy Roman rights, but a status sometimes called *isopoliteia* which allowed them civil rights (*commercium* and *conubium*) in common with the Romans, but not political rights. Nevertheless they were able to vote in Rome during the *Comitia tributa* by adding their vote to those of a tribe chosen at random, to settle there and have themselves included in the census as citizens (*ius migrationis*).

In fact they had the status formerly enjoyed by inhabitants of the cities of Latium which together with Rome formed the Latin League.[12] Naturally, these cities preserved their autonomy in relation to one another by maintaining for their citizens the possibility of having private connections, even of settling in the neighbouring town. They had also together founded cities which had spontaneously assumed the rights they shared in common. The Latin League had been dissolved in the fourth century and the cities it comprised had been annexed by Rome. But the earlier status lingered on, with the double advantage that it defined their joint civil ties and showed political separateness, and created cities whose inhabitants had all the attributes of being Roman, but without the civic rights.

Latin colonies were thus both more numerous and more populated. Between 2,000 and 6,000 colonists were settled in this way on lands confiscated from defeated peoples. For the most part they were Roman citizens who gave up their political rights in exchange for slightly larger plots of land than those given to colonies of citizens, as they ranged from 16 to 40 *jugera* (4 to 10 hectares). It would not have been possible to distribute these to them if they had preserved their original status without the risk of altering their tax-rating qualification and thus the political equilibrium obtaining in Rome. The status conferred by Latin rights allowed the trouble-free creation of communities where these former citizens found the means of living and self-administration at the same time.

They formed real civic communities, enjoying institutions inspired by Roman models, a people's assembly organized in voting units, a senate and magistrates. The hierarchy prevailing in Rome was reproduced there. When the settlement was being prepared, a distinction was made between footsoldiers and horsemen, with larger plots being allocated to the latter so that they would form the aristocracy of the new city. Thus it happened that they were given the name *socii* (allies), for as such these colonies had to participate in any Roman war effort by providing troops. They had, moreover, been founded throughout the conquests of Italy and marked a stage in Roman expansion, because in each case they bordered on conquered lands, to some extent enfolding into their network the territory of the erstwhile enemy. Like the citizens' colonies, they served to maintain Roman domination. Together they formed what Cicero called the *propugnacula imperii*, the 'bastions of the empire'.[13]

But their role was not only defensive. Because they were true foundations, they introduced into the Italian world the ideal image of the Roman town, as it was thought of in the third century. Three examples give us a good idea of it: Alba Fucens for the Marsi, Cosa in southern Etruria, and Paestum in Lucania, where the colony was implanted in the very heart of the Greek town of Poseidonia. The fundamental features of a city were in each instance preserved: the defence wall, a network of orthogonal streets marking out the various quarters, the temples, notably the Capitol, which housed the community's tutelary deities, and the forum which gave the citizens somewhere to assemble. This last, in particular, was arranged so that all the strictly Roman political rituals could be observed. It comprised several public buildings, a *curia* for example, which enabled the senate to meet, as well as a *comitium*, i.e. a circular area surrounded by steps on which the citizens could assemble and hear the magistrates; and in the ground positions were prepared for the barriers which, at times of electoral *comitia*, would be used to separate the voting units among which the citizens were divided.[14]

Colonies thus integrated within themselves people who did not all share the same origins. Certainly, most were composed of Roman citizens, but others might be settled with them: citizens who until then had only had citizenship without suffrage, and who had been enrolled among recently annexed peoples, or a few individuals who had emerged from former local communities. The conditions of recruitment were certainly fixed by the law or senatorial decree arranging the foundation of the colony. The choice of colonists itself depended on the magistrates responsible for the *deductio*. In this, they followed Rome's general political interests, but also their own, benefiting and expanding their clientele among the Roman citizens or indigenous inhabitants. They also took account of the status of the beneficiaries and would not lightly grant Roman citizenship to those who lacked it.[15] But all in all, a certain diversity came to light in these new cities, and mingled in a communal life individuals who were certainly not far removed from one another, but who blended their original features and unified them into a voluntary and ideal 'Roman-ness'.

In their turn, these new communities spread their influence over neighbouring regions which they helped to Romanize. In the fabric of Italian populations they cut out little islands of Roman-ness. So city-states appeared in regions which as yet knew only organization by *pagi* and *vici*.[16] Besides, Romans or inhabitants of Latium brought their language and all the features that defined a particular way of life; craftsmen especially, who through the articles they made introduced their techniques and tastes to societies which hitherto had been subject to other influences.[17]

In this way they replaced and Romanized old local communities which had been conquered and subdued, their lands confiscated, or which quite simply had been impoverished. It might be imagined that these populations had been destroyed or displaced, but most often they had not disappeared. They were associated willy-nilly with the newcomers in a relationship of cohabitation which varied according to circumstances. If the colony was settled directly on the same site, some rare inhabitants might perhaps be registered on the list of new citizens, but usually they remained where they were, probably organized but without voting rights, most likely with the status of simple residents, with the result that the same town might house two communities.[18] In such a case the two groups would ultimately combine in the space of a few generations. But even when towns were founded near former cities, the latter, rivalled and smothered, also ended by being absorbed in the Roman model.

The other cities and peoples who lived apart from this territorial whole kept their own identity and, as they were neither Romans nor enemies, were of necessity allies. Their relations with Rome were established by treaty (*foedus*), some on terms of equality (*foedus aequum*). These had always been friendly, though they were few in number; they included Camerinum, Heraclea and Naples. The rest, almost all the peoples and cities of Italy, were former defeated enemies whose relations were established on an unequal footing (*foedus iniquum*). The distinction was probably more symbolic than actual, for Rome's position did not allow any real show of independence. All had to contribute to the Roman war effort, the maritime states by fitting out ships, and the rest by making contributions of men and money which were regulated according to a list of each one's capabilities, known as the *formula togatorum*, which allowed overall requirements to be apportioned in the event of mobilization.[19]

In the peninsula, the Italians dealt directly with the Senate. But in the islands, Sicily, Sardinia and Corsica, things were different: Roman magistrates resided there permanently. At first they were probably former consuls or praetors whose command was extended for the occasion, then from 227 two praetors, one for Sicily, the other for Sardinia and Corsica, who regularly succeeded one another. They exercised the *imperium*, set out the law, gave judgement, commanded troops and presided over relations with local cities and populations, checking that they were properly conforming to the terms of the treaties. The term *provincia*, which originally designated the sphere of competence in which their authority lay, thus came to assume the sense of a geographic zone.

Roman rule in Italy was organized in two concentric wholes. In the centre was the *ager romanus* of the thirty-five tribes with which were mingled the territories of cities and peoples who had received citizenship without suffrage and were gradually integrated into this first ensemble. On the periphery there were a few Roman colonies, but more often Latin colonies or allied cities which, despite their autonomy, could not choose their alliances and were obliged to contribute to the Roman war effort. The nerve channels of the whole body were the roads connecting Rome to Brindisi in the south of the peninsula and to Rimini on the Adriatic, at the edge of the Po Valley.

Roman power at the end of the third century was therefore considerable. Polybius gave figures concerning the mobilization effected in 225 to counter the danger from the Gauls: the Romans had engaged more than 200,000 men, three-quarters of whom were supplied by the allies, and still had at their disposal a reserve of over 300,000 men. And in this total only the peoples of the centre of the peninsula were taken into account, excepting the Bruttii, the Greeks and, of course, the populations of the isalands. There was something extraordinary about these figures: they meant that Rome had already reached and even surpassed the greatest Hellenistic powers of the time.

Rome in the Third Century

This transformation of Italy into a general state broadly capable of rivalling the greatest kingdoms was certainly accompanied by a parallel development in the city of Rome, which had assumed some of the features that defined the cities of the Greek world at the time.

The town itself had in fact attained a size that placed it on a par with the most important of them. The defence wall, incorrectly called the 'Servian wall', which had enclosed it since 378 at the latest, embraced an area of over 400 hectares. The population it sheltered probably numbered some 200,000 inhabitants in the late third century.[20] Beginnning at the end of the fourth century, construction work had been carried out, first by the censor Appius Claudius Caecus, who had built the first aqueduct in 312; then a second had been made in 272 by M. Curius Dentatus. It was a matter of responding to the large increase in the population. Temples had been erected; the forum had been embellished. On the north side, the *comitium* had been built, allowing the citizens to assemble when summoned by the magistrates. Shops and large public buildings, *atria*, bordered it. Italy's capital was also one of the Mediterranean world's major cities.

Needless to say, all this matched a general development of Roman society. Rome similarly benefited from its important economic sphere of influence. It had opened out to the rest of the Mediterranean world and thus took part in a cultural *koine* which extended over the central part of the peninsula and testified to close contacts with Greater Greece and Sicily. The population as a whole had adopted Greek tastes and sensibilities: gods had been introduced, and theatrical and literary forms of expression had made their appearance. The aristocracy had been the principal agent in this process in which it had become completely involved, to the point where the very functioning of the state had also been affected by these changes.

Rome in this period was in fact a city that both imported and exported articles made by craftsmen. All the pottery produced at that time in Italy, notably in Etruria and southern Italy, is represented in the archaeological material that has been brought to light. Similarly, articles produced in Rome had been discovered in the rest of Italy.[21] Remember, in particular, the products of what has been called 'L'atelier des petites estampilles', with its truly remarkable quality. These were spread over a region with Rome at its centre and extending from Campania to the Adriatic and north of Etruria, and beyond as far as the east coast of Corsica, Liguria, the coasts of the Gulf of Lions and the territories dominated by Carthage.[22] But to this fist example could be added the *pocula*, which were most often goblets inscribed with the name of a deity; the design and decorative style of these objects belonged to the same artistic unity in which Roman society was completely involved.[23]

On a par with all these events, it was the development of the use of money that showed the share taken by the city of Rome in trade as a whole, including economic and cultural exchanges, in the Mediterranean world. The process occurred in several stages. Initially, the late fourth century saw the appearance of coinage minted in centres in Campania. The subjects, symbols and style of these coins were very similar to those of the Greek cities' money, which had long been in circulation in southern Italy. Later, probably dating from the war against Pyrrhus, a permanent currency was established, for a time borrowing the Greek units of measurement and value, before the appearance during the second Punic War of the specifically Roman system of the denarius, which fixed equivalents between coins in bronze, silver and gold. Of course, new coins, especially silver ones, were struck in response to the needs of war; the troops had to be paid and provisions secured.[24] But for the Romans each step in this development meant progress in setting up an autonomous monetary policy. They were becoming increasingly integrated into the Mediterranean world as a whole, more especially with the Greek cities of southern Italy and Sicily, from a variety of aspects, obviously economic though that was not the fruit of a conscious policy, but mainly cultural and political, since by stamping the coins with their own sign they took their place among the powers whose symbols circulated in the Mediterranean world.

In this way Roman society from then on infiltrated the entire Hellenized world of that period, yet retained its own personality, the more so because the Italian Hellenism in which it participated possessed its own particular features.

An episode reported by Pliny the Elder gives us some idea of the situation. He noted in fact that 'statues had been erected to Pythagoras and Alcibiades at the corners of the *Comitium*, when the Pythian Apollo, during the Samnite War (probably the third), was said to have commanded the dedication in a public place of a statue to the bravest of the Greeks and another to the wisest.'[25] In this affair, the Senate had addressed itself directly to the oracle at Delphi. The relationship was very old, probably dating to the early fourth century, and clearly showed that the Roman world belonged to the overall Greek world, regarded in its broadest sense. But the models of courage and wisdom chosen made sense only in an Italian context since they in fact corresponded to the political and intellectual history of Syracuse and Tarentum. It must be borne in mind that this Hellenism, in which third-century Rome joined, was the special and regional manifestation of a much vaster phenomenon whose centres of influence lay in the capitals of Hellenistic rulers.

Religion may provide the occasion for an initial series of comments. The list of cults introduced to Rome during the century, or to which new temples were consecrated, reveals a whole range of alterations in the religious manifestations of the time. Deities associated with victory, such as Bellona Victrix (in 296), Jupiter Victor (in 295) or Victory herself in (294) made their appearance: this innovation is quite rightly compared with the contemporary development of the same themes in the Greek world. Moreover, in 293 the god Asclepius himself was solemnly brought from Epidaurus to Rome. In this instance the relationship was direct. Gods from vanquished cities or peoples were 'evoked': Vortumnus-Voltumna from Etruria (in 264) or Minerva Capta from Falerii (in 241). Others who belonged to the traditional pantheon or, more precisely, moral entities, such as Spes, Honos (in 234), Concordia (in 217), Mens (in 217) and Virtus (in 208), received temples and became real deities identified as such, as if by giving them a temple, a statue, and thus an image, the Romans, following the example of the Hellenistic world, felt the need to actualize such concepts.[26]

Similarly, forms of artistic expression henceforth took their inspiration directly from the Hellenistic art of the period. The successful wars against the Greek cities of Italy and Sicily had certainly contributed to this development in taste, and works of art had indeed been brought back as booty. Such had been the case, notably, in the triumphs that followed the defeat of Pyrrhus and the capture of Tarentum, as well as the later victory of Claudius Marcellus, conqueror of Syracuse, which enabled him to adorn Rome's temples. But this explanation if far from adequate. The phenomenon of Hellenization had not waited for the end of the third century, nor was it confined to the pure and simple import of models which were reproduced after they had been admired. Its scope was quite different and ranged through all levels of society, which benefited from increasing exchanges and appropriated these new forms of expression while at the same time adapting them to their own taste.

Among other aesthetic examples of this assimilation, I must mention the magnificent bronze head, said to be of Brutus, which was probably part of a larger statue, dated to the third century. What other significance can it have but that the Roman aristocracy, desirous of preserving the images of its ancestors, had henceforth found the way of representing its aspirations by a technique of expression which was Greek in origin but which Rome had perfectly mastered? But it would probably be better to linger over more modest objects, mainly terracotta ex-votos, which reveal the tastes and sensibilities of the ordinary people. These were frequently heads of men or women, or statuettes which were for the most part feminine. Even if the execution was far from perfect, all of them fitted in perfectly with a Hellenistic tradition that associated rather clear-cut features with elongated body forms imbued with a vague pathos. Although we may imagine that the craftsmen who designed the moulds may have been Greeks, free or slaves, coming willingly or under duress to settle in Rome, we have to admit that such objects came up to the expectations of the city's inhabitants.[27]

In this context, we must also consider innovations of a literary nature. They too matched a change in sensibilities and expectations affecting Roman society as a whole.

It is symptomatic that the person responsible for the greatest changes in this field should have been a Tarentine, L. Livius Andronicus, who had come to Rome as a slave, probably when his town was captured. Freed by his master, he had opened a school, where he taught in both languages. We are chiefly indebted to him for translating the *Odyssey* into Latin, and introducing Greek-style drama in the form of a *fabula* which was performed for the young Romans of 240. He went on to write other works, a few comedies but, above all, tragedies, most of which borrowed their plots from Greek themes and most particularly from the Trojan cycle. A little later, at the end of the century, another author, Cn. Naevius, appeared and followed this initial trend. He was originally from Campania, one of the most Hellenized parts of Italy and, like Livius Andronicus, offered the Roman public plays with subjects drawn from the same repertoire: the tragedies favoured Homeric themes, and the comedies were inspired by Greek models. But he stood out because, to our knowledge, he was the first to offer a new type of tragedy, the *fabulae praetextae*, in which events from Roman history were celebrated.[28]

A process of appropriation had therefore taken place. The games, those collective demonstrations in which the civic community gathered to honour the gods and manifest its unity, were arranged around the celebration of events borrowed from the founding myths of Hellenism, and secondly to some extent of events which were its own. Thanks to the myths of Aeneas, the Romans had in fact long regarded themselves as full-fledged members of the line of Homer's heirs, and sought in this new form of literary expression confirmation of an identity which ranked them among the supporters of civilizing powers.

In the late third century, while belonging to the Hellenistic group of that period, Rome preserved its originality. In fact, it would seem that the forms of artistic expression borrowed from the Greek world had served only to make manifest aspirations that were deeply rooted in Roman civic reality: the bust said to be of Brutus offered a Roman senator for admiration, and it could not have been confused with a Hellenistic ruler. And if Homer was so much appreciated, it was also because in his verses people could find roots that were undoubtedly Trojan.

The Role and Place of the Aristocracy

Within Roman society, the aristocracy played the leading role in this process. Between the end of the fourth century and the beginning of the third it was transformed.

Previously, it had been split by the conflict that set patricians against plebeians. The difference between the two social categories lay mainly in the gentilitial organization of society and the fact that the patricians had the monopoly of magistracies and priesthoods. In fact, they possessed all the instruments that allowed the exercise of power: they were able to set forth the standards of law and command the other citizens (the *imperium*), and they could maintain the goodwill of the gods by observing the signs they sent and by celebrating in suitable fashion the sacrifices intended for them. The rebellion of the plebians had manifested itself in secessions which had led to the creation of their own civic officials: their magistrates, the tribunes of the plebs and plebeian aediles; their assemblies, the plebeian councils; and their laws, the plebiscites. From then on there were two states within the city of Rome, one of the People and the other of the Plebs, each having its own institutions. During the fourth century this dualism had begun to soften, in that the patricians were no longer the only ones with access to the senior magistracies. But it finally lost its importance early in the third century, when in 300 the *lex Ogulnia* opened up the highest priesthoods to the plebeians and, around 286, the *lex Hortensia* rendered plebiscites applicable to the whole of the people.

This development coincided with the appearance of a new aristocracy comprising members of both the patriciate and the plebs. Within this new dominant class, distinctions no longer rested on belonging to this or that *gens*, and therefore on birth, but on position in the state. The latter was not arbitrarily defined, but was fixed by censors who regularly recomposed the civic body by placing each citizen in its various units, the tribes which defined its territorial organization and the centuries which were arranged in hierarchies according to the different classes of property qualification for tax purposes. It was therefore wealth and especially land ownership that merited inclusion in the first class.

This criterion was not exclusive. Worthiness and respectability were equally taken into account. It was probably this period that saw the structuring of rituals, such as funerals and triumphs, that enabled people to show the entire city the marks of prestige and influence they had acquired.[29] Thus the distinctions began to appear which, within the eighteen centuries known as equestrian from which senators were usually recruited, could or could not afford access to power. Three groupings were defined, somewhat by default, and they found more precise definitions during the following period: at the summit were the nobles, known as this because one of their ancestors had held a curule magistracy; then the senators, who were not nobles, and lastly the knights, who were not senators and held no magistracies.

I will not review here all the qualitites that defined worthiness or merit (*dignitas*) and justified membership of the aristocracy that governed the state. Let us say simply that they were assessed in terms of charisma and included the prestige attached to the exercise of priesthoods, the knowledge and interpretation of the law, and military command that brought victory. But they were also measured against the yardstick of a social power dependent on the relative size of the network of clients available to each man. Patronage was, in fact, one of the most important social institutions in ancient Rome. This term meant the relationship that linked two individuals of unequal rank, the more powerful protecting the weaker and obtaining every possible advantage for him, while the latter made some return for these benefits by a gratitude that meant readiness to be of service and availability at all times. Such attachments were evidence of the aristocracy's influence in society and, above all, allowed the setting up of an efficient network of dependants and political agents.

The third century had without any doubt provided this new aristocracy with many opportunities of simultaneously increasing its economic wealth and its social power.

Research being carried out on amphorae leads us to suppose that after the first Punic War certain regions of Italy experienced a perceptible development in speculative agriculture, in particular viticulture. Some of these, called 'Graeco-Italic' have in fact enabled numerous workshops in Campania, Latium, and southern Etruria to be identified. They were most often situated near coasts, allowing the wine produced in these regions to be exported. They were also found at points on the Adriatic coast, in Cisalpine Gaul, and the Languedoc.[30] The Roman world's increased opening up to the rest of the Mediterranean, and the establishment of Roman rule over Italy and the islands were also revealed in social changes.

The aristocrats had become aware of new opportunities of acquiring greater wealth being presented to them. Indeed, probably taking their inspiration from Sicilian examples, they were the ones who set up on their domains the first villas intended to produce and sell goods whose commercialization would allow them to grow rich. But this situation was worrying, because there was a danger that they might abandon their traditional duties of protection and assistance, which called for a certain disinterestedness, to the extent that in 220–218 a law, the Claudian plebiscite, prohibited senators from owning ships capable of carrying a cargo of over 300 amphorae. No one wanted them to become purely traders.

Similarly, the members of this aristocracy were the chief agents in the process of opening up to the Hellenistic world. In their capacity as magistrates, it was they who took responsibility for introducing a god, celebrating this or that festival, or constructing this or that type of building, but by their behaviour or the display of their tastes it was also they who set new standards.

Two examples could be mentioned, which were characteristic of the cultural state of third-century Roman aristocracy. The first is a funerary painting adorning the tomb of one Fabius, perhaps Q. Fabius Rullianus, five times consul and triumphant victor, who lived at the end of the fourth century. It revealed the compostion and style of those paintings from Samnite Campania showing the power and glory of warriors, but with a quality which at the time had almost no equivalent.[31] The other, a trifle later, is the sarcophagus of L. Cornelius Scipio Barbatus, who was censor around 280. The designs which decorate it were borrowed from the world of Greater Greece and fitted in with a conception of the tomb which recalled that of the founding heroes.[32] Henceforth these aristocrats used Greek models to inspire the plastic arts they employed to demonstrate their own power. To the richness of their tombs was added the custom they adopted during the third century of erecting statues and monuments commemorating victories, also of representing in paintings the important moments of a campaign; all practices which, like the triumph and funeral rituals, firmly implanted the legitimacy of their authority in the collective memory.[33]

The enrichment of the aristocracy was not measured only in terms of gains obtained by way of changes in agriculture and commercial development. Its power was also connected with the number and importance of those under its protection.

The widening of Roman domination was perforce accompanied by an increase in the networks of 'clients', first in Rome itself, where the population had swollen. On pain of becoming isolated, these newcomers needed the protection of a patron to represent them and defend them in all those situations where the backing of a powerful personage was necessary, but chiefly in the rest of Italy, and from two aspects.

The defeated who gave themselves up to the *fides* of the Roman people did so through the intermediary of the magistrate who had just won. By accepting the *deditio*, he quite naturally became the mediator who represented to the Senate the cause of those who had trusted him, and from that time on he took a hand in all matters that concerned them. If one thinks of the extent and size of the conquests accomplished by Rome during the third century, it is easy to imagine what gains in

BELLEVUE UNIVERSITY LIBRARY

clientelae the aristocracy had been able to obtain over that period.

The other means by which members of the aristocracy won themselves large clienteles in Italy was specifically the process that had been established of creating city-states. In fact, each time a colony was founded, all the recipients of a plot of land and the corresponding status became the clients of the magistrate who carried out the *deductio* and thus granted them a recognized place in the new community as well as supposedly improved living conditions. Generally speaking, however, the establishment of Roman rule over the whole of Italy and the neighbouring islands forced all these populations to have dealings with the Senate and the Roman magistrates who governed them. The rules of law or fact that these authorities followed were completely their own and it was quite out of the question that all these peoples of Italy, whose culture and traditions were often different, could manage without intermediaries to represent and protect them, in short, to exert all the pressures needed to avoid the harm that the exercise of a discretionary power was always likely to provoke.

In all these aspects, the Roman aristocracy lived through a period of great expansion and the broadening of its power, matched also by a certain modification of the ways in which political life functioned.

At that time the institutional structures of the city quite simply reflected the growth of Roman domination. Conquered territories needed to be governed, and the increase in population and intensification of trade had to be faced. New praetors were created. In 242, one of these was appointed to take care of jurisdiction over affairs concerning foreigners in Rome and their relations with Roman citizens; two others were appointed for Sicily and Sardinia in 227, when those islands began to be governed through regular magistrates. And the number of their assistants was increased, whether they were prefects representing them in Italy, where Roman citizens were to benefit by administration, or *triumviri capitales* (superintendents of public prisons and executions), created in 290 to supervise day-to-day penal law, which probably grew more burdensome because of the increase in population. The number of quaestors was similarly increased by the creation of two for Rome and two others for the provinces. And, as if all that were not enough, it began to be the custom to extend the *imperium* of consuls and praetors leaving office in

order to entrust them with command duties in the various military operations which were being conducted.

In parallel, measures were introduced into the organization of civic life which tended to regularize it. The centurial arrangement was adapted to the new situation in which the state found itself. The greater importance of transferable capital[34] was taken into account and the system of centuries was adapted to that of the tribes. The number of the latter had grown, in fact, as Roman citizens had been installed in the various conquered parts of Italy. In 241 it had reached thirty-five, and was not subsequently altered. By fixing the number of centuries of the first class at seventy, two centuries were thus allocated to each tribe, one of *juniores* and the other of *seniores*, and to some extent the electoral map of the principal voters followed the lines of regional solidarities. All this tended towards the preservation of the interests of the aristocracy who relied precisely on these centuries of the first class,[35] but also towards a better control of the regions of Italy, as well as a rationalization of civic life, as if the entire state were adapting to its new context.

Generally speaking, it would appear that political life during the third century was not marked by any major internal conflict. The periods of war had probably proved relatively testing times for Roman society, but the resulting expansion certainly compensated for the losses and difficulties. The foundation of colonies and concession of lands had eased social tensions, wherever necessary. The development of trade, at least at the beginning of the century, had brought a certain amount of prosperity. The aristocracy had benefited from the new situation and a certain equilibrium had been achieved, which had contributed to the setting up of new rules for the functioning of the state

In the same way, relations between Rome and the other peoples and cities of Italy found their definitive organization in the hierarchy of status and duties ranging from total integration to alliance with respect for self-government. Common communication had been established in the sharing of Hellenistic cultural features which, to varying degrees, henceforth belonged to the peoples of central and southern Italy and of Sicily. At the end of the third century, neither the city of Rome nor the empire it headed lacked power or cohesion. The aristocracy which governed this fine ensemble was determined. Hannibal, who arrived in Italy at that time, would be able to put it to the test.

3

HANNIBAL IN ITALY: CONSEQUENCES OF THE SECOND PUNIC WAR

There is no need here to refer to the causes of the second Punic War. The question is much debated and, in any case, pointless. Although the fate of Italy was at stake in this episode, it was only because in the autumn of 218 Hannibal descended on the Po Valley at the head of the army he had brought with him across the Alps. At that time, the whole system of alliances and solidarities that Rome had formed around itself was threatened. Hannibal's ambition had probably never been to destroy Carthage's rival which, in any case, he did not really seek to capture, but to restore the power and field of influence of his own city over the western Mediterranean. For that all he needed was to overthrow Roman domination, ruin the bases of that territorial state and win for himself the loyalty of those he could wrest from the power of his enemy. Did he almost achieve this? Probably not. Following the defeat at Cannae, it is true, Roman rule wavered. But defections were limited and the majority of the allies remained loyal. And following its victory, Rome knew how to reward those who had kept faith.

It also knew how to punish betrayal. Operations had lasted over fifteen years, and the losses had been terrible. There had been moments of great anguish, and victory had been dearly won. Tensions and a spirit of revenge weighed heavily on relations between the Romans and their allies. Among those who defected, in fact, there were certainly the age-old enemies who had barely been subdued, such as the peoples of Cisalpine Gaul, but also *municipia* populated by Roman citizens, such as Capua. All would be treated as vanquished enemies; such harshness brought many consequences, concerning both demography and the organization of rural land, through losses, displacement of population and confiscations, and also involved the relations henceforth linking the population of Rome to unreliable and weakened Italians.

The War in Italy

Before analysing its consequences, let us take up the thread of events which, throughout Hannibal's war, caused so many upheavals in Italy.

In the autumn of 218, Hannibal arrived in Cisalpine Gaul. He was welcomed by some of the Gallic tribes, the Boii and the Insubres, who had just been quelled by the Romans and had not waited for his arrival before attacking the colonists installed that very year in Cremona and Piacenza and pursuing them as far as Modena, which they besieged.[1] He was therefore able to rebuild his army, after the losses he had suffered during the crossing of the Alps, and victoriously confront P. Cornelius Scipio's troops, which he defeated on the Trebbia. Even in these initial operations, he made quite obvious the strategy he intended to follow in order to bring down Roman rule.

Polybius indeed recounts that Hannibal had seized the town of Clastidium thanks to the treachery of the head of the garrison, originally from Brindisi, a Latin colony founded in 244. 'He at once made use of the wheat to feed his army and, as for the men who had fallen into his hands, he took them into his service without doing them the slightest harm. . . . He also granted great honours to the man who had handed the place over to him, in order to encourage men in positions of authority to side with the Carthaginians.'[2] Then, a little farther on:

While he overwintered in Cisalpine Gaul, Hannibal, who had taken Roman citizens among the prisoners, gave them rations with scrupulous fairness. As for those who belonged to nations allied with Rome, first he treated them with every consideration until the day when he assembled them to make a speech in which he said that he had come to make war not on them but on the Romans, and that they would consequently be acting wisely if they became his friends. His main aim, he said, was to restore liberty to the peoples of Italy and give them back possession of the towns and lands confiscated by the Romans. Then, having addressed them in this fashion, he sent all the prisoners home without ransom. By doing so he hoped to draw the Italian populations into his camp by detaching them from the Romans, and to push into rebellion those who considered that their cities and ports had suffered from Rome's domination.[3]

The danger to the Romans was considerable. As we have seen, even a leader from a Latin colony, that is, an individual belonging to the local aristocracy, who had obtained land in a city that had recently been founded and shared *isopoliteia* with Roman citizens, was capable of being tempted to betray. It meant that what was at stake in the ensuing operations was truly the preservation or collapse of Roman domination in Italy.

It is known that the first years of the war were catastrophic for Rome. In the spring of 217 Hannibal resumed his march towards the centre of the peninsula, then, some weeks later, crushed the Roman legions on the shore of Lake Trasimene in the dawn fog of a June day. During the period that followed he stormed through Italy, first eastward in Picenum, then following the Adriatic coast as far as Apulia, to turn back to the west in Campania. Needless to say, by following this course he gave himself the advantage of living off the resources of the Italian populations and forcing them either to rally to him or to oppose him, and thereby to have to fight him without in any way obtaining the assistance of a defeated Roman army which could only counter him with the tactics of Q. Fabius, sometimes called Cunctator ('the delayer'), precisely because he awaited his opportunity. The year 216 was nearly decisive. The Romans thought they could win in the battle they fought near Cannae, but they were massacred. Only then did Hannibal obtain the support he hoped for, and a large number of cities and peoples of southern Italy rallied to him.

Livy certainly gives a list of them, but it includes other defections which took place afterward: 'The Campanians, Atellani, Calatini, Hirpini, some of the Apulians, the Samnites with the exception of the Pentrians, all the Bruttians, the Lucanians, and the Uzentini besides, and nearly all the coast occupied by the Greek cities, the Tarentines, the Metapontines, the Crotoniates and the Locrians, and all the Gauls of the Cisalpine region.'[4] We should not imagine, however, that these decisions were easily taken by the leaders of those cities. The stakes were very high. On both sides the procedure was similar. Those who rallied and remained loyal were honoured and rewarded, but resistance and betrayal were ferociously punished. For instance, Hannibal deported the inhabitants of Herdonia, burned the town and executed the aristocrats who had dared to negotiate with the Romans, but the latter, in the course of a single campaign, killed or enslaved 25,000 Samnites, Lucanians and Apulians who had gone over to the adversary's side, though at a time when they would hardly have been capable of resisting.[5]

Among the arguments in favour of staying loyal to the Romans, there was, of course, the respect owed to former commitments, sometimes family ties which had had the opportunity and time to be established, and often a common adherence to the same civic and cultural entity, made all the stronger because Hannibal's armies also included Gallic contingents that repre-sented a fearsome enemy, one that had always been fought. But there was the certainty, too, that the Romans would remain in Italy when Hannibal departed and that their desire for revenge would then have to be reckoned with. It was therefore necessary for Hannibal to employ arguments other than those available to him from his position of force in order to win the support of those he wanted to carry with him. Among the conditions some cities laid down when they defected, some of the aspirations governing their choice were revealed.

In particular, the Capuans insisted 'that no Carthaginian commander or magistrate would have jurisdiction over a Campanian citizen, no Campanian citizen would be forced to serve in the war or bear any of the costs, and that Capua would have its own laws and its own magistrates'.[6] Such conditions made sense only when compared with those which Roman domi-nation meant to the Campanians. It was because they were citizens without the vote that the inhabitants of Capua had to obey Roman military leaders and participate in the military and fiscal charges on the city. They did not even have access to honours, although some of them were socially very close to the

Roman aristocracy. Livy cites the Romans' refusal to let them become magistrates as one of the causes of the betrayal.[7] But perhaps that was to anticipate the later situation in Italy, when precisely that demand lay at the origins of the Social War. At all events, however integrated they may have been in the Roman civic community, the Capuans preserved the memory of their erstwhile independence, longed for it, and saw in the Punic alliance the hope of regaining it and even, by this means, of achieving leadership over Italy.

With the obliteration, albeit temporary, of Roman domination, old lines of cleavage surfaced again, for example, between city and city. It is indeed probable that if Capua went over to Hannibal's side, Cumae and Naples had good reason to stay loyal to Rome. And if the Italiot states favoured the Romans, it was also because the Bruttians had become their enemies again.[8] It happened within states as well. Despite what the Latin historians say, especially Livy,[9] the lower classes were not at the root of the defection, but local aristocracies. In Capua, the town senators, Vibellius Taurea, Vibius Virrus and Pacuvius Calavius, the very one who was connected with the greatest families in Rome, were the organizers of the treachery. They were not alone; when the Romans recaptured the town, twenty-seven committed suicide while fifty-three let themselves be taken prisoner. Similarly, among the Bruttians, it was the noblest, Vibius and Paccius, who went over to Hannibal, or at Arpi, it was an aristocrat, Dasius Altinius, who dragged his city into the Carthaginian camp.[10] However, other aristocrats remained partisans of Rome and tried either to keep the communities they dominated toeing the line of loyalty, or to bring them back to it when Roman victories made such a course possible.

Here, for example, is what Appian says about Salapia:

> In the city of the Iapyges of Salapia, which was subject to the Africans [i.e. Carthaginians], there were two men who stood out from the rest by birth, wealth and power, but who had long been opposed to each other. Of the two, Dasius had sided with the Africans, Blatius with the Romans. While Hannibal's affairs prospered, Blatius kept himself apart; but when the Romans recovered and regained most of their power, Blatius made an effort to persuade his enemy to come to an understanding with him in order to protect his homeland, so that it should not fall victim to irrevocable harm if the Romans took it by force . . . [Dasius revealed the

plan to Hannibal, who after judgement acquitted Blatius, believing him to be the victim of Dasius' enmity] . . . Even after escaping trial, Blatius did not give up trying to make his enemy change sides, for he considered that the man had not kept his word. [A little later, he surrendered to Rome.] Having given his son as hostage to the Senate, he asked for a thousand horsemen, with whom he hastened as quickly as possible . . . [He then seized Salapia, massacred the small Carthaginian garrison, and waited there for Dasius who had fled to Hannibal's camp and obtained some troops, laid an ambush for him and killed him].[11]

This episode serves to reveal the mechanism of the divisions that influenced the cities of Italy which were caught up in the contradictory choices of the second Punic War. Old conflicts, which had long set rival factions or warring families against one another, resurfaced. The two foes, the Romans and Hannibal, obviously sought to take advantage of them to gain or keep control of the cities of Italy whose alliance was necessary to the success of their enterprise. When they chose their side, the local aristocrats were of course trying to maintain or regain domination over their own city. But all this did not take place without demonstrations of local cohesion, or mistrust between the chief protagonists and their allies. A new organization of government was being set up in the Italian cities: henceforth it increasingly relied on the power that possessed hegemony over the whole of Italy, and would delegate the means of exerting it to those who seemed to be its most trustworthy dependants. But that obviously brought about the resurgence of conflicts between simultaneous and sometimes contradictory solidarities, those of long standing and those which were dawning.

At all events, the years following the first period of Roman defeats were marked by a kind of jockeying for position between the two camps, during which the Romans gradually tried to take back from Hannibal the cities he had won, while at the same time other, no less important, operations were taking place in Spain.

Thus in 213 Arpi once more came under their domination, Capua in 211, Salapia in 210, Tarentum and part of Lucania in 209. In Sicily, in 211 they recaptured Syracuse which, after the death of Hieron in 215, had gone over to the Carthaginian side, and in 210 Agrigentum. In 207 in Picenum, on the Metaurus, they defeated Hasdrubal, Hannibal's brother, who was bringing reinforcements. In 206 they regained control of the whole of Lucania. In 205 it was the turn of Locris, then in 204 of Consentia and a large part of Bruttium. When Hannibal had to leave Italy in 203 to fight the threat which Scipio had succeeded in bringing to the gates of Carthage, he had lost everything that had made him dominant. The war continued, in fact, in Africa and was in essence over at the battle of Zama, in 202.

In the following years, however, the Romans undertook to reconquer the regions of Cisalpine Gaul that had eluded their rule throughout this period, adding all the mountains on the Ligurian coast which had hitherto not been subdued. They were lengthy and, in certain instances, difficult operations. The Gallic tribes, notably the Boii, who had supported Hannibal and could expect no mercy, fought on until 191, and the Ligures, who occupied virtually impregnable positions, held out until 172. Similarly, the putting down of the last rebellions in Sardinia and Corsica continued until 176 for the former and 173 for the latter.

The Roman Effort

For the Romans, espeacially when they were fighting Hannibal, the war years had been very difficult. They had had to mobilize many troops, collect large sums of money and confront with determination all the setbacks that had occurred. There remained a feeling of revenge which, once peace was re-established, could not fail to find expression.

Thanks to a few indications provided by census figures, which are nevertheless very hard to interpret, attempts have been made to assess what the demographic cost of this war meant to the Roman population. Total Roman losses had been quite considerable, in the region of 50,000 citizens,[12] and the consequences were certainly felt for a long time. For the moment, however, difficulties were chiefly concerned with recruitment. Requirements in terms of men were very large. The Roman legions still comprised between 50,000 and 80,000 men. And it may be supposed that, with the defection of southern Italy, the share taken by allies in the overall strength of the armies was declining. It was therefore necessary to place an increased burden on those who had stayed loyal, and in Rome itself to go outside the normal rules of recruitment: not to take account of the conditions of property qualification or, the sign of an extreme situation, to mobilize slaves to form rowing crews for the navy or even to make them fight as infantry (the *volones*) in return for a promise of emancipation.[13]

Financial difficulties were no less heavy, in the face of considerable needs. It is estimated that the war might have cost around 4.5 million *denarii* per annum – a sum that could not be supplied from taxes, although they had been increased, or from booty. Money was thus devalued, the relationship between precious metals was altered – it was then that the system of the *denarius* appeared – and gold coinage was struck, a measure practised in exceptional circumstances. There was borrowing, from Hieron of Syracuse, from the tax-gatherers, who were asked to make advances, from the owners of slaves, who were required to supply them for the army and continue to pay for their unkeep, from all senators and knights, who were invited to give gold, silver and jewels. Lastly, large portions of the *ager publicus* were sold off.[14]

The entire population was affected by the crisis situation in which Rome found itself. Anxiety surfaced everywhere, as the religious life of the city during those years bears witness. The number of prodigies rose continually, and with them the consultation of the Sibylline Books. After Cannae, and also after the supposed incest of two Vestals, resort was made to an extremely rare practice envisaged only in the case of tremendous threat: a Greek couple and a Gallic couple were buried alive in the Forum Boarium. New religious practices were called upon, especially the *ludi Apollinares*, which were introduced after consultation with the oracle at Delphi, and above all the cult of Cybele, which in many aspects remained very foreign to Roman standards yet was installed even within the *pomoerium*.

In the general climate of tension, however, the aristocracy had to shoulder special responsibilities. In this period it still formed the part of the entire civic community most able to be mobilized and taxed. It also found itself subjected to a kind of very strong moral pressure which impelled it to cohesiveness and resolution. Several examples bear witness. As was their role, the censors, especially those of 214, punished those who had failed in courage, notably those who after Cannae had contemplated leaving Italy, or the knights who had avoided being enlisted.[15] The tribunes of the plebs, moreover, used their office to support the war effort instead of challenging the Senate's authority,[16] as was customary. The times did not allow even symbolic forms of conflict to divide the city. Laws also appeared, aiming to maintain the aristocracy in its traditional role. I have already mentioned the Claudian plebiscite of 220–218, which prevented senators from becoming shipowners. But others might well be cited, such as the *lex Oppia* of 215, which restricted luxury in clothing and domestic articles, or the *leges Publicia de cereis* of 209 and *Cincia de donis et muneribus* of 204, which regulated the relationship of patronage by limiting the size of gifts that clients might give their patrons; as if, in this period of troubles and dangers, it was feared that not every person would play the role assigned to him in the state.

Needless to say, the attitude of the Italians created another cause for worry. Hannibal controlled the south of the peninsula and, with the exception of Cisalpine Gaul, the north did not defect. That possiblity was nevertheless feared, as is shown by the fact that from 212 to 200 two legions were maintained in Etruria, and by the measures taken in 209 concerning the city of Arezzo, where potential treason was suspected.[17]

At Arezzo, 'Hostilius immediately brought a legion into the town . . . made the senators come to the Forum, and demanded hostages. When the senate asked for two days in which to deliberate, he declared that they were to be handed over at once or that the next day he would take all the senators' children; then he commanded the tribunes, prefects of the allies, and centurions to guard the gates.' Seven senators managed to flee. 'The next day, when their absence was noted their possessions were confiscated; 120 hostages were taken from among the other senators, their own children who were handed over to C. Terentius to be taken to Rome.'[18]

Anxiety was great, therefore. The Senators of Arezzo might even be said to be lucky. Elsewhere, at Nola or Enna in Sicily, whole populations were massacred for fear that they would turn traitor. Similar testimony is given by the action taken when, also in the year 209, twelve Latin colonies announced that it was impossible for them to meet the demands of mobilization.

'When the consuls had in turn argued at length,' Livy recounts,

the envoys, who had remained unshaken, replied that they had nothing to report to their fellow-citizens, and that their senate could take no other decision, since there was no soldier left to recruit and no money to contribute. Seeing their obstinacy, the consuls informed the Senate: such terror gripped their minds that a great number of senators declared the empire doomed, that the other colonies and then the allies would copy this example; that all of them seemed to have agreed to hand Rome over to Hannibal.

Then, as the other colonies agreed to supply what had been asked of them: 'As for the other twelve which had refused to obey, the Senate forbade any mention of them, and ordered the consuls neither to take leave of the envoys, nor to retain them nor to summon them: this silent punishment seemed to be most in keeping with the dignity of the Roman people.'[19]

The attitude of acceptance and discretion in this last instance is an obvious contrast with the extreme brutality of the actions taken against Arezzo. The Senate would certainly have acted much more firmly with regard to the Latin cities if it had believed it had the political or military means to make itself obeyed, and if it had not feared the contagion of example or the disastrous results such information might have provoked had it been known by the people, allies and, of course, the enemy. In both cases, anxiety, tension and, it must be said, fear dictated behaviour.

Moreover, in 204 when the war was on the point of ending, these same cities were treated with scant ceremony:

they were each ordered to give double the largest number of foot-soldiers they had supplied to the Roman people since the enemy had been in Italy, as well as one hundred and twenty horsemen; if any of them could not fulfil this last condition, it could offer three footsoldiers for one horseman; the richest footsoldiers and horsemen were to be chosen and would be sent outside Italy, wherever reinforcements were needed . . . . An additional contribution of one *as* per thousand would be imposed and levied each year; the operations of the property qualification assessment would be carried out according to the method used by the Roman censors.[20]

Reading these terms, which were harsh for allies who had in no way betrayed, the attitude among the ruling circles in Rome towards cities and peoples who had defected may be imagined. These, as we have seen, made up a large part of the south of the peninsula. And for the most part they were treated as enemies; this once again meant destruction, confiscation of lands and sometimes reducing part of the population to slavery. But there was a hint of a shift in the relations between local populations and a Roman aristocracy which, in the thick of the war effort, had been forced to experience betrayal. These two aspects must be taken into account when examining the consequences of the second Punic War in Italy.

The best-known example of the fate of defeated cities after they had defected is probably that of Capua. Livy tells us:

> So seventy of the leading senators were executed; nearly 300 Campanian nobles were thrown into prison; others, entrusted to the keeping of allied towns with Latin rights, died of various accidents; what remained of the mass of Campanian citizens were sold as slaves. There followed deliberations on the fate of the town and its territory. Some were of the opinion that a powerful, nearby town, hostile to Rome, should be destroyed. Immediate concerns, however, won the day: because it was recognized that this was some of Italy's most fertile soil, the town was preserved so that those working the land could have somewhere to live. To populate it, they retained the mass of non-citizen residents and freedmen, as well as traders and labourers; the entire territory and all public buildings became the property of the Roman people. It was decided that Capua would no longer be anything but a dwelling-place, and that it would have neither state, nor senate, nor assembly of the plebs, nor magistrates: deprived of the instruments of decision-making and leaders, the mass of inhabitants would be unable to unite on any matter or agree upon any plan. A prefect would be sent every year from Rome to exercise jurisdiction.[21]

The fact that this repression was inflicted on the aristocrats who had been responsible for the defection was perfectly logical. They in fact formed the milieu from which the city leaders were recruited, since they were the families with wealth and legitimacy at their disposal. Having been the most responsible, they were the more culpable. They were therefore the first to be affected, as in the case of the Latin colonies, where care had been taken to specify that the richest were to bear the increased cost of mobilization.

Confiscation of lands was central to the arrangements. Obviously, they were not left uncultivated and, while waiting for probable reallocation in the form of sales or concessions, by distribution or colonization, they were rented to their former owners. Above all, every decision taken, either by the Senate or magistrates on the spot, was the equivalent of destroying the state, not as a town, as Livy emphasizes, but as a political entity. All the functioning organs of the civic community were suppressed. Capua had lost the means of its existence.[22] However, its situation was not quite as Livy described it. Not all its inhabitants had disappeared. Some were displaced to southern Etruria and Latium.[23] The majority of the poorer people stayed where they were. Nor had all the aristocrats been executed. A small troop of 300 horsemen serving in Sicily at the time of the defection, who belonged to the worthiest circles, had remained on the Roman side. They kept their Roman citizenship – probably without suffrage – by express vote of the people, and were enrolled in the municipium of Cumae. Perhaps they were not the only ones, and it may be supposed that others benefited from the same arrangements. Later, all these survivors of the former Capua were admitted into the community of Roman citizens.[24] But the city-state itself was not really reborn until the foundation of colonies, one very transitory in 83, the other which, in contrast, lasted being established in 59.

Elsewhere, the measures adopted by the Romans were perhaps not quite so final, but they went in the same direction. Frequently, part of the population was reduced to slavery: 30,000 in Tarentum, 5,000 among the Hirpini. Generally, the leading men of the city were executed: at Agrigentum, and again among the Hirpini, since they had been responsible for the defection. Vice versa, the allies who had stayed loyal were rewarded. For instance, Petelia had put up a stout resistance against Hannibal during the siege he had inflicted: people died of starvation and, after the town fell, barely 800 survivors were left. But after the victory, the Romans undertook to seek them out and restore their city to them. The inhabitants of Nuceria, whose town had similarly been destroyed, were allowed to choose between rebuilding it or settling in Atella, which had defected at the same time as Capua. They opted for the second solution, so that the Atellani had to move to Calatia and crowd in with the original inhabitants who had also failed the alliance.

The Consequences of the War

These few examples are the proof: the consequences of the second
Punic War were heavy for Italy, though it is difficult to assess
them with any precision. There is no lack of analyses of the
subject, yet agreement is far from being reached. Nevertheless,
the main aspects deserve some emphasis.

One of the first results of the conflict was certainly the damage
to relations between the Romans and the cities and peoples of
Italy. Mistrust and contempt tended to surface in Roman attitudes. I have already mentioned the case of Etruria, where legions
were maintained until the reconquest of Cisalpine Gaul. One
could add the procedures known as *quaestiones*, i.e. of enquiry
and repression, which were conducted in 206, 204 and 203 into
possible conspiracies of Etruscan aristocrats, and the fact that in
200 Etruria was still designated a province, as in the old days of
the conquest.[25] Similarly, also during 203, a dictator was
appointed, assisted by a master of cavalry, to carry out in the
towns of southern Italy which had gone over to the Carthaginian
side a further procedure of *quaestio* against all those who might
have harmed Roman interests.[26] The choice of such a magistrate
was not without importance, for it implied that Rome was not
going to let itself be deterred by the rights of the *provocatio* which
protected Roman citizens, and that consequently all individuals,
even the most highly placed, were under threat. Nothing must
interfere with the Romans in their concern to punish everyone
who had betrayed them.

Once this first result was obtained, relations could not immediately and easily resume their normal course. Unless they were
destroyed, as in Capua's case, former allies, even when they had
become enemies again, regained the status of allies, since there
was no intermediate stance. In many instances, however,
there could never be the same trust as before. That probably
explains the fate reserved for the Bruttians: for a while Rome
refused to mobilize them except to use them as public ser-
vants.[27] The position itself was not very honourable; compared
with that of soldiers it was downright degrading. There were
certainly other instances of this nature not mentioned by our
sources. Let us simply say that the conditions accompanying
the reintegration of defaulting allies into the Roman order

were deeply humiliating for some of them.

Should one go further in the train of events and consider that the allies' defections would weigh heavily for a long time on Romano-Italian relations? Possibly. At all events, that was the opinion of Arnold Toynbee,[28] who explained in this light two incidents which later revealed the contempt felt by Roman magistrates for the towns of Italy. In 173, indeed, the consul L. Postumius Albinus arbitrarily demanded from the city of Praeneste lodgings and a transport service which it did not owe.[29] This action was as good as an overt declaration that the rights and autonomy of allied cities need not be respected. Around the middle of the second century, a consul had a municipal magistrate of Teanum Sidicinum birched because there had been a delay in evicting men from baths which the consul's wife wished to visit.[30] At that time the second Punic War was well in the past, and it is unlikely that the tensions it had provoked were directly at the root of these attitudes. Other events had had time to work, widening the gap between the members of the Roman senatorial aristocracy and local aristocrats. Nevertheless, it would probably not be wrong to see in the pride the Romans felt about the victory they had won, despite betrayals, one of the first cracks which later gave rise to the conflicts resulting in the Social War.

Among the measures systematically adopted by the Romans to punish allies who had defected, we must of course count the confiscation of lands. Apparently, such arrangements were made even when the cities that had defaulted had returned to the Roman side and had not immediately suffered heavy sanctions. Such was the case for the inhabitants of Arpi who had fought and, when they returned to the Roman side, had allowed the men of the Carthaginian garrison to escape, but also for certain Hirpini and Lucanians who had handed them over, though not for the inhabitants of Salapia, who had massacred them.[31] In the time of their alliance with Hannibal, voluntary or not, they had in fact become enemies once more.

One may well suppose that a large part of the peoples and cities occupying southern Italy thus became the Roman people's *ager publicus*. Confiscation, of course, affected only part of a city's territory, a quarter or a third, as far as can be estimated.[32] Not all, then, suffered Capua's fate. Nevertheless, the areas concerned must have been very large, and entire regions were deeply affected: Campania, Samnium, Apulia, Lucania and

Bruttium, and of course Cisapline Gaul.[33] Some, such as Apulia[34] and the most southern parts of the peninsula, seem to have been lastingly impoverished. Others, in contrast, experienced a new prosperity thanks to the opportunities which were thus presented.

These somewhat general remarks suffice to reveal the upheavals that confiscations wreaked in Italy's agrarian structures. The *ager publicus* could be sold, given or leased for the benefit of the Roman state. In all cases, the property changed hands, which in itself had heavy consequences for its former owners. But depending on what the Romans did with the land, the fate of the farms could vary. When they were leased to the members of local communities, the general organization might hardly be changed. But when land was granted to Roman owners, two possibilities might present themselves: either they in their turn rented it or they started to work it themselves, and the Italians were then completely dispossessed. Needless to say, that was what happened when individual allocations were made or when a colony was founded. But it is clear that on the whole it was the Romans who largely benefited from the new situation, but to varying degrees. Working-class Romans could do so only in so far as they profited from the allocations of land. There was no shortage of these, as numerous colonies were created after the war. But they concerned only a part of the people and, above all, formed only small units for development whose prosperity was sometimes very uncertain.

In contrast, the aristocrats found there was much more in it for them. First, on repayment of a loan raised in 210 among the richest, because they had contributed most they likewise received most: for a third of what they had advanced, they were awarded permanent ownership of lands situated less than 50 miles from Rome. Next, because when land was sold, they were the ones in the best position to take advantage of the opportunities offered. Last and most important, they were able to set themselves up as the state's farmers, notably when it was a matter of vast stretches of territory intended for livestock breeding; or to take possession of areas that had not been surveyed and were unoccupied, even encroaching on neighbouring properties, belonging to the state or private individuals who were less powerful than themselves, following a practice which, if we are to believe the early writers, was extremely widespread.[35]

It was because these changes in ownership and in the organ-ization of farming developments were part of a general context of partial, yet perceptible, destruction of the social fabric of Italy that this situation affecting the land was possible.

We must take the strictly quantitative point of view. Roman losses during the war have already been mentioned. As far as can be assessed, they corresponded to 6 per cent of the total civic population.[36] As in all wars of comparable size, the decline in births must be added, due to the length of campaigns and the remoteness of the troops, since many fought for a long time outside Italy. Yet, if one imagines what the total toll of the war might have been, the Romans were not the ones who suffered most. The Italians who went over to Hannibal's side were, of necessity, more affected than they because the losses – which may be presumed equivalent – were complemented by those incurred in reprisals, notably the enslavement of the defeated. The rare figures available on this last point indeed lead us to suppose that the number was far from negligible: the 25,000 Samnites, Lucanians and Apulians already mentioned in 214,[37] the popula-tion of Agrigentum in 210,[38] and the 80,000 Sardinians killed or sold in 175.[39] It may therefore be assumed that, although certain regions, especially those in the centre of the peninsula, were affected only by the burden of mobilization due to the war against Hannibal, others in the south – Samnium, Apulia, Bruttium and Lucania, of course – and in the north – Cisalpine Gaul, Liguria, Sardinia and Corsica – probably lost a large portion of their popu-lation at the time of their defeat and in the ensuing years.

In addition to these brutal losses, there were also the conse-quences of the transfer of population. Human beings in Italy endured enormous upheavals through the enforced or voluntary displacement of sometimes large numbers of people.

We may recall the fate of the inhabitants of Capua and neigh-bouring towns, some of whom were forced to settle in southern Etruria. There were other instances, for the Romans proceeded with deportations that enabled territories which had previously been devastated to be repopulated. The Ligures, for example, who in 180 were installed in the lands of the Taurasini on the border of Samnium and Campania, numbered 47,000, including women and children. If we add other figures, about which we have scant information, we may suppose that the demographic and, even more, ethnic balance was altered.

From this viewpoint, the process of colonization played the leading role in Italy's social transformation in the aftermath of the second Punic War. Territories had been laid waste, lands had been confiscated, and sometimes extensive zones needed to be reoccupied. Roman citizens and certain of their allies might well be rewarded for the war effort they had made.

The founding of colonies were therefore resumed after the second Punic War and continued after the reconquest of north Italy. The year 194 saw the creation of Pozzuoli, Salerno, Volturnum, Liternum, Sipontum, Buxentum, Crotona and Tempsa; 193, Copia on the territory of the Thurii; 192, Vibo Valentia on that of Hipponium; 189, Bologna; 184, Potentia and Pesaro; 183, Saturnia, Modena and Parma; 181, Graviscae and Aquileia; 180–178, possibly Lucca, and 177, Luna.[40] As it stands, the list is already impressive, but one must add the former colonies, abandoned or depopulated, which received new colonists who were to give them fresh vitality: in 200, Venusia; in 199, Narni; in 197, Cosa; in 190, Cremona and Piacenza, and still others to follow. Added to this was the construction of new roads linking all the cities to one another as well as to the centre of the peninsula: the Via Aemilia from Rimini to Piacenza (187), the Cassia from Rome to Arezzo (154?), the Annia from Bologna to Aquileia (153?), the Postumia from Genoa to Aquileia (148), and the Annia from Capua to Rhegium (131?), to name only the main ones;[41] so that all Italy found itself far more subject than in the past to the presence of Roman dominion.

Needless to say, it was mostly the regions which had been affected by the war that benefited from these additions of population. Over 50,000 colonists and their families appear to have been moved and settled in this way between 200 and 133, in the territories of southern Italy, Etruria and Cisalpine Gaul, over areas of as much as 250,000 hectares.[42] And mention should also be made of all those, such as Scipio's veterans following the Punic War, who profited by the individual allocations (viritim) that accompanied the colonization process. These figures are high, and the phenomenon they reveal obviously had an important effect on the agrarian and social structure of Italy.

Somewhat more exact indications that may be gleaned here and there leave room to suppose that to the large number of beneficiaries was added a perceptible increase in the size of the plots of land allocated. In Cisalpine Gaul, notably, areas attained unprecedented sizes: 50 *jugera* (12.5 hectares) at Bologna and Aquileia; and,in the last instance, even 100 *jugera* (25 hectares) for a centurion and 140 *jugera* (35 hectares) when the person concerned was a horseman. We are speaking of Latin colonies, where allocations were traditionally always more generous than in the Roman colonies. But the increase was also confirmed in the case of colonies of citizens, since the inhabitants of Potentia and Pesaro received 6 *jugera* (1.5 hectares), which was slightly more than the figures customarily known for this type of city.[43]

Nevertheless, Cisalpine Gaul was the recipient of special treatment. It was indeed as if Roman ruling circles had decided to turn it into a vast frontier region, where it was necessary to install a great number of Romans and Italians from the centre of the peninsula, both to ward off any Gallic menace and to keep for themselves the lands confiscated in the southern region. The colonies founded there were really for populating, and often imposed large-scale work in order to develop them. Land that had certainly been little used till then had to be cleared, drained and improved.[44] This was an attempt to attract volunteers to carry out such pioneering work, especially veterans who were richer than the others, centurions and cavalrymen, who would form the aristocracy of these new city-states.[45] It was very likely during the course of work on the founding of these towns in the Po Valley that Roman surveyors perfected their techniques and began systematically to use the method of land measurement known as centuriation, which consisted of setting in place two lines at right angles (the *cardo* and the *decumanus*) and creating a grid of equal square plots by the projection of equidistant secondary axes.[46] The entire region thus underwent a vast process of agricultural development which integrated it with the rest of the peninsula.

Throughout Italy, however, the displacement of population was large enough to have noticeable effects on the populace as a whole. The war and subsequent sanctions had in many places destroyed the traditional social fabric: the population had dwindled, lands had been confiscated, part of the peasantry found itself uprooted and footloose. These conditions had without any doubt made such a policy of colonization feasible.[47]

But so many lands changed hands, so many families changed their dwelling-place, from Latium to Cisalpine Gaul, from Liguria to Campania, that the ethnic and social composition of the peninsula could not help but be altered. These changes took place in varying degrees, obviously, depending on the number of immigrants, the size of the plots of land assigned to them, and the sites on which they were settled, in the heart of indigenous populations or on the fringes of their territories. In some regions, such as the part of Cisalpine Gaul lying south of the Po, the process was such that the Gallic populations vanished as a result of colonization. Elsewhere, on the other hand, as in northern Etruria where the Pisans themselves asked for the colony of Luna[48] to be created, these movements probably had the effect of maintaining a certain demographic equilibrium. At all events, the consequences of this process were of necessity a greater cultural and political homogeneity in Italy under the sole and acknowledged domination of Rome, on the one hand, and the growth in weight, depth and extent of that same domination, on the other.

All these happenings in fact gave Rome's aristocrats increased strength and wealth, together with the means of obtaining even greater economic and political power. We shall return in the next chapter to the specific conditions that gave rise to new methods of land development being put into practice, sparking off a speculative type of agriculture that contributed greatly to their wealth. But here we can examine how the organization of economic life was affected by the efforts of financial and logistic mobilization which the Roman government had to make.

Mention has already been made of the creation of the monetary system based on the denarius, and this supported trade in almost all the Mediterranean world until the end of the Republic and the start of the Empire. On the other hand, it must also be emphasized that during the war years needs in provisions and materials of every kind largely favoured the expansion of what might be considered the infrastructure of finance and trade.

We must refer here to the companies of *publicani* (tax-gatherers) who make their appearance in our sources precisely during the second Punic War. This name covered the financial associations formed among themselves by citizens who took on leases either the revenues of the state, or the public works it was carrying out. In the first instance, they advanced to the treasury resources that they counted on recouping, for example, from customs duties or income from the *ager publicus*. In the second, they tendered for the construction of roads or buildings and were paid by the city. All these undertakings, of course, involved large sums which it was beyond the scope of a simple private individual to gather. The publicans were therefore organized in companies, kinds of fiscal and financial businesses, in which shares could be bought. Only the wealthiest could take part in such operations. Since the members of the senatorial order were excluded from public tendering, the majority of publicans were recruited from the knights, that is, members of the aristocracy who, though not senators, were still worthy enough to take part in civic responsibilites and thereby to acquire wealth in the service of the state.

This technique of leasing predated the end of the third century and had certainly improved on the model of the kingdom of Syracuse's fiscal organization. But the conditions created by the demands of war, then by the massive increase in revenues gained from the *ager publicus*, gave the institution its decisive development. On two occasions Livy referred to companies such as these when speaking of supplies for the Roman armies: first in 215, when the navy and army of Spain had to be equipped, and second in 212, when it appeared that one of these publicans, M. Postumius of Pyrgi, had cheated the city by having himself reimbursed for cargoes which he falsely claimed had been lost.[49] These people were rich enough to be able to invest several tens of thousands of *denarii* each in the enterprise. In fact, the annual needs of the legions in Spain have been estimated at 1.5 million *denarii*. The publicans were also powerful enough to be able for a time to prevent the holding of their associate's trial. Possibly, they had not yet attained the power and influence they would enjoy during the subsequent decades, but it is likely that they had already laid the foundations of their future might.[50]

To oppose Hannibal, Rome had to mobilize all the necessary resources, including those of the whole of Italy and the surrounding islands. One of Livy's texts makes us aware of the importance of the event. In it, the historian describes the supplies that were assembled when Scipio left for Africa. For example, Caere provided wheat, Populonia iron, Tarquinia linen cloth for sails, Volterra lengths of timber for boatbuilding and wheat, Arezzo weapons and equipment, Perugia timber for boats, etc.[51] It may be supposed that, at every important moment in the war, the farmers and craftsmen of the cities who were in a position to contribute to the efforts of the combatants were widely called upon. Some cities thus reaped the benefits of an important stimulus whose effects lasted well after the war.

In two cases at least, this is very noticeable. In Sicily, the

Roman authorities keenly encouraged the growing of cereals. Once the island had been reconquered and peace restored, the consul M. Valerius Laevinus took all the measures he could to assist the reinstatement of farms and the development of production which, as Livy emphasizes, 'served to feed not only the island, but also Rome and Italy'. And his efforts were carried on by his successors.[52] They seem to have been effective as, in 209, 205, 204 and 203, as well as after the war in 198, 191, 190, 187 and 171, the Roman armies were provisioned from Sicilian and Sardinian grain, and until under the Empire, Sicily, with other regions, such as Sardinia, was one of the chief zones that met the needs of the town of Rome.[53]

In the same way, Campania owed part of its later development to the situation created by the second Punic War. Although to a noticeably lesser degree, this area also supplied grain to Rome and its surrounding region. Consequently, Pozzuoli, the port through which it was exported, assumed strategic importance. In 215 it was fortified.[54] In 197 a decision was taken to found a colony there. It eventually became Italy's chief port, through which passed the essential part of trade at first with the Tyrrhenian Sea, and then with the Orient during later years.[55] Campania thus without any doubt became the region that was most open to the rest of the Mediterranean world; this could not fail to play a role in its development.

So the remarks prompted by the consequences of the second Punic War result in a contrasting picture. Demographic losses and the uprooting of populations brought certain regions to the brink of ruin. But, in contrast, the war effort that the Roman aristocracy was obliged to make to fend off Hannibal created the conditions for a development which really blossomed in the following decades. Everywhere, the founding of colonies and the allocation of lands aided the ethnic mixture and the cultural unification of Italy. Many factors converged at that time to allow an expansion which would give this same aristocracy the means of further entrenching its superiority over all the communities in the peninsula. In many respects, Hannibal's campaign thus proved to be the decisive episode which led Italy along the path of unification, and Romanization.

4

TRANSFORMATIONS IN THE ITALIAN ECONOMY

The consequences of the second Punic War were already weighing very heavily on the economic and social life of Italy when, during the second and first centuries, the effects of the increased opening of the peninsula to the Mediterranean world also made themselves felt. Every conquest led Roman armies to Spain, Greece, Asia Minor, then North Africa, Syria, Gaul and lastly Egypt. This military expansion was the major factor that contributed to the destructuring of traditional Italian society and brought about a crisis in Roman civic institutions, which became totally unsuited to managing conflicts that extended through the whole of the ancient world.

Here I will not go into the chronology of events, which would take too long to recall. Let us say simply that several phases must be distinguished. The first immediately followed the second Punic War and ended in 133 BC. This was the one that saw the most rapid expansion. In the space of a few decades, indeed, the greater part of Spain was conquered and annexed, on the one hand, and most of Greece, Macedonia and Asia Minor on the other. At that time Roman rule over the Mediterranean world was truly established, and the opening up of Italy had major consequences for the economic and social balance of the peninsula. Conquests did not really start again until Pompey's great campaigns in the East and Caesar's in Gaul, finishing with the incorporation of Egypt ino the Empire after Octavian's victory over Antony and Cleopatra.

The Influx of Wealth

The consequences of this process obviously revealed themselves at a different, broader pace, but because of the lack of statistical data it is difficult to distinguish their various stages. They took many forms, and for the time being I shall emphasize the immediate economic aspects, keeping for further consideration an examination of the social and cultural expansion that could not fail to result from such an increase in the area henceforth under Roman domination. The economic effects were essentially financial and demographic. Among the former, we must of course note the extraordinary enrichment of the city of Rome and individual citizens, Roman or not, who took part in this process of expansion.

In the first decades of the second century BC, when one after the other the chief Hellenistic rulers of the time were reduced to subjection, the flood of wealth to Rome took a spectacular turn. The example of the triumph over the Galatians celebrated by Cn. Manlius Vulso in 186 allows us to grasp some measure of the phenomenon:

> In his triumph, Cn. Manlius had borne on chariots 212 gold crowns, 220,000 silver librae, 2,103 gold librae, 127,000 Attic tetradrachmas, 250,000 cistophori, 6,320 gold philippi, together with many Gaulish weapons and spoils; fifty-two enemy leaders were marched in front of the chariot. He had forty-two denarii distributed to each of his soldiers, double for a centurion and treble for the cavalry, and he gave them double pay . . . a senatorial decree decided that, thanks to the money which had been brought in at the time of the triumph, the people would be reimbursed for the tax they had paid into the public treasury. With scrupulous care the urban quaestors paid twenty-five and a half *as* per thousand *as* of tax assessment.[1]

Following the customary idea of antiquity, all citizens had the right to benefit from the wealth of the state. Reimbursement of a tax was therefore a perfectly normal measure which allowed the whole community to profit from a victory. For all that, Roman citizens stopped paying after the victory of 168 over Perseus, the last king of Macedonia. As we see, the soldiers also received a share of the booty, according to rules respecting their hierarchy.

And it may be supposed that the superior officers and Manlius Vulso himself had not been forgotten. Among its first consequences, war would thus remunerate the Romans.

To the booty were then added the tributes imposed on the defeated: 15,000 talents, for instance (or 90 million denarii) from Antiochus III, to be paid mainly in twelve annual instalments. Then there were the taxes imposed permanently: customs taxes and duties, direct taxes (*stipendia* and tithes), and lastly the revenues from properties confiscated to the profit of the Roman people: the lands of the *ager publicus*, for example, or the mines in Spain or Macedonia. All this constituted a vast total income which people have tried to evaluate, but such an attempt is difficult. Some revenues were exceptional and occurred only once. The others were regular, but with no indication of their amount. However, it may be supposed that the Roman treasury could have received some 610 million denarii between 200 and 157, or an average of 14 million a year.[2]

With time, and the spread of Roman domination, profits continued to grow. Thus Plutarch tells us that state revenues were already some 50 million a year before Pompey's conquests, and that the latter raised the sum of 85 million. In one century the increase had been considerable, even taking into account an inflation which may have tripled the price of wheat.[3]

Of course, not all Roman citizens profited equally from these riches. The greater part of the people – but what proportion? – benefited only in the form of grants of land that accompanied the various agrarian arrangements decided during the period, or distributions of wheat at no or low cost which were also part of the so-called *populares* measures claiming to meet the real or supposed needs of the lower classes. The only ones who truly had their share in this collective enrichment were the members of the aristocracy who, for one reason or another, were likely to divert part of the inflow to their own profit, therefore mainly magistrates and tax-farmers.

The former were better placed. When they had command of armies they were the first beneficiaries of victory and unstintingly took their share of the booty or gifts that the vanquished were bound to offer. Tigranes, for instance, the king of Armenia whom Pompey had subdued in 66, presented 6,000 talents (36 million denarii) to his victor, even extending the donation to the entire army, since each soldier received 50 denarii, each centurion

1,000, and each tribune 6,000. Taking part in these victorious campaigns which allowed the Romans to dominate the whole Mediterranean world was obviously a profitable affair. Livy notes that this motive alone was sufficient to provoke combats during the third Macedonian War.[4] But the takings were very unevenly shared since, regarding the civic hierarchy, distributions were to the advantage of the highest and most meritorious members of the aristocracy, who therefore received far more than ordinary soldiers from the common people.

When these same magistrates administered provinces, they could also profit from all the generous gifts, voluntary or enforced, that the allies and the defeated were induced to concede. The exchange of presents or services was normal practice in Roman society. A governor was also called upon to become the host and patron of the cities under his administration, and they had to recompense him for his protection and benevolence. Only extortion was reprehensible. But the borderline between the gift received and the gift demanded was very tenuous. The most famous example, because of the speech made by Cicero against him, was that of Verres, praetor from 73 to 71 in Sicily, where he grew scandalously wealthy. There he made – claimed his opponent – over 10 million denarii in embezzlement and swindles of all kinds.[5] Cicero, who had the ambition to govern Cilicia while fully respecting the law, earned only 550,000 denarii in a year. Even so, that was quite a good sum, and one may assume that the two figures marked the extreme limits, of legality and illegality, of the ordinary gains of a Roman magistrate governing a pacified province.

The tax-farmers were the other large-scale beneficiaries of the system of exploitation that had been set up. Their chances of getting rich had grown with the increase in the revenues of the Roman treasury and public expenditure. The sums at stake had become considerable. Asia's tithe, to cite only one source, was bringing 6 million denarii annually into the coffers at the beginning of the first century. Of course, the advance of such sums made it all the more essential to have recourse to companies which allowed the concentration of the necessary capital. They had probably thus reached a larger size than in the past, using their own administration and their own staff, who levied amounts on the spot and also kept higher profits for their partners.

C. Rabirius Postumus was one such. This is how Cicero

describes him during a trial in which he defended him: 'He was engaged in a mass of business deals; participated to a large extent in the state's tax-farms; made loans to foreign countries; had interests in many provinces and even served kings,' notably Ptolemy Auletes to whom he lent a considerable sum and whose offficial he agreed to be in order to levy the necessary taxes on his behalf.[6]

It was indeed difficult to distinguish between all the financial operations that accompanied the payment of taxes due to the Roman state. The tax-farmers were committed to the state but also made loans to the provincials, who had to pay them and then sought to recover their dues. It was a very speculative but highly profitable procedure. The rate of credit was at least 10 per cent per annum, often far more, and interest was capitalized, which produced comfortable profits. As for the profit realized by merely levying the tax, it was at least 1 per cent, but could swell to 6 per cent, depending on circumstances.[7] Being unable to assess the phenomenon with the requisite statistical nicety, one is thus led to assume that the various sources of income levied in the provinces by the Roman state contributed greatly to the enrichment of members of the senatorial or equestrian aristocracy: they helped themselves to a large share of this regular flow of wealth.

To these first two categories of direct beneficiaries of the exploitation of the Empire must be added all those traders and businessmen who took advantage of the fact that it was impossible for members of the senatorial order overtly to obtain money by usury or commercial speculation. Such activity in fact contradicted the system of aristocratic standards on which their prestige and authority relied. It was certainly not due to lack of keeness on their part. But since they were unable to get rich directly by these means, they were obliged to deal through associates who represented them in all matters, even the shadiest, in which they had interests. They were therefore incapable of becoming the kind of entrepreneurs who could have led Roman society along the path of market capitalism.

Others, who remained their subordinates in the hierarchy of status, did it for them. There were tax-farmers, of course, whom nothing prevented from financing any imaginable commercial enterprise but who, on the other hand, could not cope alone with the new volume of trade. But there were also bankers, usurers, shipowners, large and small traders in wheat, oil, wine or slaves, their number and importance always increasing, who spread through the provinces as early as the second century BC. Unlike the others, these individuals did not need any special civic qualification, as they looked after functions that had no direct relationship with the management of the state's interests. They might or might not be Roman citizens, and there were many Italians among them.

In fact, one of the consequences of the establishment of Roman rule and tax levies in the provinces was to create a financial flow that began from the periphery of the Empire, chiefly the East, to become concentrated in Italy. It flowed back again, however, for the aristocrats who thus acquired their wealth made use of it to buy the products they wanted, mainly works of art, slaves and land.[8] These flows of money were matched at the time by those of people. Some left Italy to take part in the conquest or make their fortune by it, as others arrived: slaves, for the most part, destined for the properties of the moneyed Italians.

Movements and Changes in Population

Changes in demographic balance and especially migrations were another consequence of the conquest of the Mediterranean world. Attempts have been made to evaluate what these main flows represented, first from a quantitative aspect, since qualitatively the various populations did not occupy the same place in the peninsula's social organization.

Italian emigration embraced two categories of people: the soldiers who took part in the conquests and the traders who set themselves up in the provinces.

During the first half of the second century BC, campaigns were repeated in three theatres of operations, Cisalpine Gaul, Spain and the East. On average, between seven and ten legions were sent off; if one adds the allies' troops who necessarily accompanied them, this represents 120,000 men who were annually withdrawn from Italian society and, in part, sent overseas.[9] During the second half of the century, the number of mobilized soldiers decreased. Nevertheless, their number remained at five or six legions of citizens on average, which, together with the allies, made troops of between 60,000 and 70,000 men. This is quite a considerable number, especially if it is related to the free population of Italy (excluding Cisalpine Gaul), about 3 million inhabitants, and bearing in mind that this demographic toll affected the males of the active population. This could not fail to have perceptible repercussions on the organization of labour and also, naturally, on the renewal of the population.[10]

The period of mobilization must also be borne in mind. It corresponded to the duration of the campaigns, and these could last for years, for even if the generals changed the men mostly stayed where they were. Some therefore spent very long periods on active service and did not return home for many years. This was particularly the case for those fighting in Spain. The legion sent there in 196 was not relieved until 180, and the one that joined it in 187 was relieved only in 177. And these two replacement legions were still serving in 168.[11] The example could equally be cited of the troops sent to Asia in 86 who did not return until 66. Such spells of duty were, however, exceptional. The more usual periods were of a few years, between four and six;[12] and even those had awkward consequences.

The absence of these men in fact weighed heavily on the farms to which they would normally supply their labour, whether or not they were the owners, not to the point of bringing about the complete ruin of traditional agriculture in Italy, as has sometimes been said, but certainly to the point of weakening the frailest among them, subjecting them still further to all the hazards of subsistence farming with its feeble capacity for resisting both climatic and human vicissitudes. The permanent mobilization which kept men away from their native region for several years was at least a strong contributory factor in the disintegration of the fabric of Italian society. Only the sturdiest communities, therefore, could afford to witness the regular departure of a large number of their members, and show themselves capable of ensuring their reabsorption on their return.

On the other hand, when they were demobilized, some troops remained in the provinces where they had fought. During the second century, this occurrence mainly affected Spain, gathering somewhat in volume only during the first century, when the great military leaders created colonies for their veterans. The first to organize the large-scale settlement of his soldiers overseas was Caesar, who gave them lands in Africa, Spain and Gaul.[13] To these must be added the colonies of Carthage and Narbonne, founded respectively in 123 and 118, which were intended to receive Roman citizens who thus benefited from the distribution of land. But if we consider that in total only around ten cities were created before Caesar's foundations, and that the highest population figures reached were between 4,000 and 6,000, we must conclude, particularly if this fact is related to the length of the period, that it is no basis for assuming a strong emigration movement. These shifts of population reflected the uprooting that successive mobilizations or economic imbalances had brought in their wake rather than provoked.[14]

In contrast, the emigration of the Italians who settled in the rest of the Mediterranean to trade and do business was a phenomenon of far greater scope, perhaps not so much for the number of people involved as for the effects produced on the peninsula by this opening up. It is certainly difficult to establish figures. Those of the early writers are always quoted in connection with the massacre committed in 88 by the inhabitants of the cities of Asia and Greece when they rebelled at the instigation of Mithridates. It is thought that the Italians who had settled in those regions were often traders or businessmen. In antiquity, estimates varied between 80,000 and 150,000 dead,[15] but they were certainly wildly exaggerated. The general estimate of the overseas Italian population, based on recruitment in the civil wars, was 125,000 adult males in 69, and 150,000 around 49, that is, total population figures of 375,000 and 450,000 respectively.[16] If one omits the inhabitants of the colonies just referred to, the provincials who in that period had received citizenship and the freedmen of Roman citizens, the most reasonable figures in the middle of the first century should not exceed between 200,000 and 300,000 spread through the entire Mediterranean basin.

Some of these people, however, played a role that was more important in other ways for the history of Italy than the colonists who had settled in the provinces. Those who remained in contact with the peninsula, because they derived the main part of their wealth from trade and business with it, contributed largely to opening it up to the outside world.

Merchants and traders had spread through all the provinces. The phenomenom was by no means new, but the establishment of Roman rule had given it a very considerable impetus and development. In the aftermath of the second Punic War, merchants made their appearance almost everywhere in the Mediterranean basin. They were certainly in the West, in Spain, Africa and Narbonensian Gaul, though there is no precise information on the stages of their settlement, but chiefly in the East, in Illyria and north-west Greece, notably Ambracia where the Romans obtained fiscal immunity in 187, central Greece, Euboea, Corinth, Athens, and lastly in Asia Minor, and above all in Delos, where a great many installed themselves. After the third Macedonian War, in 166, to punish Rhodes for its hesitancy, the Senate made Delos a free port exempt from taxes. It then became a commercial and financial centre of major importance.

It is here, in the inscriptions of the second and first century BC preserved there, that the scale and diversity of the Italian implantation are revealed. Indeed, over 220 individuals have been counted, bearing around 150 different names, which onomastic analysis enables us to identify as originating from this or that region of Italy.[17]

Several areas may thus be distinguished which supplied their contingent of traders or businessmen who were settled in Delos: Romans from Rome or Latium first, for instance, the Aemilii, Caecilii, Claudii or Clodii, and among them a small group of names to be found at Praeneste, which provide a third of the total names represented; and chiefly an important collection of family names known in the south of the peninsula, some of indigenous Oscan and Samnite families, like the Staii or the Pettii, others of Latin origin and thus families who at some given moment had settled in southern Italy. To these must be added all the names of Greeks from Italy, who represent a fifth of the total, and Sicilians who also traded and did business with Delos. In the group as a whole, however, two polarized areas predominated: Rome itself and the city-states of Campania, especially the port of Pozzuoli, where there were several families, the Granii, the Cossinii and the Cluvii, for example, who are clearly seen to have maintained important relations with the East.

These inscriptions similarly teach us that, of some 220 people who appear in them, only slightly more than a third were free-born. The others were either slaves or freedmen, and were therefore not of Italian origin themselves. In other words, some of the enterprises founded by these Italians had been sufficiently prosperous for individuals who were basically only employees to appear in documentation, or even sometimes for masters to absent themselves, leaving their subordinates to run their branch or trading post in Delos.

As an instance of the organization of these businesses, take the one identified with the Cossutii, whose network extended all over the Oriental world. Its founder was probably Decimus Cossutius, an architect, perhaps a *praefectus fabrum* of the Roman army, who lived in the middle of the second century BC. At all events, his name suggests that he originated from southern Latium. He worked on the construction of the Olympeion at Athens and possibly also the aqueduct of Antioch. After him, other Cossutii appeared in Greece at the end of the century: one M. Cossutius in Athens, another at Eretria, an L. Cossutius at Delos, accompanied by two more who were probably freedmen or slaves, and above all in the first century, Greek sculptors who bore the name M. Cossutius and were freedmen of a member of the same family. We have to add the interests that these people possessed in marble-quarrying in the East. Here we find the traces of a business made up of descendants or relatives of the first Cossutius who, with the help of their slaves and freedmen, grew rich in the manufacture and trade in works of art that they imported into Italy. In the early first century, it is no more surprising to see the documentary appearance of a Cossutius launching into a senatorial career, and a Cossutia who is rich and worthy enough to Caesar's fiancée for a time.[18]

In the latter instance, family connections seem to have structured the business. In others, it could have been those born of longstanding exchanges of services, or those that extended earlier links of friendship, proximity or patronage.[19] The links that were established most frequently reposed on networks that had already been set up, allowing greater solidity and mutual trust to be introduced into business affairs. A large number of enterprising Italians thus took advantage of the establishment of Roman domination and the appearance of trading circuits created between Italy and the rest of the world to grow rich by building up companies of relatives, freedmen, friends and partners of all kinds, who extended the framework of their businesses throughout the Mediterranean.

This commercial dynamism had two consequences for the history of Italy. The first was the opening up of Italian society to the world by the action of these networks of businessmen. The members of the Roman aristocracy, magistrates and financiers, were not the only ones to crisscross the road and sea routes, to make contacts with conquered populaces, acquire their wealth or be inspired by their way of life. Others belonging to more modest strata of society, and obviously not all Roman citizens, followed the same path, came and went, exchanged information, became Hellenized through contact with Greek culture and thought and brought back home, notably to southern Italy, moral and intellectual values which further contributed to unifying these different regions.

The other consequence was that, outside the peninsula, ethnic or civic differences which distinguished Italians from one another tended to become blurred. First, because the terms in which they appeared in Greek inscriptions were uniform, either 'Italici' or 'Italikoi', or 'Romaioi', but used synonymously to encompass all Italians, including Greeks from southern Italy, whether or not they were Roman citizens, freedmen or freeborn, all lumped together under a single appellation. That of course indicated that the Greeks made no differences among themselves, but even more that they felt no need to make distinctions, whereas in Italy even belonging to this or that community and, even more, the possession or not of Roman citizenship was the subject of the closest attention.[20]

Why should this have been? Plunged as they were in a Hellenic and Oriental milieu, they tended to draw near to one another and emphasize their points of resemblance. They used Greek in their inscriptions, rarely Latin, and never another language of Italy, although some differences remained, as revealed by some linguistic deviations that have been noted in inscriptions from Delos: a 'Marcus' written 'Maarkos', or a 'Decimus' transcribed as 'Dekmos', as that is how it was pronounced in the Oscan tongue.[21]

Furthermore, these colonies of Italians had their own forms of organization. Still in Delos, there were *collegia*, the Poseidoniasts, the Hermaists, the Apolloniasts and the Competeliasts, who borrowed their names from deities. These societies with religious purposes also functioned as craft or trade guilds: they brought together Italians who were engaged in the same activities and could thus unite them and display their solidarity. In other cities, other associations of the same kind brought Italians together and enabled them to enjoy a rudimentary collective organization in the face of local or even Roman authorities. And although it is true that sometimes certain brotherhoods, such as the

Competeliasts in Delos, gathered together individuals of lower rank, slaves or freedmen, never were distinctions made on a basis of ethnic or civic differences. All over the Mediterranean world, Italians from a variety of origins merged in cities, elected the *magistri* who ran the *collegia*, honoured the gods and met for banquets and festivals.[22] In these forms of sociability they probably found the means of defending their interests, but also, by drawing closer together, of compensating for the feelings of exile or rootlessness which their situation forced them to experience. The unity they established among themselves was also influenced by a certain assimilation of the cultural values of the Greek society whose guests they were. The emigration of the Italians into the Mediterranean area certainly contributed to preparing the way for unity in the peninsula, by creating the conditions of new solidarities and diminishing the gaps that separated various peoples from one another, but it also worked in the development of another type of identity which would draw a large part of its characteristics from the Hellenistic world.

In the same way that the Italians left the peninsula to go and make their fortune elsewhere, others came to settle there: traders and certainly also craftsmen who, having the advantage of special skills and abilities, could see the likelihood of profiting from the new luxury markets opening up in Rome and other towns in Italy. But they were not the most numerous. The influx was chiefly of slaves, whom Roman victories and the aristocracy's consequent increase in wealth caused to arrive in Italy in impressive numbers.

The first were, of course, prisoners of the second Punic War, then the wars of conquest that followed: over 5,000 Istrians in 177, for example, 150,000 Epirotes in 167, 10,000 Spanish in 147, 140,000 Cimbri and Teutons in 104, 1,000,000 Gauls in 52, who were sold in the slave markets then directed mostly to Italy, the chief market for this new labour force. From around the middle of the second century, to this necessarily irregular flow was added that of the constant supply offered by a trade that found its main source in the piracy that ravaged the coasts of the eastern Mediterranean, or in the traffic in which certain kings and princes of Asia Minor indulged. It was a large-scale phenomenon and centred precisely on Delos.[23]

All in all, this represented a demographic and economic occurrence that people have tried to measure. In fact, it may be supposed that at the end of the first century, the body of slaves in Italy amounted to between 2 and 3 million people out of a total of 7½ million (including Cisalpine Gaul), or roughly one-third of the population. In other words, if the population at the beginning of the second century was 5 million inhabitants for the same geographical area, a large part of the demographic growth in Italy itself had been the result of this immigration. Also, more or less roughly, the natural increase in the Italian population had fed emigration.[24] This had serious consequences.

First, the demographic and cultural ones. It meant, in fact, that this same Italian population had lost part of its capacity for reproduction: the diminution or uprooting of the male population, voluntary birth control. The phenomenon could be explained in a number of ways, but the fact still remained that traditional society was losing its vitality, albeit very unevenly. Cisalpine Gaul, which had been systematically colonized, had received an influx of free population which wanted only to prosper, if historical and geographical conditions allowed. Elsewhere, in the Centre and the South, by contrast, the proportion of free men who had come from the old stock of the Italic population was dwindling. Some rural estates were abandoned. Networks of family and clients (of patrons) grew weaker. Regions that did not benefit from the new forms of economic activity became depopulated and the aristocrats who ruled them lost their power. Old values, local languages and traditions declined.

Another society therefore tended to get into position, especially in the towns and regions where slaves were most numerous. Replenishment of the free population was henceforth brought about largely through emancipation. All these individuals of slave stock had certainly become adapted to Italian rules of life, but the majority were of Greek or Oriental origin. It was easier to free slaves who belonged to urban households and who were often more cultivated, that is more Hellenized, than the rest. The procedure in this way contributed to the cultural unification of Italy by favouring the adoption of both Roman and Greek standards to the detriment of traditional local values; the former because they had been dominant in Italy since the late third century, and the latter because they were becoming so in their turn and were in any case shared by both Roman aristocrats and the newly freed. This process tended to favour the concentration of local government and social authority. A freedman remained strictly dependent on his master or patron. At the same stroke, wealthier slaveowners became the most powerful patrons, with the fullest and most extensive networks of clients. Traditional hierarchies were upset by them. In Rome especially, the number of citizens of slave origin similarly increased and alarmed the rulers who tried to confine them in urban tribes.[25]

Transformations in Crafts and Farming

The massive import of slaves was only one of many factors which, throughout the second and third century, accompanied a profound transformation in Italy's economy. Both in farming and craftsmanship, practices of an unprecedented type appeared and gained in importance: farms and workshops increased in size and the number of employees, the organization of labour called for a specialization in types of work, and a process of concentration came into being which aimed at the rapid enrichment of owners by getting standardized products onto the market with sales that would be highly profitable.

This phenomenon was certainly most noticeable in the artisan class and is clearly revealed in two fields: building techniques and pottery production. We can see that, from the second century BC, architects turned increasingly often to a new technique that replaced the building of walls with large hewn blocks of stone that were fitted together (*opus quadratum*) by the use of a lime mortar and smaller stones which were at first crudely cut (*opus incertum*) and then more regularly, so that the external appearance of the walls thus constructed presented a certain aesthetic quality (*opus reticulatum*). In the last instance, however, the work was greatly simplified since the size of the stones was completely standardized and building walls no longer called for the expertise of masons whose task was to put the blocks in place one by one, but merely for unskilled labourers directed by foremen.[26]

Pottery production experienced the same kind of evolution. The standardization of certain items allowed production costs to be lowered and favoured their export far from Italy. We are talking of lamps, like those known as 'Esquiline biconic', which were produced in Latium, Campania and Apulia and distributed, from the middle of the second century, to northern Italy, Narbonensian Gaul, Spain and Africa;[27] and above all a type of pottery which made its appearance in the late third century, first in Campania and then Etruria and which, for this reason, archae- ologists termed Campanian or Etrusco-Campanian.

This glazed pottery was of high enough quality to deserve the interest of populations who lacked such articles, and was suf- ficiently simple to manufacture for it to be profitably commercialized. There was therefore a standardized mass production: the quality of the clay was consistent, paint was applied by immersion, there were not many shapes and they were widely repeated, the decoration remained uniform, identical in the same model, with no innovation or reduction. Workshops using many well-organized slaves in a hierarchy were perfectly able to ensure the manufacture of these articles which called for only repetitive work. The marketing was then effected in the simplest possible way: the products were used as supplementary cargo on boats carrying amphorae of wine. They were thus distributed through the provinces of the West to such an extent that now there are enormous finds of this pottery in a very large number of sites in Narbonensian Gaul, Spain and Africa.[28]

A completely new organization of labour was growing in importance, and benefiting precisely from the import of a cheap and unskilled slave labour force. It is quite probable that similar forms of concentrated production through specialization and standardization were also occurring in other sectors of artisanal activity, notably in wool production, which henceforth became a speciality for certain towns in Italy that were situated on the periphery of livestock-raising areas, for instance, Canosa, Luceria or Fregellae.

It was in farming that this boom in the economy, with its massive blend of slave labour and capital investment, was most clearly seen and certainly had the weightiest social consequences.

There were indeed other factors contributing to the establish- ment of a process of transformation: the increase in the wealth of the Roman aristocracy and that part of Italian society which could take advantage of the new trading trends; the existence of large areas of the *ager publicus* offering those with the means to make use of it the chance to expand their farms or create new ones; the decline in traditional rural society which allowed people to break free of old rules and old structures; and lastly the

continual wars, social then civil, which provoked more confiscations and still further accentuated the concentration of
properties. Prompted by the possibility of launching easily
saleable products onto the market, therefore, a number of people
embarked on profitable speculative farming.

Thus there developed in central and southern Italy an industry
of livestock-breeding practising transhumance, extending on a
large scale from north to south, which created a noticeable boom
in wool production. Of course, the Samnites, Bruttians,
Lucanians and Apulians had been using this method of farming
for a long time. Some communities probably lived by it alone. But
it was precisely in this region that the consequences of the second
Punic War had been the hardest; the population had dwindled
and lands had been confiscated. This ancient practice had been
able to gain in importance, for large areas of the *ager publicus* had
been cleared that could be used, against payment of a tax to
Rome's treasury, and because the former populations no longer
had the same ability to ensure that their grazing or even occupation rights were respected as they had been in the past. Lastly, for
those who had the means to pay, imported slave labour provided
shepherds to watch over the flocks.

It is not surprising, therefore, that among all those to whom our
sources attribute this type of enterprise, we meet Roman senators
like Licinius Lucullus, who was accused of making improper use
of *ager publicus* land,[29] or M. Terentius Varro, who boasted in his
agronomy manual of owning huge flocks of sheep in Apulia,[30] and
knights like P. Aufidius Pontianus, a rich landowner of
Amiternum, who bought – as the same Varro tells us – herds in
'deepest Umbria' to have them driven 'to the pastures of
Metapontum and [sold] in the fair at Heraclea,'[31] and who was
perhaps connected with other Aufidii who appear as *negotiatores*
in the Orient.[32] As these few examples show, all these persons had
the means to invest large amounts of capital in buying livestock
and to make use, legally or not, of public lands as grazing. Their
profit was assured: the animals were resold, probably much more
for their wool than for their meat, and this was processed and
then exported through the markets of southern Italy, especially
those in the Tarentum region, which was famous for the quality
of its fabrics.

So speculative farming took up its position, but its chief
products were at first wheat, wine and oil, which in their turn

became goods with commercial value and thus likely to make a profit. The constraints of the second Punic War had brought about a constant supply in grain between Sicily and Sardinia on the one hand and Rome on the other. Oil began to be exported during the second century. The wine trade commenced in the late third century but expanded considerably from the middle of the second, when its consumption increased and new markets were created, notably as a result of the migratory movements in large towns in Italy and the overseas provinces.[33]

Of course, the development of these products did not affect all regions of Italy in the same way. The export of wheat really concerned only Sicily and Sardinia. The oil merchants to be met principally in Delos originated from Apulia and Lucania. The amphorae used to transport it were manufactured in the same regions, where olive-growing had gained sufficient importance for the product to be commercialized widely outside the peninsula.[34] Above all, the development of viticulture was considerable: massive vineyards extended along the Adriatic coast, and even more, for quality wines, in Latium, Campania and Etruria. In this domain profits were surely the highest, for they provided a large part of Italy with the impetus that allowed it to emerge in a profound alteration of its economy.[35]

As in the case of livestock-breeding, the chief participants and beneficiaries of such alterations were the selfsame Roman or Italian aristocrats who were able to invest or reinvest in land the profits they extracted both from political domination and commercial progress. The owners of properties that can be identified belonged to these circles. Especially in Sicily, alongside local landowners, we meet Roman senators and knights, but also Italian merchants whose names similarly appear in Campanian towns, at Pozzuoli, Capua and Minturnae, for example.[36] Among those who profited from the development of the wine trade, we find members of local, and chiefly Roman aristocracies. This is because either, according to our sources, some of them, M. Aemilius Lepidus, L. Cornelius Lentulus Crus and even Pompey, were the owners of large vineyards, or because the Sestius whose name can be seen on a range of amphorae unearthed in great numbers all over the western part of the Mediterranean basin, notably in Gaul, is believed to have belonged to the senatorial family of the Sestii.[37]

Throughout the second and first centuries there was a

deepening of the process which had first revealed itself at the end of the third century and which included the concentration of ownership and specialization in certain types of farming, bringing profits to Roman elites and those who, like them, could take advantage of the new forms of economic activity. Two fields of evidence enable us to confirm and throw light on this process: the first Latin agronomy manuals, whose publication corresponded to this period of renewal in Italian agriculture, and the remains, which archaeology has allowed us to study, of the estates and villas that exported all these commercialized products to the markets.

The importance of these agronomy manuals must be emphasized; they proliferated particularly during the second and first centuries BC. The first was by Cato the Elder, in the middle of the second century. It was followed by those of the Saserna, father and son, Cn. Tremelius Scrofa and M. Terentius Varro in the middle of the first century. Only the works of Cato and Varro have been preserved. Between one and the other ideas as a whole evolved; reflections became more rational and synthetic. But in both instances the aim remained the same: to offer the reader the means of managing his properties more efficiently and more profitably. Naturally, the public targeted by these works included members of the aristocracy who possessed estates of fair size. Cato described ideal estates with an area of between 100 and 250 jugera, or 25 and slightly over 60 hectares, depending on whether olive groves or vineyards were the subject, and later authors quoted comparable figures.[38] In both instances it was matter of carefully evaluating the equipment, the number and ability of slaves and agricultural workers necessary to farm relatively specialized cultivatable areas. It was thus a far cry from a food-producing agriculture, even if the estates as a whole must have been sufficiently diversified to allow a means of subsistence to those working on them. At all events, their main function was still to enable goods to be produced for marketing, whose sale would achieve a good rate of profit.

Fortunately, certain archaeological research pursued lately in Italy has brought to light buildings which housed some of these farms, and has thus provided a greater understanding of the way in which they were run.

The best-known example is certainly the villa of Settefinestre, in southern Etruria, on the territory of the Cosa colony. It had been built somewhere in the forties BC and represented a perfect stage in the evolution of the agricultural estates under scrutiny here. The area farmed was about 500 jugera or 125 hectares of land and perhaps the equivalent in woods and pastures on the surrounding hills. It comprised a series of grouped buildings, the main one, as in all villas, being divided into two: the *pars urbana*, which formed the owner's house when he was staying on the estate and comprised an atrium, peristyle, bedrooms and a portico overlooking the countryside, and the *pars rustica*, which formed the part more specifically intended for agricultural production. The latter was composed of cowsheds and stables for the animals, lodgings for the slaves and overseer (the *vilicus*) and premises to house the presses and stores necessary for the production of oil and, above all, wine.

It was in fact from the marketing of the latter product that the owner of the villa derived his profits, the remainder of the farm produce being used to ensure self-sufficiency. It has been calculated that at least half the cultivated area of this estate was given over to vines, that about forty slaves were employed and that annual production of wine was over 1000 hectolitres, at a minimum value of 16,000 denarii.[39]

Furthermore, among the many amphorae distributed throughout the Mediterranean world, some originating from the territory of Cosa have been identified. These are amphorae of the Dressel I type, marked 'Sest' or 'Sext', from the name of an important landowner. They have been found along the whole Ligurian coast and that of Narbonensian Gaul, especially in one of the shipwrecks of the Grand-Congloué, near Marseilles, as well as inland, along the valleys of the Rhône, Saône and Loire. It is known that the Gaulish aristocracy bought large quantities of wine, thus making the fortune of Italian producers. In this instance, it is supposed that Sest(ius) belonged to the family of P. Sestius, a tribune of the plebs whom Cicero had defended and who is known to have possessed property in the region of Cosa. People have even gone so far as to imagine that he was also the master of Settefinestre. Bricks marked 'L.S.' would lead us to suppose so. However that may be, the most important fact remains that members of the senatorial aristocracy were the ones to benefit from the development of the wine trade and to get rich from its production.

We may then understand how powerful the consequences of

the advance in such speculative farming must have been in the regions of Italy which underwent this profound transformation in its structure.

In some instances, small peasant farmers were threatened with the loss of the tiny plot necessary for their very survival. In many regions, indeed, the traditional social fabric had been destroyed or at least gravely weakened by the results of the second Punic War, and almost everywhere it was still tending to disintegrate because of the conflicts of the first century and demographic developments. It was then difficult for peasant communities, let alone individuals, to defend themselves against the pressure from often powerful aristocrats who were trying to set up new forms of farming with profit-making in view. This happened in regions where collective lands were the means of tradtional livestock-rearing or formed an essential complement to smallholdings of barely one or two hectares, which just about prevented their owners from starving to death.[40] It may be supposed that these were the lands most frequently confiscated after the second Punic War and incorporated into the *ager publicus*. Roman senators and knights thus often had the means of taking possession of them, legally or illegally, to establish livestock-breeding with transhumance in a programme that attained the size just mentioned. In contrast, the situation was different in other regions. Where the development of speculative farming involved production which, like vineyards and olive groves, necessitated reliance on a plentiful and easily mobilized labour force, slaves would not suffice, and the employment of farm-workers favoured the maintenance of a free peasantry *in situ*.

All this resulted in a process of transformation in the human and economic rural equilibrium that was far more complex[41] than the abandonment and population drain which have sometimes been described. In regions unaffected by the development of speculative farming, because, for example, they were too remote from markets and communication routes, traditional structures were probably able to persist without too many difficulties.[42] In others, everything depended on the type of development taking place. Extensive wheat production or transhumant livestock-breeding, notably in Sicily and southern Italy, exerted a great deal of pressure on smallholdings; But elsewhere intensive crop-growing favoured their upkeep. The few specific researches carried out, notably in south Etruria,[43] show in fact that for a long while small farms coexisted with villas, their number dwindling noticeably only during the first century AD. The resistance of traditional agriculture was helped by several factors: the strong level of self-sufficiency of the peasant population, the growth of the urban population, which brought in its wake the development of urban food markets, and the effects of the policies of land distribution carried out by the *populares* authorities or military leaders.

Nevertheless, the general trend, over a long period, was a weakening of the old structures of agriculture. Although small farmers were not always threatened, small properties were more so because, subjected to all the constraints described above, they could either disappear as a result of the increase in size of great estates or be changed into a form of indirect farming which, while maintaining the old organization of production, made those who were known as colonists subordinate to the landowners.[44] Contemporaries were keenly aware of this evolution, as we find echoes of it in many of the early writers, who simultaneously stressed the cupidity of the wealthy, the ruin of the peasantry and the disappearance of the free rural population.

The end result was to encourage, if not provoke, a rural exodus that revealed itself in two main ways: on the one hand, the emigration of a large number of Italians from the centre of the peninsula, either to Cisalpine Gaul where they could benefit from the distribution of land, or to other regions of the Mediterranean where they sought to take advantage of Roman domination and, on the other hand, a move to Rome and several other large towns, where they hoped to find better living conditions, and where they formed a sizable increase in the population. We obviously lack the information that would help us appreciate the magnitude of this event, but we know, for example, that in 177 envoys from the Samnites and Pelignians complained that 4,000 families had installed themselves in Fregellae, no doubt attracted there by the development of the wool industry.[45] The same sort of thing occurred in the port of Pozzuoli and other towns, which new economic activities were making prosperous. Above all, the number of inhabitants in Rome grew immensely, passing from some 200,000 people at the end of the third century to a figure somewhere between 700,000 and 1 million at the end of the first century. The regular provisioning of this great metropolis thus became one of the major headaches that its rulers had to try to solve. Obviously, these newcomers were not all peasants who had deserted their lands; among them were large proportions of slaves and foreigners.[46] Nevertheless, even with those qualifications, the problem must have been one of some amplitude.

The other consequence was related to the influx of slave labour into rural areas. The hundreds of thousands of slaves who arrived in Italy during one and a half centuries were mainly employed in the new structures of agricultural production, in a variety of ways. Among this slave population there were, of course, skilled workers, wine-growers or estate stewards who enjoyed a certain autonomy and who in any case were probably not badly treated, if only because they were valuable. But one must also take into account the masses of chained wretches in *ergastula* who supplied a brute labour force. Lastly we must add the bands who were more or less left to their own devices, for example, the teams of woodcutters or, especially, the shepherds who accompanied the flocks in their moves to other pastures. They presented a certain danger for the people around about, as they were armed and often obliged to live off the land to keep their animals and themselves from starving.

This massive slave presence had heavy consequences for the social life of Italy. One thinks first of the slave rebellions that regularly erupted between the early second century and the middle of the first: in Etruria in 196, Apulia in 186–80, Sicily in 135, Campania and Sicily again in 104–102, and the whole of Italy with the uprising led by Spartacus from 72 to 71. In every case, there were profound movements which rapidly mobilized tens of thousands of men, sometimes bringing free men with them, who organized themselves, come what may, behind charismatic leaders and showed themselves capable, at least initially, of fighting the Roman armies sent against them. These rebellions impinged on people's minds to the point where the fear of slave revolts became one of the recurring themes in the political discourse of the end of the Republic.

But even more, the uprisings revealed how different this population was from the rest of Italy. Their leaders were, like themselves, Gauls, Cimbri, Syrians or Cilicians, who had preserved their language, religion and political models, around which they tried to organize their government. Moreover, the ease and rapidity with which they recruited large bands underline the poor level of their integration. The fact that free men joined them confirmed that in some parts of Italy and Sicily traditional societies had fallen apart to the extent where uprooted or marginalized individuals could participate in these movements of rebellion which had no solution or prospects. If we reflect that throughout this period their number continually increased, we may imagine the destructive effect of such immigration on social structures and the ethnic balance of regions in which they were concentrated, precisely those where changes in the economy were taking place, namely: Latium, Campania, Sicily, the whole of southern Italy and coastal Etruria.

The same transformations, however, had a unifying effect on the peninsula as a whole. They certainly helped to bring it into a trading economy which it had hitherto only partly penetrated. The ports experienced increased activity: Pozzuoli, Minternae, certainly Ostia, and also Rome where, beginning in the 190s, a whole series of buildings was constructed along the Tiber. The use of coinage spread. The denarius became the dominant method of payment in Italy from the middle of the second century. It spread throughout Italy and even to Sicily where, at the end of the century, it tended to supplant local money. The inscription 'Roma' disappeared from coins which no longer needed to be identified since they were in use by all.[47] The phenomenon was not only economic, but also political and ideological. It meant the Rome's domination henceforth extended everywhere, not only in its relations with the other cities of Italy, but also in people's consciousness and systems of reference, as if from then on nothing could couterbalance Roman authority.

But this omnipotence was by no means purely psychological. The same regions that underwent a transformation in economic activity were also those that above all else benefited from the investments and the increased presence of Roman aristocracy.

In some instances, the process contributed to the impoverishment and depopulation of rural areas; but in contrast, a new human landscape was formed in others. The Roman landowners installed themselves in the region where they had acquired their possessions. This was true of Sicily, where Roman senators, knights and merchants bought lands and created great estates given over to the production of wheat. It was also true of Campania or Etruria, where they built villas in which they spent at least a little time during the year. Even if they were not in fact resident there, these new Roman masters replaced the old ones in the social structure and representation, becoming both the men of power whose wealth and authority formed a threat, but also potential patrons who, if one agreed to join their clientele, could turn out to be effective protectors.

Through the upheavals in the forms of property ownership and farming, the whole of the profound Romanization of Italy was thus being made ready and gradually put in place. The two trends described above fitted in with each other to produce this result. On the one hand, the demographic weakening of traditional society and, on the other, the establishment of new structures of craft and agricultural production plus the import of hundreds of thousands of slaves, in fact combined in the disintegration of the social and ethnic fabric of the regions most affected by this process. Society's new organization placed side by side the new rulers, who were very often Roman, their slaves and the former inhabitants who continued to make their old civic structures work.

The problems raised by this new situation had to be resolved by the relationship between a Roman government, increasingly gaining strength, and local authorities. The Italian aristocracies were the first to be involved in these changes, either because they could boost their own power by taking advantage of them or, on the contrary, because they had lost their supremacy by falling victim to them. For even if the situation varied considerably from one people or city or another, it was the aristocrats who, by their presence, their dynamism or their weaknesses, bore witness to the deep-seated changes in Italy.

5

ITALIAN MUNICIPAL ARISTOCRACIES

I have already stressed several times the importance of the role played by municipal aristocracies in Italy in the first two centuries BC. In fact, they constituted the dominant classes which locally governed the various cities and peoples in the peninsula, managed their political life and imposed their methods of representation. Through them, fundamentally, was instituted the Romanization that gradually incorporated all these different societies into a single cultural and political whole and united them.

Of course, they were the first to be affected by the profound changes influencing Italian societies, whether they stood to gain from them or were their victims. They either grew rich by taking part in the new commercial trading or the developments in speculative farming that were under way – and strengthened their position – or, on the other hand, became impoverished and these very transformations removed part of their means of dominance. It should not be imagined, however, that wealth was the only element to define them as a dominant class. Other aspects also played an important part: the networks of clients and friends they controlled, for instance, or the image of themselves that they presented to reassure the fellow-citizens they intended to govern.

Their power depended on the position they occupied in the new hierarchy that had been established in Italy, and it was not solely concerned with their respective riches. Since Rome ruled the entire peninsula, that was where most of the important decisions directly affecting the life of the city-states were taken. The authority of an aristocrat was thus measured by his ability to influence the deliberations of Roman magistrates and senators in one direction or another. Moreover, since Italy in its entirety had been incorporated into a cultural ensemble dominated by Greek methods of representation, the aristocracy's prestige and the evidence of its superiority relied on its talent for presenting an image of itself appropriate to what was henceforth expected of anyone aspiring to rule the city. All these aspects were connected, although they were sometimes marked by contradictions; in any case, they varied considerably from one people to another, according to the degree of independence they maintained with regard to the Roman government, or their feeling of self-worth and dignity, which may or may not have saved them having to seek their standards of conduct elsewhere.

To get a good overall view of the relative influence of the various factors, I will first analyse these municipal aristocracies in a general way, especially as they were in the second century, and to this end try to identify the means that enabled them to exert their dominance locally. In the ethnic and cultural diversity that still existed in Italy, we must similarly recognize the behaviour they adopted in their desire to preserve or increase their power still further in the midst of all the changes affecting the life of the peninsula.

Municipal Politics

What first defined an aristocrat in an Italian city-state was that he governed or could claim to govern it, and also that he possessed the means to do so. Not everybody could do this. Everywhere, inscriptions reveal that those individuals who held magistracies belonged to a few families whose names often recurred from one generation to the next. This does not mean that situations were rigidly set or that advancement and decline were ruled out, but rather that only the members of the minority at the summit of the local hierarchy might hope to govern their fellow-citizens.

This social fact was equally valid for colonies, *municipia* (or free towns) and allied cities. Everywhere civic organization required a senate and magistrates to govern the community, and that the individuals holding such offices should meet certain specific requirements of wealth and social status.

In the Latin colonies and those with Roman citizens, at least when the latter had acquired enough autonomy, the magistrates were organized in various hierarchies called *collegia*, following the model of what prevailed in Rome. The most important generally had the title of *praetor*, and later of *duumviri*. It was their responsibility to set out the legal standards specific to the new city, to see that they were applied, to organize elections and preside over assemblies. They or others, as sometimes the title *censor* appears in sources, carried out censuses. At regular intervals, every five years if one had to abide by Roman rules, they reviewed the list of citizens and chose from their ranks the members of the local senate. Lower-ranking magistrates, *aediles* or *quaestors*, sometimes assisted them in the less important duties: managing provisions or finances. Priests were responsible for religious matters. All had a particular position in the city's administration. Ushers, scribes, lictors, stewards, soothsayers were at their service. Attributes, such as a court, a purple band on the toga, reserved seats at the theatre, marked them out from the ordinary people.[1]

As in Rome, the senators, who were often known as *conscripti* or decurions, were responsible for the permanent running of the community. They exercised the rights that had been left with the city in the matter of external policy, which were of some interest and importance as they allowed relations of patronage or good neighbourliness to be established and maintained with individuals or other cities. They controlled finances and decided on the public works that needed to be implemented. They also had a say in all important matters involving public order. All this constituted a group of high-level posts from which decisions frequently emanated on measures that seriously affected the lives of the inhabitants, so it would be wrong to underestimate their power.

Elsewhere, in cities that had their own history and had not been founded by Rome, municipia incorporated into the community of Roman citizens or allied cities which preserved their own laws, the constitution varied from one town to another, but in general still respected the tripartite division distinguishing between the people, the senate and the magistrates. There were scarcely any exceptions. Peoples like the Samnites, who were organized in *pagi* and *vici*, nevertheless held assemblies, and were in any case governed by magistrates, the *meddices*. Even the old Capuans, whose city had been broken up, had preserved a local organization centred around people in charge known as *magistri*.[2]

But apart from these general rules, titles and competences varied from one city to another. I have already mentioned the different magistracies found among the various peoples, and I must add that the disparities could be sizeable. In the agreement between Abella and Nola, for instance, over the running of a sanctuary situated on the frontier of the two cities, the first was represented by a quaestor and the second by a *meddix*. Both, however, exercised the same function.[3] Even the municipia were far from having adopted all the Roman constitutional principles since in Capua, before the second Punic War, the senate seems to have been elected by the people.[4] All this reflected Italy's deepseated heterogeneity at that time. Each city's institutions were the outcome of a different history; they were the sign of its identity, and also of the vitality of its civic traditions.

We do not have the documents to enable us to appreciate the forms and intensity of political life in Italy's city-states. But, for example, was it less strong at Pompeii in the second century, when this town had not yet undergone the establishment of a Roman colony, than in the following years during the electoral campaigns to which the grafiti that can still be read on the walls bear witness? Some inscriptions from those distant times remain: they refer to a people's assembly (*kumbennio*), a senate (*kumparakion*) and magistrates who, as in the Oscan areas, bore the title *meddices*.[5]

Nevertheless, the best example one can quote is provided by Cicero, recounting an episode from the history of Arpinum, his native town. In 115 BC a certain M. Gratidius proposed a law to introduce a secret ballot in people's assemblies. This procedure had already been used in Rome since 139 BC. Arpinum had been a municipium with full Roman rights since 188. This meant that Rome's laws were not necessarily applied in other cities, even when they were composed of Roman citizens, since the people of Arpinum themselves had to decide on measures determining the functioning of their institutions. In his town M. Gratidius thus conducted a policy said to be *popularis*, which consisted of promoting measures of a democratic kind. He was probably trying in this way to find favour with the common people. But he was opposed by Cicero's grandfather, M. Tullius Cicero, who for his part held a conservative position. There was violent conflict and the matter was referred to the Senate in Rome.[6] The two men were related by marriage, however, because the second had married the sister of the first. But they were also the representatives of two of the greatest aristocratic families dominating the city of Arpinum. For them the family connection was as necessary as the conflict: they needed to join forces to ensure their own dominance, even if it meant clashing when their rivalry was revealed and they had to gain the votes of the people or the esteem of their fellow-citizens.

This affair is a fair illustration of a situation which, setting aside ethnic and cultural differences, must have prevailed in the majority of towns in Italy. Aristocratic families dominated local political life, and enlivened it with their conflicts and competitiveness. As soon as our information becomes rather more plentiful, indeed, this series of individuals appears who, bearing the same name and therefore fathers, sons, brothers or cousins, forebears or descendants across several generations, succeeded one another in local magistracies, sometimes dropping out of sight for a while then reappearing a few decades later, their wealth and prestige rebuilt.

Among the native families at Pompeii, we could thus quote the Popidii, who provided the city with at least four magistrates, including one of its *meddices*; the Satrii, whose name was borne by one aedile, and the Suttii, who were similarly situated and whose members reappeared in the early first century AD among the notables, magistrates and candidates for election.[7] One could carry out the same exercise at Aquileia, this time a Latin colony, where among the rulers of the city there are several instances of Babrinii, Gavillii or Vibii, who were still governing it after it had become a municipium.[8] We might also recall that at Praeneste, at the end of the second century, the Dindii, Feidenatii, Magulnii, Orcevii and Saufeii were the ones with the monopoly of power.[9]

As at Arpinum, these families formed alliances among themselves. The exercise of power relied on both the fortune that could be amassed and the services that could be rendered by relatives or family connections. All those instruments of domination had to be assembled and concentrated, at all costs avoiding their dispersal, which was the more to be feared in cities with Roman rights because the rules of inheritance made provision for sharing legacies. So we see that at Chiusi, in the second century, the town was controlled by a handful of families who were all connected with one another, chiefly the Seiante, but also the Tlesna, Tetina, Larcna, Pulfna, Tutna, Velu and Velsi, to name only the main ones, who through trade and reciprocity controlled the ownership of land and power over the city.[10] Elsewhere, at Larinum, in a family we know well because Cicero described their history in one of his defence speeches, the Abbii, Aurii, Cluentii and Vibii were connected, early in the first century, by ties that were sometimes intensified, causing first or second cousins to marry over several generations or forcing a couple to unite the children the spouses had had by former marriages.[11] So both sides could maintain the capital of wealth and social relations that formed their strength, by means of strategies which certainly had more to do with violence and rivalry than with tenderness and affection.

The Criteria of Worthiness

It was at all events a constant feature of the method of Roman representation that an aristocracy was necessary to the constitution of a city. It may be recalled that at the time of the founding of colonies following the second Punic War, notably at Aquileia, the allocations of land served to establish in the new city the social hierarchy intended to be reproduced there. The plots were in fact of varying size, depending on whether the recipients were footsoldiers, centurions or cavalrymen. The difference in property ownership, but also the difference in worthiness that separated the leaders from their subordinates, served as means of establishing the new social ladder. When we learn that the magistrates whose task was to set up a colony selected the members of the first local senate, we may easily imagine that they recruited them from these new aristocrats.

This ideal situation, of an aristocracy in its native state so to speak, obviously did not occur everywhere. But there was always the double requirement of wealth, especially in the form of landed property, and worthiness.

Let us start by examining the former. Again we lack the information to present exact rules. But two inscriptions from the first century BC may be quoted which confirm this requirement, two fragments of laws organizing the institutions of some cities; with Roman rights it is true, which puts certain limitations on the conclusions that may be drawn. First, the law known as that of Tarentum, since it established the constitution of that city. On pain of a fine, it obliged every decurion to own, either in the town or on adjacent territory, a building comprising at least 1,500 tiles.[12] This was confirmed by another text of the same type, contemporary with Caesar's government, concerning the town of Urso in Spain, though it probably borrowed its regulations from a model common to all Italy. In this case, there was an obligation on the senator to possess within the town or less than a mile (about 1.5 km) distant, a house 'that may be used as security'.[13]

To meet these demands, by the ownership of possessions that could be verified, senators had to provide guarantees that would suffice for the exercise of their responsibilities. They had to participate in the management of public funds, but also contribute to the prosperity of the community. When they entered the local curia, or when they held a magistracy, they were asked to pay into the treasury or spend on public works or games a certain sum of money (*summa honoraria*) which obviously varied according to the size of the city but corresponded overall to the level of wealth of the local notables. They were frequently expected to be public benefactors who, by their largesse, contributed to the well-being and prestige of their community.[14] It was desirable that they should be accessible and available and therefore that there was some assurance of their residing among their fellow-citizens.

The facts yielded by archaeology mainly verify this initial evidence. Some of the houses found in the heart of Italian towns were rich dwellings, often abundantly decorated, arranged around one or more *atria* and other reception rooms that would allow the master of the house to receive his dependants. There are many examples, but we shall take just one, precisely because it is marginal. At Saepinum (Sepino), in Samnium, on the site of what would later be the forum, during the second century, two types of buildings made their appearance: wool-processing workshops (*fullonicae*) on the one hand, whose presence is easily explained by this region's important sheep-rearing and transhumance industry, and indicates a certain degree of wealth, and on the other a house adorned with a mosaic representing a hunting scene, which suggests that its owner had the rudiments of aristocratic tastes. We may thus see the association of these few buildings as heralding the process of municipalization that would be completed at the end of the first century.[15]

The aristocrats' town houses, however, were not the sole constituents of their wealth; the lands they owned and the various manufacturing businesses that made them rich must be added.

Here again, a handful of examples will suffice. Among the families who formed the aristocracy of Pompeii, the Holconii had given their name to one of the most celebrated vineyards in Campania. One Corellius was known for having been the first to cultivate chestnuts in order to market them. The Lassii and the Eumachii were associates. The former produced wine and the latter the amphorae used to transport it.[16] Obviously, they were all totally committed to speculative farming and found the way to get rich by it. Elsewhere, artisanal activities made it possible to acquire the necessary wealth: Cicero's maternal family owned *fullonicae* that had certainly contributed to setting up the family heritage.[17] In yet other cities, the rulers grew rich through trade and business deals. This was obviously the case of Campanian towns which profited largely from trade with the East, notably Pozzuoli where the Annii, for instance, who had grown rich by trafficking with the most distant places, continually advanced in the town's social hierarchy.[18]

Not all activities carried the same cachet, however. It was not considered suitable to make one's money through craft industry. The share of his wealth which his relatives had acquired from wool production earned Cicero insulting comments on the lowliness of his origins.[19] Commerce was acceptable only if conducted on a grand scale, and the Annii just mentioned took several generations to reach the summit of local society. In reality, there was no truly honourable wealth except in landed property. It was by the evaluation of estates, in the Roman system, that tax assessment was established and, in the hierarchy resulting from different economic activities, it was agriculture that really dominated: 'Of all the profit-making enterprises, nothing is better than farming, nothing is more productive, nothing more pleasing, nothing more worthy of a man and of a free man,'[20] explained Cicero himself, thus resuming an everyday theme among the authors of antiquity.

Worthiness was the second condition which had to be met in order to be admitted to the ranks of local aristocracies. Here again, a law that is known from an important inscription, the so-called table of Heraclea, allows us to pinpoint the principal features defining it. Among the arrangements it envisaged were those excluding from local senates a whole range of people whose shared characteristic was to have been condemned for crimes of common law or to have lost their integrity.[21]

This last word, rather vague it is true, in fact embraced a real aristocratic *ethos* which allowed a man to be truly his own master. The concept covered all fields, from the most concrete to the most symbolic. Prostitutes and gladiators, who had allowed someone else to make use of their bodies, were obviously ruled out. They dragged with them into their infamy procurers and the buyers and trainers of gladiators who organized the combats. But to them must be added those who had failed the trust that had been placed in them: the bankrupts, debtors incapable of repaying their debts, dishonest guardians, the authors of slanderous accusations, and even soldiers who had been discharged from the army for having fled or disobeyed, in fact, all who had shown themselves to be failing in their obligations and who had lost their credit (*fides*). This last idea was important: it was represented as a kind of resource that extended the person of the citizen, incorporated bodily in the right hand which was proffered to seal an agreement. Not to measure up to it meant infamy and degradation.

From this dual aspect of landed wealth and integrity we are given a good understanding of what constituted an aristocrat in Roman eyes. It was necessary to be rich to have credit, but also to be capable of respecting one's own word in order to continue to enjoy the confidence and trust of one's fellow-citizens. One had to be loyal to oneself, one's relatives, one's allies and one's neighbours; to aid and succour those who sought help; to become their patron, if it was a matter of inferiors who needed protection. What was received in exchange far outweighed mere esteem. Whoever was capable of protecting others could protect the city as a whole. Being a powerful and trustworthy aristocrat enabled one to lay the foundations of a charisma that earned its possessor the alligiance of his fellow-citizens and a sphere of influence that would enable him to be known and esteemed beyond his own community.

To all these requirements must be added other criteria, which may not appear in the documents but are well attested in Roman tradition. The charisma defining the superior individual was also related to certain abilities that reassured and reinforced the community who put their trust in him: knowledge of the law and military worth.[22] In the early days, the first was hardly distinguishable from a knowledge of the standards that enabled the rules governing the relations between gods and men to be respected. The whole balance of the state depended on it and one can understand why it received so much attention. The importance of the second goes without saying: it allowed individuals like Pompey and, above all, Caesar to turn themselves into monarchs.

All these values counted, even in Italy's smallest states. They were spread through the whole of society and shared by all. For although, for Roman citizens, attention was drawn first to the great personages who dominated the political stage in Rome, judgements made at a local level on this or that person who showed a desire to govern obviously relied on the same criteria. This was what happened at Arpinum, where the two protagonists borrowed their standards of behaviour from Roman models and joined directly in the same political semantics as they did. It is easy to suppose that Roman citizens enjoying all civic rights and, in some cases, belonging to the equestrian order, should themselves attain magistracies that were specifically Roman. The consul Aemilius Scaurus had said as much to Cicero's grandfather, when regretting that he had not been able to grace the senatorial order with the qualities of courage which he had proved so well at Arpinum.[23]

All the same, M. Tullius had shown no such desire. He remained devoted to his own city. He was evidently not alone, for the running of all Italy's towns relied on those aristocrats who found in the government of their homeland the necessary instrument for the continuance of their status and the satisfaction of their desire to fulfil the expectations of their fellow-citizens.

However, of necessity the ideal image of the aristocrat varied from one region to another, because of individual local history and cultural differences. From the Sardinians who operated the suffetate to the Samnites who aspired to be *meddices*, values could not be identical, even though in their main characteristics the definitions given above were generally conceded. There is not sufficient documentation to allow this aristocracy to be pinpointed precisely in every instance, but some evidence can be picked up here and there. For example, on the urns found in large numbers in the cemeteries of the Etruscan town of Volterra, when the dead were represented it was often in the guise of magistrates surrounded by their attendants and accompanied by the symbols of their office.[24] Moreover, the frequency with which the instruments of divination or worship of the gods were depicted suggests that, in Etruscan society, the charisma legitimizing the exercise of power was rooted in the practice of civil and religious laws. This was probably also true of the Marsi, who were very proud of their knowledge in matters of divination. Military achievements[25] were highly prized there too, as they were among the Samnites. Elsewhere, in the Greek cities of southern Italy and Sicily, other forms of virtue probably held greater importance, notably public benefaction, by which a rich citizen used his wealth to the advantage of his fellow-citizens.

These variations in the scale of aristocratic values had their importance: they led individuals to adopt different ways of behaviour depending on their ethnic origins. As long as they lasted, they were the sign of people's identity, and also of the allegiance they felt towards it.

Tastes become Hellenized

During the second half of the second century, however, there were various manifestations of a continuous Hellenization of these social and cultural values, evidently extending an earlier process but which, stimulated by Italy's opening out on to the external world, favoured the aristocracies' trend towards uniformity. In the main, this development concerned the central regions of the peninsula, Latium and Campania, but it heralded and prepared the ground for a process that was to continue in other regions, so we must have a clear understanding of what was at stake. Adopting Greek-style tastes and cultural practices did not stem from a simple change in people's sensibilities; it was also a matter of people's position in a developing society, at the heart of which rivalry for possession of the means of pre-eminence compelled the adoption of its most up-to-date and keenest expressions.

For instance, although there is no evidence to show that the Italian world, with the probable exception of the Greek cities, was well versed in the art of rhetoric, this spread and grew in importance, certainly in Rome, but also in other cities in the peninsula. Cicero made precise notes of the phenomenon. In his *Brutus*, one of the dialogues in which he described Latin eloquence, he quoted a whole series of orators of municipal origin, mostly contemporary with the late second century, who came from the Marsian region, Campania, Cisalpine Gaul or Picenum, and bore witness that in that period the art of eloquence was already widely spread among the peoples of Italy.[26] And he was mentioning only the most important personages for, if we examine the documents, there were many others who in those years bestowed the benefits of their talents on their contemporaries.

There were many contributory factors. Rhetoric was fundamentally a technique whose rules had constantly progressed in the Greek world, thanks to both the work of its practitioners and the subjects and methods of reflection that had been introduced by philosophy. It enabled those who had been trained in it to utter speeches that were much richer, more ornate and more moving. It provided them with the means not only to persuade, and thus to triumph over, their adversaries in all the political and legal jousts that were the essential part of aristocratic activity, but also to increase their stature by its power to captivate and move, and acquire the extra charisma which would further justify their aspirations to govern their fellow-citizens. It is easy to understand why it spread in all cities where political life at that time relied on the use of words.

There do not appear to have been any significant time lags between Rome and the other regions. The first generation of Roman aristocrats to be truly schooled in rhetoric was born after 180. Indeed, a famous episode provides an important point of reference. In 155, on the day when ambassadors from Athens, who had been chosen precisely from among representatives of the foremost philosophical schools, were profiting from their stay to hold lectures, young people rushed up from all sides to listen to them and, recounts Plutarch, it was 'as if an impetuous wind filled the town with its noise'.[27] There must, therefore, have been an extraordinary novelty in this event to provoke such a reaction.

Similarly, during the latter half of the second century the first Latin-speaking orators originating from the municipia began to make themselves known.[28] Most often they were from Latium or Campania and mainly contemporaries of the orators who really founded the art of rhetoric in Rome. The process that had taken shape worked at roughly the same pace in all that part of Italy. The reason was that apprenticeship was undertaken either with Greek masters who had come to Italy, cultured slaves employed as tutors or learned men invited by rich families, or – though the custom did not really catch on until the early first century – by the travelling which some of these young people did in Greece to get their training at the very founts of rhetoric and philosophy. The Campanian aristocrats, engaged as they were in relations with the East, had easy access to these intellectual resources even if, as we shall see a little later, they remained under the domination of the model instituted by the Roman aristocracy.

At the same time as the art of speech-making, other forms of Hellenistic taste and expression in the plastic arts invaded the homes and towns of Italy. Here again, it would be wrong to perceive nothing more than the strictly aesthetic dimension of this occurrence, for the decoration and pictures which peopled both the public and private backdrops to social life equally introduced evidence of prestige and superiority.

It was not the sole function of an aristocrat's dwelling, for example, to provide him with a roof over his head. It was also the place where he received his friends and dependants and therefore allowed him to make a clear statement of his position in society.

It had long been true, but a remark by Seneca discloses that during the latter half of the second century some important changes in customs and habits made their appearance.

> It is an ancient practice among kings and those who wish to emulate them to divide a company of friends into different classes; and a characteristic of arrogance to set a very high price on the right to cross, or even touch, the threshold, and to grant as an honour a position near the entrance, to set foot ahead of others in the house, wherein lies a series of doors to deny further access even to those who are allowed to enter. Among us C. Gracchus, then Livius Drusus, first of all established the custom of separating the crowd of their friends into categories, receiving some in private, others in a small group, and the rest all together. Those men, therefore, had first-class and second-class friends – never true friends.[29]

Leaving aside the last remark, which concerns philosophy, and keeping only on the allusion to Gaius Gracchus and Livius Drusus, the others enable us to date this borrowing from the customs of Hellenistic sovereigns to the last decades of the second century. At that time the residence of Roman aristocrats became the instrument in a courtly ritual which demonstrated their civic superiority. Naturally, this practice had an effect on domestic living arrangements. The hierarchy of admissions to the house had to be matched by a hierarchy of rooms allowing the 'filtering' of visitors. Once can understand why, in these conditions, dwellings, houses or villas, grew larger; to be precise, they were developed by the addition of rooms, a second *atrium* or a peristyle, as in the noblest houses in Pompeii, which, when added to the succession of areas to be crossed, probably elevated the majesty of the owner still further.[30]

Thus we get a better grasp of the process of adopting Hellenistic models in the field of architecture and decoration: these were imitations of the houses of aristocrats of the East, even the palaces of their kings. They provided the inspiration that gave rise to the appearance of peristyles and *atria* with columns, the porticoed façades of the villas dominating the countryside[31] and the mosaics with their heroic themes.[32] Some of these mansions attained or even exceeded the size of the buildings from which their architects drew their inspiration: the house known as that of the Faun at Pompeii covered 3,000 square metres. That was more than the palace of the kings of Pergamum. It was also decorated with mosaics of unprecedented luxury. The mosaic occupying one of the rooms giving onto the peristyle represented Alexander in combat, and was composed of one and a half million tesserae.[33] Its owner was, however, no more than one of those notables I mentioned before. Here imitation assumed the air of identification: by appropriating Hellenistic values one increased one's standing through the prestige of those kings who had just been vanquished.

To be even more precise, the implicit claim to the glory of Alexander and his heirs through the use of Hellenistic plastic arts also appeared in the representations left by these individuals showing themselves or their exploits. There are not many examples, but one could quote fragments of reliefs found in aristocratic houses at Fregellae, recalling the battles in which their owners had taken part in the East.[34]

Among some statues and protraits that have been preserved, the statue of C. Ofellius Ferus is particularly worthy of mention. It adorned the agora of the Italians in Delos, which is sometimes thought to have been used as a slave market. The man belonged to a well-known family of notables of Capua and Beneventum. He was one of those Italians who made a fortune in the East, possibly in this trade, and he had contributed to the construction of the building. As a gesture of gratitude, his statue had been erected. It was larger than life-size, and he was shown in the nude. There was nothing ordinary about this style; it denoted gods and heroes, and had been used for Alexander, his successors, saviours and founders. Although it had since become quite commonplace, chiefly in Greece, it is nevertheless an interesting sign: it would seem that these merchants had learned the lessons of the East and had appropriated its symbols and languages.[35]

So there should be no surprise that very often, in Italy itself, the representations of themselves which aristocrats wanted to convey similarly used this Hellenizing style that idealized the model.[36] Here, it was not a question of taste alone. The self-image one presented meant a claim on the social ladder. It was one of the means that enabled these notables to affirm themselves as the natural and legitimate leaders of their communities.

Public Benefaction and Changes in the Urban Framework

Still under the influence of the Hellenistic world, there was another increasingly widespread and important means of displaying one's position and status in society: public benefaction. It enabled one to become the benefactor of one's city.

Gifts could be made in a variety of ways: games, banquets, construction of buildings, embassies to other cities, especially Rome, carried out without charge. They could be offered in wills, or in the lifetime of the donor, during the holding of magistracies or not. The man who showed such generosity was first defined as a superior individual because he was both rich and unselfish. But he also caused the community to which he belonged to benefit from his prosperity, helped it by his influence, beautified it or gave it the opportunity for collective festivities. He thus acquired renown as a benefactor in exchange for the recognition and gratitude of his fellow-citizens, who demonstrated this by erecting statues to him or placing inscriptions that bore witness to his distinction and would justify for future generations the claim of his descendants to rule the city.

One example will give us the measure of this phenomenon. It is the inscription which was raised to the Alatri around the end of the second century in honour of L. Betilienus Varus, a notable of the town:

> L. Betilienus Varus, son of Lucius, on the advice of the senate, has undertaken to have the following built: all the streets in the town, the portico giving access to the acropolis, the ground for the games, the clock, the market, the whitewashing of the basilica, the seats, the bathing pool, the reservoir near the gate, supplying water to the town by raising it to 340 feet high, he had the arches built and the water ducts strengthened. For all this, he was made censor for the second time, the senate decided that his son should be exempted from military service and the people offered him a statue and gave him the name Censorinus.[37]

Here was a man who must have spent a fortune for his town, and it is understandable that he was rewarded for it. It is also true that the honours he was awarded were the highest possible, on the scale of his community. Censorship was the most elevated magistracy of all. It gave its holder the right to recruit senators and to put each citizen in his proper place, downgrading some and promoting others. He himself must therefore have been regarded as the most respectable. The inscription, the statue and the surname he had received entrenched the event in the collective memory, and he was judged, together with his family, to have deserved enough of his city for his son to be exempt from military service.

But the works he had accomplished could not be ascribed to mere embellishment. Reading the list of all these operations, one realizes that it was not simply a decorative undertaking. The entire urban lay-out of Alatri was restructured in such a way that henceforth the self-image presented by the city would match the model provided by the most beautiful towns in the East. All the works financed by Betilienus tended to adorn Alatri with the attributes of an ideal town: water supplies for the baths, grounds for the games, the market and the restoration of the basilica. Still more, as they were combined, they constituted a real programme of reshaping the urban landscape: the streets that were constructed, adapting their plan wherever possible to the new rules, and the portico which, lending the aspect of Propylaea to the entrance to the citadel, increased its majesty; all these works were directed towards the same end.[38]

Betilinius Varus was not an isolated instance. Others were carrying out comparable works in their own cities. During the latter half of the second century, temples, basilicas, baths and theatres were built in many places, chiefly, it is true, in the regions of central Italy that were most involved in trade with the rest of the Mediterranean world and the establishment of speculative farming: Latium and Campania. It was here, in fact, that the aristocrats who were expected to take charge of their communities had become rich enough to be able through their generosity to alter the architectural surroundings of their own cities. Naturally, those who financed all these buildings introduced their personal tastes. As in the case of those houses in which the style of decoration helped to display their owners' status, the grandiose edifices thus constructed combined gratitude and aesthetic feeling in the same sense of admiration, proclaiming at one fell swoop the superiority of the benefactors and the need for a style.

The most spectacular examples were without any doubt the great sanctuaries in southern Latium, erected at the end of the second century or the beginning of the first, especially the one at Praeneste. It was an ancient oracular sanctuary devoted to Fortune, and seems to have been built with public money rather than the gift of a benefactor. But if the town of Praeneste was so rich that it was able to raise such a building, it was because the Praenestians were well represented among the merchants acquiring wealth through trade with the East. Some were to be found mainly at Delos; and it is obviously not by chance that the cult of the goddess Fortune adopted certain aspects of the worship received on the island by the Egyptian goddess Isis.

The early religious sites scattered over the side of the hill dominating the town were incorporated into a single architectural ensemble composed of a series of terraces bordered by porticoes, dominated on the highest stage by the *cavea* of a theatre and the *tholos* of the temple. The design of the entire construction was arranged to allow the visitor's gaze to fall on one aspect after another, following clever rules of perspective and a principle of adhering to an axial plan that decided the urban lay-out of Praeneste, which it dominated. The model was of course Hellenistic, but here it assumed a strength and coherence it had perhaps not as yet enjoyed. This was probably also related to the fact that during the second century, exactly in this part of central Italy, techniques concerning the use of mortar had appeared which permitted bolder responses to architectural challenges.[39]

The arrangement of a succession of terraces and porticoes, and above all the combination of a temple and a theatre in a single architectural whole, were not isolated. Other examples could be found between the middle of the second century and the first few decades of the first century, imparting a new majesty to old traditional sanctuaries: in Latium at Gabii, Tibur or Terracina, for instance; also in Samnium, at Pietrabbondante. When it was not a matter of Roman aristocrats maintaining personal links with these cities, members of local aristocracies, made wealthy by the new developments in agriculture and the opening up of trade with the East, ensured the funding of this building work either collectively or by private benefaction. At that time these regions of central and southern Italy became centres which, in their turn, spread their influence through the rest of the peninsula. To quote just one example, we may remember that it was in late second-century Campania that baths received their standard criteria and perhaps the first stone amphitheatres were built, whereas in Rome the first building of this type was not erected until the end of the first century.[40]

When municipal aristocracies grew rich, an extraordinary civic vitality swept the towns of which they were in charge. There was no reason for a crisis in local identity to occur when this happened. Cities that prospered preserved a pride in themselves.

There has been some speculation as to the nature of the entertainments which could have been given in the theatres that were built here and there. There is no easy answer as, of course, Latin literature completely obscured local literatures, but a few traces reveal that traditions had survived. The cities of Italy had their own foundation myths which, like those of Rome, often went back to the Trojan War, the event to which all the civilized inhabitants of the Mediterranean world were connected, or other myths that allowed the re-creation of a common history of the ancient world. And if their town had not been founded by the descendants of Aeneas, as in the case of the Romans, it had been by Diomedes, for the Daunians or the inhabitants of Spina, or by Marsyas for the Marsi, or Hercules, Ulysses or some other hero had passed through, founding the city and leaving a posterity that had produced the local noble lineage.[41] Local identity and patriotism were not idle notions for the peoples of Italy and they could boast sufficient claims to distinction and venerability to preserve a powerful image of themselves that strengthened their self-worth.

This overall picture of Italian municipal aristocracies nevertheless deserves some shading. The changes did not occur everywhere in the same way. They were dependent on the ability of certain families to grow rich and to enter or not into contact with the Hellenistic world. For that there were two principal means, which in no way contradicted each other: to take advantage of the opportunities offered by the new forms of economic activity, and to take part in the Roman military campaigns in the East. Differences were established depending on whether or not people had access to these resources. First, within the cities, some families advanced while others fell back. Some rose to the point of attaining the level of the Roman aristocracy while others merely benefited from a local sphere of influence. These variations occurred from one region to another, too, for what has just been described applied chiefly to the most open and developed parts of Italy, those most in contact with the Greek Orient.

According to such assessment as has been attempted of building work carried out during the last two centuries BC, the regions with the greatest density were Latium and Campania, followed by Samnium and Picenum, then Etruria and Cisalpine Gaul. To be more precise, if one takes only the major construction operations, building aqueducts and restructuring urban road systems, which are the most representative of local aristocracies' concern to meet a model of town planning, Latium and Campania are in the lead with twenty of the forty-five attested sties, followed by Samnium, Picenum, Umbria and Etruria, with sixteen sites, while the other regions in the peninsula shared the remainder. And we find a fairly comparable division in the case of theatres as, out of some twenty constructions, half the buildings were situated in Campania and central Italy.[42] In this distribution of large-scale works we again find the regions that derived the greatest benefits from Italy's economic changes, those where speculative agriculture and trade with the East developed. Latium and Campania were in the forefront, the others in their wake but with variations over which we must pause for a moment.

Some, in fact, borrowed their models directly from the Greek world, whereas others remained subject to the influence of Rome, which to some extent served as a relay point in the Hellenization of Italy.

Nevertheless, the former had not attained the same degree of artistic flowering as Latium and Campania. In Sicily, for instance, the architecture of public buildings and the decoration of houses shared the trends that were encountered in Greece and Asia Minor. There was no time lag here. The influences were identical and brought to bear at the same time. But the houses in Syracuse were more modest than those of Campania, and the style of the paintings ornamenting the tombs of Lilybaeum did not attain the quality of the originals they imitated.[43] In central Italy, the constructions adorning the great sanctuaries mentioned earlier, like the one at Pietrabbondante, were inspired by those to be found at the same time in Campania, but they remained isolated. In these regions, aristocrats who were capable of such foundations were less numerous. Certain cities in Cisalpine Gaul also found themselves subject to Greek influence by way of the trade with eastern markets in which some of their inhabitants were engaged. It is noteworthy that, in the late second century, chiefly at Aquileia, architectural features, especially capitals, revealed styles and manufacturing techniques of great similarity to contemporary articles in the Hellenistic world. But it is also true that, here again, this was an isolated example.[44]

Etruria belonged to the second category. There, artistic production had declined somewhat during the third century. The second century experienced a revival, but the models that were imitated had already been given a welcome in Rome and it was from there that they, in their turn, extended their influence, in the pediments of the temples at Telamon and Arezzo, or in the portraits at Caere.[45] There is an explanation for this. As far as we know, trade movements had turned towards the West, notably wine exports, which enabled some estate owners to grow rich. And it may be supposed that the populations of the region took less part than others in the conquest of the East.[46]

All in all, however, the dominant models remained those of

Hellenism and imposed themselves everywhere. Italy as a whole was totally engaged in a process of unification through the adoption of common civic and urbanistic models. Only the routes and paces varied by virtue of the relations maintained by local elites with the peninsula's capital. Some showed themselves capable of profiting simultaneously from the new opportunities of enrichment and mastering for themselves the cultural forms coming from the East, others taking longer about it or revealing themselves as more dependent on Rome in choosing the new values.

Nevertheless, they all remained under the domination of one city-state, which had made itself master of Italy and a good portion of the known world. A curious relationship seemed to become established between a Roman aristocracy, on the one hand, which had the monopoly of power but not of culture, and those Italian aristocracies who, though they relied increasingly on Rome for the management of their political affairs, did not always need it in order to acquire wealth and assume the extra prestige bestowed by participation on the world of Hellenism. And it is obviously by taking account of this curious situation which ruled the relations between them that we must try to evaluate the efforts and constraints determining the incorporation of the different peoples of Italy in a culturally and politically united whole.

6

THE MECHANISMS OF UNIFICATION

Subjected as they were to the pressure of the economic and social transformations affecting the entire peninsula, the various peoples of Italy were led to commit themselves to a process of unification and incorporation into a single political whole, an enlarged state of Rome, expanded to the dimensions of the whole peninsula. Such a development was bound to encounter many obstacles, the most serious of which was connected with the difficulty experienced by peoples in antiquity in grasping the concept of a civic community consisting of millions of members scattered over a vast territory. It took many years for the actors on the stage of Italian political life to become truly aware of the need for unity.

At the beginning of the second century, the Italians did not dream of demanding a citizenship which was not theirs and which the Romans would certainly not have imagined it possible to grant. But in the early first century, the need was so great that the majority of the peoples in the centre and south of the peninsula rebelled in order to obtain it, and in the years that followed all were gradually incorporated into a political ensemble of new dimensions. Meanwhile, the stakes represented by whether or not one possessed citizenship had increased. Those who benefited from it, on condition of course that they had also been integrated into the Roman political class, could take part in deliberations or exert some influence on political choices that would determine the future of Italian populations: the allocation of the lands of the *ager publicus* which, from the time of the Gracchi, there were plans to take back from those who occupied them, the major decisions on external policy that could have grave consequences for the state of affairs. Acknowledged aristocrats who, by their honourable status and the size of their fortune could hope to exert some authority in Rome, might well in such a case give up their own civic identity. That was made all the easier because differences had lost their relevance, since everyone adopted more or less the same tastes and attitudes and local government carried ever-decreasing weight when faced with the decisions of Roman magistrates, who did not hesitate to intervene here and there when the Senate considered it necessary.

The question which then arose was one of the relations that had to be maintained with the Roman aristocracy, the real holders of power, who certainly had no intention of sharing it easily. Traditionally, the means available to the Italians of taking part in Roman political life were those conferred on them by the custom of patronage. They could, in effect, appeal to the patrons who protected their city to avoid decisions being taken that might adversely affect themselves or their people. Social rules demanded that great attention should be paid to such requests. But the importance of what was at stake and the harshness of political conflicts largely removed the effectiveness of this means of recourse. Henceforth, the decisions taken in Rome concerned all the peoples of the Mediterranean. Government became increasingly concentrated in the hands of the most powerful. To avoid being marginalized, it was necessary to be able to take a strong and direct hand in the real mechanisms of political decision-making.

Roman Aristocracy

The changes experienced by Roman aristocracy during the second and first centuries BC played a considerable role in Italy's social history. The same factors that affected Italian aristocrats touched them as well, but with wider-ranging results.

We have already noted the vast increase in their wealth. I have also mentioned, rather cursorily, their cultural development. It hardly differed from that of the municipal elites we have studied, except in its size and the importance of the consequences it brought about.

Intellectual life was transformed. Literary genres as yet unknown were revealed, notably history with Fabius Pictor who, at the time of the second Punic War, described in Greek the first annals of the Roman people, probably attempting in this way to justify Roman policy to the Hellenistic public. Others followed him, writing in Latin when the need to read such works had spread. Beside the dramatic and epic poetry whose emergence during the third century has already been mentioned, other forms were born, involving a more intimate circulation reserved for learned aristocratic circles: satire, given its rules at the end of the second century by Lucilius, and elegy, a little later, which drew its models from the Alexandrian world.

But rhetoric and philosophy enjoyed the greatest importance in the social and political life of Rome. The former upset the workings of political life because it introduced means of persuasion which no longer relied solely on the authority of the orator. In fact, it was no longer enough to bear a great name or to have held prestigious magistracies in order to convince an increasingly bored audience. Under pressure from clever competitors, it was necessary to find fresher and more moving arguments, thus to learn the rules of invention and composition which had been perfected over decades by Greek practitioners of the art of oratory. Above all, philosophy won minds. It was simultaneously the source of morality and knowledge. By its virtue the organization of the universe could be understood, and its precepts adapted to the nature of men and of objects. For those who were responsible, even collectively, for governing an empire that covered almost all the known world, there was no longer any question of dispensing with the rules proposed by philosophy for both action and reflection.

Thus, from the middle of the second century, Roman aristocracy was permeated with these new ways of thinking. The first reaction, as we saw in connection with the embassy from Athens in 155, had been one of enthusiasm among the younger members. It was one of reluctance among the older members, notably Cato, who managed to have these disruptive people given their marching orders. However, this same Cato published the first work with encyclopaedic pretensions – which amounted to subscribing to the Aristotelian tradition – undoubtedly to demonstrate that Rome, too, was not without a certain degree of knowledge, and to undermine an influence which he probably judged would lead to dependency. After him, however, Hellenistic ways of thinking continued to make progress in people's minds.

This phenomenon showed itself in various ways, one of which was encyclopaedic study, for it allowed all natural sciences to be embraced. This approach also fitted in very well with the interest in agriculture, for instance, but it went even deeper. Some values by which social superiority and the legitimacy of the exercise of power were defined could no longer be justified except in their relation to truth and morality. The knowledge of the law on which the authority of those known as jurisconsults was based, and which enabled them to set out formulas and standards that had their own efficacy, was no longer a matter of revealed wisdom which, like religious rituals, permitted observance of the balance between men and gods: thoughtful reflection led people to look for justice in rules that were in keeping with the nature of man and the world. Political thinking could no longer be content with the conformity systematically demanded from precedent and custom that was defined by the name *mos maiorum*. There had to be another value to justify attention being paid to social equilibrium within the state, or even contemplation of reforms that would affect the organization of government.

Of course, not everyone was capable of such lofty thought, so distinctions appeared between those who had acquired the means of knowledge and reflection and others who held fast to tradition. All this did not happen without conflict. But in the same way that mastery of rhetoric enabled some to win the day over their rivals, that of philosophy allowed the same people or others to pose as scrupulous moralists or politicians prepared to restore a threatened balance.

All members of the senatorial aristocracy were engaged in a bitter rivalry imposed on them by the need to preserve their family's position in society. In effect, they had constantly to reproduce the conditions that had enabled their ancestors to make a name for themselves, a network of clients and the wealth that allowed them to maintain the entire situation. There was no other way of doing so than to continue to exert power and thus to justify their pre-eminence. Here precisely, Hellenistic models played an increasingly important role because of the boost in superiority they offered to those who were shrewd enough to make use of them. It is true that some showed resistance and took the line of Cato, who had tried to deny them any validity. In the main, they failed, and even though traditional Roman mores, or rather the archaistic ways that were passed off as such, could still help to provide the basis for an image of self-worth, the values of the Greek Orient increasingly ruled representations and attitudes.

Nevertheless, these new values assumed the greatest importance of all in the exercise of military command. The model held up to all was Alexander, who had conquered an empire so vast that it extended almost to the limits of the known world. His successors had reinforced the image of the ideal leader, combining strength, intelligence and a divine protection that revealed itself in victory, and it is easy to understand why the most ambitious Romans, Scipio Aemilianus, Sulla, Pompey, Caesar and Agustus, to name only a few, should have sought to identify themselves with this paradigm in order to legitimize the power they intended to exercise.

All in all, a new archetype of Roman aristocracy was thus formed in a series of veiled conflicts in which loyalty to the past was in combat with the dazzle of novelty. Some ancient features of Roman *virtus* remained, but revived and enhanced by the possession of qualities that imparted further resonance and majesty to the exercise of government. I cannot go into all the manifestations of this renewal here. It passed through an increased personalization and an exacerbation of competition which led to a profound modification in the conditions of political life themselves. It also involved a cultural enrichment which, going beyond specifically Roman society, in its turn extended its influence over the whole of Italy.

Under the impetus of the great leaders who sought to entrench their renown in its monuments, the architectural landscape of the town of Rome was altered. I will not list all the monuments erected during the second and first centuries BC.[1] I will simply stress that major trends were towards a multiplication of public amenities for which aediles were responsible: the construction of aqueducts, the establishment of port installations along the Tiber, which accompanied the growth in population and the opening up of Mediterranean markets; the building of temples, which served the dual purpose of thanking the gods for a victory and keeping it in people's memories; the organization, though not yet completely unified, of the Forum, where the renovating of temples and the building of basilicas were added to one another to mark, in the area of political life itself, the right they all had to collective recognition.

Similarly, there was an evolution in the setting. These monuments were situated in the artistic context of Hellenism. The architects and sculptors working there were Greeks who had come to live in Rome. Some have been identified, like Polycles and Dionysius the son of Timarchides, Athenian in origin. They introduced a neo-Attic taste to Rome, well suited to an aristocracy happy to assume classicizing airs that helped to legitimize it.[2] It was not, in fact, unintentional that the statues representing great men or scenes recalling such and such an important event were presented in a style which, simply by the effect of identification produced by the use of the same artistic language, admitted these Roman magistrates and senators into the lineage of those who had brought fame to the history of Greece. Naturally, other artists followed suit, especially early in the first century BC when, after the capture of Athens that coincided with the repression of Mithridates' rebellion, it became increasingly evident that Rome was henceforth the cultural capital of the Hellenistic world. Styles also developed and were liberated from their oriental models. Artistic creativity in Rome became powerful and fertile enough to find its own forms of expression.

There were hardly any differences between the rulers of Rome and the kings they had formerly subdued, except for the fact that there were several of them who together had to manage the whole of the Empire they had conquered and the rivalry which set one against the other made their task more complicated. The same social necessities were imposed on them: they had to gather round them a court of friends and clients who would guarantee their power, but also turn their residences into the seat of their own sphere of influence. Like the other Italian aristocrats, they enlarged and embellished their houses according to arrangements that were not structurally different from those we have already noted, but were even larger. Above all, they introduced a new way of life and sociability in so far as they developed the use of their *villae* as places for receptions and social life. So from the middle of the second century, in southern Latium and on the Campanian coast, appeared those palaces where the wealth and refinement of the new dynasties were put on show.

The best example is datable to the last decades of the first century. It is a villa near Herculaneum, known as that of the *papyri* because of the discovery there of a philosophical library that was especially rich in Epicurean works. The overall construction comprised several alternating *atria* and peristyles opening onto gardens. The lay-out of Hellenistic gymnasia was thus reproduced, as if this aristocratic residence should equally appear to be the place for acquiring and displaying the rules of philosophical training and reflection. The artefacts and statues of gods, heroes or famous men which adorned each of the rooms in this house were placed according to a vast decorative programme in which, by means of various extremely subtle plays on thematic contrasts which, for example, put nature and culture, or *otium* and *negotium*, in opposition or association, the figure of the ideal Statesman was defined, with whom one may suppose that the fortunate owner of this palace would have liked to be identified.[3]

Such edifices thus became the new Lyceums or the new Academies of aristocrats who, perhaps already in the second century but above all in the first, reproduced in their own homes the atmosphere of the intellectual courts they had observed among the kings of Pergamum or Alexandria. The principal schools of philosophy and rhetoric remained in Athens and Rhodes, but some philosophers, among them the most renowned, did not hesitate to follow those Roman nobles who turned their homes into libraries and places for teaching and intellectual exchanges: for instance, the Stoic Panaetius, who lived in the entourage of Scipio Aemilianus, Diodotus who lived in Cicero's, Athenodorus Cordylion with Cato of Utica, Blossius of Cumae, the academician Philo of Larissa, the Peripateticians Alexander and Staseas of Naples, and the Epicureans Phaedrus and Philodemus of Gadara, whose writings were particularly well represented in the villa of the *papyri*.[4] And to these names must be added, of course, those of poets such as Archias or historians like Polybius, who enabled these aristocrats to add to the power conferred upon them by government of the Empire the prestige and superiority they earned by transforming their entourage into circles where literary debates mingled with political and moral reflection.

Patronage and Social and Cultural Integration

In their turn, the aristocrats extended their influence over the whole of Italian society, leading it to become incorporated into a more and more culturally and politically unified ensemble. The process was certainly not effected by a gentle and spontaneous diffusion of values, with the aristocrats themselves setting the example, but used the routes imposed by the very concrete realities of political domination and social subjection.

All Italian communities found themselves, in fact, included in the ramifications of clients that enabled members of the Roman senatorial aristocracy to intervene in depth in society as a whole and to dictate to it. The relationship of patronage, as we have already noted, was perfectly natural. It allowed the most deprived to benefit from the protection of those who were more powerful. In return, it offered the latter the opportunity to have at their disposal a sometimes extensive collection of dependants. Between the Italians and the Roman politicians this type of relationship was absolutely necessary. By its means, the former obliged the latter to take account of their wishes and demands in every stituation where their interests were at stake. All important decisions concerning the cities and peoples of Italy were henceforth taken in Rome. As they were not citizens, Italians were for the most part excluded from the debates on which their future hung, so their sole means of intervention was to appeal to the patrons who would defend their interests.

There were two distinct aspects to the organization of clienteles. One was collective: a city or an entire community became dependent upon a powerful personage. The other was individual and concerned families taken separately.

In the first instance, the relationship might arise from a de facto situation. A town surrendering to the Roman general who had besieged it spontaneously entered his clientele: he became the intermediary who, from that moment, would represent it to the Roman people and would continue to do so well after the peace settlement. In the same way, a colony found its natural protector in the magistrate who had created it. The connection could also be the result of the free choice of a city which, subjected to the pressure of difficult events, might decide to entrust its fate to a powerful man who would intercede on its behalf. There were many differing situations, but consider, for example, all the conflicts with neighbouring cities that would require the intervention of the Senate, or the necessity which some communities experienced to protect themselves against the abuses of a magistrate or to obtain redress. Quite a few Roman orators, notably Cicero, built up a plentiful clientele for themselves in this way.

There was generally an official aspect to the relationship. The city chose its patron by a decree, the text of which was engraved and made public.[5] Henceforth the two parties were bound and had to provide help and protection for the one, availability and political support for the other. The patron also had to give the city that had entrusted itself to him the benefit of his prestige and wealth, for example, by holding a local magistracy or performing works of public benefaction so that, from this viewpoint as well, the bond of patronage contributed to the spread of cultural at the same time as social standards.

Let us take the example of the town of Brescia. In this small Cenoman city in the Transpadane region, the early first century saw the construction of a monumental ensemble, Hellenistic in inspiration, composed of four temples placed side by side, which formed the same type of spectacular adornment as that of the sanctuaries of southern Latium and Campania. The person who funded this undertaking was probably P. Servilius Vatia Isauricus, consul in 79, who fought the Marianists in this region. No doubt he became the city's patron on this occasion and organized the building of these temples, which had the triple merit of honouring the gods who had protected him or the deified virtues associated with his victory, embellishing, in keeping with current taste, the city of which he was the benefactor and thereby fixing in the landscape imperishable testimony to his success, might and refinement.[6]

One of the consequences of this privileged relationship was also that patrons had an almost institutional role to play when the interests of the community were at issue. We find this when conflicts set city against city. The debate came before the Senate, which would then intervene by appointing a commission most often composed of the patrons of the various parties. Such was the case when there was need to arbitrate between Pisa and Luna in 168[7] or when in 117 Genoa and various Ligurian communities were in dispute: an appeal was made to the descendants of the Q.

Minucius Rufus who had conquered the region.[8] These networks, therefore, played an outstanding role in the control and political running of the peninsula.

But Roman patronage over Italy found its strongest and most varied expression in individual relationships. Local communities had, in effect, no concrete existence except through the aristocrats who governed them and personally managed these relationships. The two parties had an equal need of these direct contacts. In them the inhabitants of the cities of Italy found protection and the additional influence and power necessary to safeguard their interests, both in their own town and in the rest of the world. In return, the Roman aristocrats created networks of supporters, increasing their own power and capacity to acquire wealth. Among friends and associates of Cicero, for example, were N. Cluvius and C. Vestorius, both from Pozzuoli, both important merchants, the second even making money from his invention of a new form of colouring. Both rendered him considerable services, as they did to their other Roman patrons, for instance, serving them as agents in their business affairs and informers, and lending money to third parties on their behalf, and above all by making them their heirs, to the extent that from Cluvius' legacy Cicero obtained an income of between 20,000 and 25,000 denarii annually.[9]

On both sides, patrons and clients, the connection was normally passed on by inheritance. But there were many circumstances that could lead to the establishment of new links, either because the old one no longer met the expectations of the present parties, or because it was preferred to make an appeal to a nearer or more effective protector. Relations based on proximity created extremely favourable conditions of familiarity. The running of the city's affairs and embassies to Rome might supply some specific opportunity. An appeal to a competent orator that would enable a lawsuit to be won might provide another. Wars and army service could again offer favourable new opportunities.

In the latter instance, the Italians obviously took part in Roman campaigns. Their troops were led by officers belonging to the military staff of great conquerors such as Aemilius Paulus, Scipio Aemilianus, Lucullus, Marius, Sulla, Pompey and Caesar, to name only the principals. It is easy to imagine the kind of relationship that might have been established between these generals and their Italian subordinates.[10] The bonds created in battle must by themselves have been powerful enough, but if in addition success rewarded the efforts of both, the benefits of victory, both material and symbolic, must normally have been shared by all those who had fought. It is true that some magistrates showed far greater favour to Roman citizens, thus alienating their Italian allies,[11] but others were not so tactless and won the esteem and affection of the allies who had served under their command. In exchange, the latter received the advantages of a protection that found various ways of expressing itself.

Sex. Digitius for example, who was probably from the colony of Paestum, had fought in Spain in the army of Scipio Africanus. He was praetor in 194, the same year as the consulship of his former leader. His rise was rapid, and it may be supposed that he owed it to the Scipios. A little later, in 190, he fought in the East as a legate of Scipio Asiaticus. The bonds were strong and enduring. It is possible that they were also evident in the benefits obtained from two other patrons whom the colony celebrated in its coinage and who similarly belonged to the same circle of those loyal to the Scipios, Cn. Cornelius Blasius, also a praetor in 194, and M. Tuccius, praetor in 190. Colonies with Roman rights were, in fact, founded in the region, and Paestans probably obtained Roman citizenship by this means. In the contemporary architecture of the city we find decorative motifs that were directly inspired by the architecture of Dium, the capital of Macedonia. It is thus tempting to think that none other than Sex. Digitius and his circle who, strong in the wealth and status they had acquired thanks to their protectors, caused the city of Paestum to benefit from their influence and inscribed in the urban landscape the dual testimony of their culture and benefaction.[12]

This example highlights the various aspects of the connections of patronage, its special contribution to the incorporation of local elites into a Roman society which, in parallel, expanded and was renewed by their presence.

The backing of a powerful patron facilitated access to the chief sources of wealth, war booty, ownership of the *ager publicus*, or the network of connections that could lead to fruitful business affairs. It was thus possible to redistribute locally part of the resources one had acquired and to elevate oneself in the hierarchy of one's own city. The man who was a client in Rome became, in his turn, the benefactor and patron of his fellow-citizens, who were able to profit by his influence. He was proud of the prestige of his protectors and spread his influence in turn, deriving his strong position from their renown.

This type of relationship had several consequences. In the first place, the networks of friends and clients which Roman aristocrats built up for themselves in the peninsula became powerful instruments of Romanization, because everyhere they introduced the values that defined the Roman model of aristocratic behaviour. And as these values were revived by the prestige of Hellenistic examples, they also contributed to the Hellenization of Italy. Above all, far from being defined in an abstract fashion, they were made flesh in those personalites who dominated Roman political life and whose sphere of influence thus extended throughout the peninsula and far beyond.

Moreover, the rivalry that put all the notables in opposition to one another for local government was upset by the intrusion of these external influences. It was no longer enough to inherit a name or a fortune. They had to be preserved or increased through the support of some powerful Roman. Some took this path to grow rich and climb higher on the social ladder. Thanks to the protection they had acquired, they were able to obtain Roman citizenship if they did not already have it and sometimes, like Sex. Digitius, the tenure of a magistracy. Others, with the benefit of solid wealth and an esteemed name, sought to keep their rank and play their role suitably. They contented themselves with their position of *domi nobiles*, as they were sometimes defined, and maintained an authority that stayed local.[13] The hindmost, who did not manage to attain this, fell back down the social ladder, putting up with a steadily diminishing position, or even disappearing. There were therefore several aristocracies;[14] some were close to Roman ruling circles and, when they enjoyed Roman citizenship, notably supplied the equestrian order with a good many of its members; others were more distant, but none was sure of maintaining his place without making every effort and seeking the necessary backing.

In fact, it had long been realized that among the Roman senators and magistrates were quite a few individuals originating from Italy's cities, who had succeeded in becoming integrated into the political class in Rome. Having arrived at the summit of the state, in their turn they became patrons of their native city and thus helped it to derive benefits from their advancement. It was not an easy process, however: generally speaking, from the moment when the city was created or incorporated into the Roman community, it took two or three generations for some of its inhabitants to be able to reach the Roman Senate. To get into the government, one needed wealth, relatives and a fine reputation; then it was necessary to obtain an alliance with a well-placed family and start by holding some lower commands in the army or a few minor magistracies in Rome.[15] Lastly one had to reconcile two needs that could sometimes be contradictory: to have the advantage of an aristocratic patron and faction, who demanded something in return for the benefits they provided, and to make oneself known to the Roman people by proving one's own qualities.

The most exceptional example was that of C. Marius, who came from Arpinum. He belonged to the clientele of the Caecilii Metelli and fought under the command of Caecilius Metellus Numidicus. However, at a very early stage he had shown himself to be an independent man, highly popular both for his challenges to the aristocracy and his reputation as a soldier. It was therefore despite the opposition of his patron, who suggested that he should be consul at the same time as his very much younger son, that he succeeded in being elected: 'The plebs welcomed him immediately as the man they wanted. One of the tribunes presented him to the assembly. There, after making numerous accusations against Metellus, he asked for the consulship . . . Appointed consul with a tremendous majority.'[16] Nevertheless, this success was quite unexpected and was also connected with the conditions of the period. Respect for the rules of belonging to a clientele dependent on a patron was in fact the best guarantee for an Italian of gaining access to Roman political power. One had to accompany the patron, go to his home, include oneself publicly in the circle of his friends in order to obtain backing and assistance from him; these aristocratic entourages thus acted as instruments of integration which brought their members closer together in a courtly social life.

The military headquarters staff which, on campaign, assembled Roman and Italian commanders under the authority of a supreme leader, were among those privileged places where everyone shared the same enthusiasm for military science, values and glory. Others were the houses and residences devoted to the celebration of culture, where young people who wanted to make a career for themselves came to have the enriching experience of frequenting the most prestigious learned men and philosophers.

Cicero had been one of them. At Arpinum, his was among the most important families, and his grandfather might well have been able to benefit from the support of M. Aemilius Scaurus to make a career in Rome if circumstances had allowed. He was barely 15 or 16 when his father entrusted his training to Q. Mucius Scaevola, consul in 117, a famous jurisconsult, but chiefly the father-in-law of L. Licinius Crassus, censor in 92, one of the chief orators and politicians of the time whom he admired and had already visited. For a while he had a close relationship with Scaevola, but the latter died. He then joined his cousin, Q.Mucius Scaevola, consul in 95, another jurisconsult from whom, by observing and imitating him, he eventually learned Roman aristocratic ways at the same time as the law.

This type of training was known as *tirocinium* because it was akin to military apprenticeship under the tutelage of an older man. By admitting the young man into the intimate companionship of a master, he simultaneously established the foundations of a lasting client relationship and of an education that had more to do with initiation to the rules of conduct which make a senator than with the acquisition of precise areas of knowledge.

If we consider that these residences housed rhetoricians and philosophers as well as students, friends, clients and neighbours, Romans and Italians paying visits, that everyone frequented the master's library, that banquets were given, and science, morality, minor and major politics were debated,[17] it is easy to imagine that through its power, prestige and the sociable ambience it created, Roman senatorial aristocracy represented a major instrument of social and cultural unification.

There was one field in particular where the process was very noticeable: poetry. If we make a list of those who have left their names in the history of this literary genre we discover that, with the exception of a few Greeks already mentioned, they were nearly all from towns or villages in Italy: Plautus from Sarsina in Umbria, Ennius from Rudiae in Apulia, Pacuvius from Brindisi, Accius from Pesaro, Lucilius from Suessa Aurunca, M. Furius Bibaculus from Cremona, C. Helvius Cinna from Brescia and Catullus from Verona. Living in Rome or Campania, they took part – or we know that most of them did – in this aristocratic sociability. Such a polarization of literary life clearly reveals the range of influence of these Roman nobles who attracted municipal elites around them and helped to integrate them into a single society that was both Roman and Italian.

The integration was uneven, however, depending on the distribution and size of the networks. The most Romanized regions were those where promotions were most numerous. An examination of the number of Roman senators who originated from towns in Italy reveals that during the second century Latium supplied 16 families of new senators; Etruria, 5; the Sabine region, 3; Campania, 2; Picenum, Umbria and Venetia, 1 each. Then the movement accelerated during the first century. All cities in the peninsula received citizenship and were incorporated into a united Italy. The losses of the civil wars also imposed the need for a replenishment of the political class, and favoured the emergence of newcomers. The figures went up: Latium provided 89 families; Picenum, 24; Campania and Samnium, 22 each; the Sabine region and Etruria, 20 apiece; Venetia and Istria combined, 15; Umbria, 13; Apulia and Calabria combined, 12; Aemilia, 8; Lucania and Bruttium together, 8; Liguria and Sicily still zero.[18]

Could these figures be used to indicate Romanization? Certainly, provided some precautions are taken. The chancy nature of our sources makes them very open to question and, moreover, many of the senators coming from this or that region were not indigenous but the descendants of colonists who had settled there. Nevertheless, the indications they give are fairly coherent. They enable us to discover that, throughout the republican period, the regions supplying the greatest number of senators were the most central and those with the longest-standing ties with Rome – Latium, the Sabine region, Etruria and Campania – and that subsequently the recruitment area gradually widened to take in new, poorer or more heterogeneous regions which until then had remained outside the initial circle of Roman-ness.

The Romanization of Institutions and Men

Can we go further and, in the detail of the political and cultural life of the peoples of Italy, try to follow the stages in the acquisition of all those features which, in language, mores and a civic way of life, defined Roman citizens and accompanied or anticipated political integration? It is a difficult attempt. The sole reasonably plentiful information available is provided by inscriptions. In one region or another, it is possible to pinpoint changes in the use of language and, with them, the appearance of Latin, variations in onomastic usage and therefore the adoption of a Roman-style civic status, and in the use of various titles we see the introduction of magistracies borrowed from the Roman constitution.

This kind of research enables the phenomenon of Romanization to be examined in depth. For even if local elites were surely the elements that contributed most to the unification of Italy, the process was too extensive and too intense not to have carried all strata of the population in its wake. For instance, Latin was the language of the Roman army in which all Italian contingents served. All officers and most of the ordinary soldiers came to be familiar with it. It had also become the common language that facilitated communications and trade within the peninsula. Population movements eventually imposed its use, especially when during the first century there was an increase in the number of colonies aimed at giving veterans of the great military leaders the lands they had been promised.

There were differences, however. Roman-ness was not uniform, and perceptible variations in mores and habits remained. The language and culture of the Hellenized aristocrats of Rome were challenged by far older forms, features which had vanished in Rome itself. This has been the subject of much study, notably at Pesaro. In this Roman colony, founded in 184, Marica and the Novensides were still honoured, though the cult had disappeared in Rome, and people spoke a Latin that was elaborate and learned but different from that spoken in Rome in the same period.[19]

Such heterogeneity was obviously not without its effects. The first was that, within Roman society, various models were in confrontation. The Hellenized Romans, who at every opportunity displayed their knowledge of and liking for Greek thought and art, were in sharp contrast with those who gloried in, or were reassured by, an archaizing Roman-ness, the sign of strict discipline and reliability. It was mainly the Italians who bore the brunt of these divergences. They lived, in fact, in contact with groups of Romans who already differed among themselves; on the scale of the whole peninsula, that could obviously not produce a homogeneous acculturation. Besides, when they undertook to fit into Roman society they found themselves caught up in these conflicting attitudes, of which they were both the agents and the victims, since such disparities, being the source of distinctions, played their role in the hierarchy of aristocratic conformity.

Q. Arrius, for example, probably came from Campania. By dint of arguing and upholding the interests of Crassus, the triumvir, he attained a praetorship. His promotion, however, was a source of amusement and he was mocked for his efforts to speak good Latin: '"Hadvantages," Arrius would say, when he meant "advantages", and "hambushes" instead of "ambushes"; he imagined he had done famously when he had said "hambushes" at the top of his voice. So, I believe, spoke his mother and the freedman, his mother's brother, and his maternal grandparents.'[20]

These scornful remarks were probably commonplace in Roman society. There was one overriding concept that defined those who belonged to the body of true Romans, the *urbanitas* which Cicero said would enable any inhabitant of Rome to win the day, 'by the sweetness of the voice, the manner of articulating and forming sounds', over even the most cultivated individuals from anywhere else in Italy.[21] It may be imagined that it was also complemented by various stereotypes which systematically marked the differences and, emphasizing both cultural and linguistic gaps, justified reluctance and multiplied the obstacles to integration. We can understand that it took time and solid demographic, economic, social and political factors to bring Italian society to a state of homogeneity.

Generally, however, the use of Latin spread, first as a second language, then as the main and finally the only tongue, but with rules and at times that varied from one region to another.

In Umbria, for instance, the Latin alphabet began to be used during the course of the second century, whereas texts remained written in Umbrian. The first inscriptions in the Latin tongue are datable to the end of the century and Umbrian disappeared during the first century when, after the Social War, all the inhabitants of Italy became Roman citizens. In Etruria events were rather different. The first Latin inscriptions appeared perhaps as early as the third century for certain regions, and certainly during the second century. Bilingual inscriptions were carved in the second and, chiefly, the first century. Latin spread in the same period and became predominant after the Social War. Etruscan, however, did not truly disappear until much later, during the first century AD.[22] It was as if in Etruria, the richest and most open region, Latin had spread earlier but the inhabitants, proud of their traditions and culture, had not abandoned their own language until fairly late, whereas in Umbria, although acculturation was belated it took place more rapidly. This can certainly not have been an isolated occurrence. Similar remarks could be made when comparing the inscriptions of the Lucanian sanctuary of Rossano di Vaglio, which were written in the Oscan language and Greek characters until the beginning of the first century, then in Latin,[23] with those of Locri, which remained written in Greek well into the first century.[24] Members of Greek communities, when the latter stayed active and suitably structured, did not easily give up their identity, even when they had in fact already obtained Roman citizenship.

Instances of resistance thus appeared in the heart of the process of Romanization. Some parts of the population had no intention of renouncing what gave them their specific nature or their identity. Such opposition could be connected with many aspects of social life, not just the political organization of the city or the cultural features of the whole of the group. The example of the women of Este makes the point well. The Venetian onomastic system was such that they all had their own names, whereas that was not the case with the Romans. When the masculine population broadly adopted the rules of Latin nomenclature by choosing a Roman name and altering their indigenous name to a surname, the women, who doubtless refused to efface themselves like Roman women behind the identities of their fathers, retained *their* names, most often taking them as forenames.[25]

Generally speaking, however, the tendency was to adopt Roman standards, for both communities and individuals. We even find that cities, while sometimes preserving part of their originality, did not hesitate to adopt Roman institutions even before the political integration that followed the Social War made the process more generalized.

It is true that our sources are fairly inexplicit. Apart from a mention by Livy which informs us that in 180 the city of Cumae asked the Senate's permission to use Latin for public bills and especially auction sales,[26] literary sources remain silent. Inscriptions tell us slightly more. They enable us to note that in many places magistrates of Roman type appeared in cities that had not had them previously. The best example is provided by the Eugubine tables, which regulated certain rituals in the city of Gubbio: allusion was made to a *kvestur* in an Oscan text written in native characters and contemporary with the second century BC. Elsewhere, at Aufidena and Pompeii, *aideles* appeared, and because of the form of the name we can be certain they were of Roman inspiration. The presence of censors at Pietrabbondante and Histonium is also worth noting.[27]

The organization of Roman government certainly had a hand in these transformations. Since, for example, the allies had to supply troops according to procedures that were similar, if not always identical, to those employed in Rome, censors acquired a certain usefulness. But the model played its part: magistracies became steadily more numerous and were organized according to a hierarchy. Local magistracies were translated into their Latin equivalents. Little by little, where Rome's prestige was strong, the organization of the city was inspired by its constitution, though not everywhere. In other places, traditional structures tended to persist, notably in Etruscan and Greek cities which had a sufficiently strong past and were secure enough in their identities to be unwilling to exchange them for another's, even if they were as powerful as Rome.[28]

Overall, the process of Romanization touched the whole of Italy, but not in a homogeneous fashion. Certain strata of the population in some regions, notably aristocrats, felt the need to merge into the dominant culture and become identified with those who henceforth governed the Empire. They apparently belonged to those peoples who were closest to Rome and the least cultivated; in their view the Roman model was the strongest and enabled them to contemplate giving up an image from which they could easily detach themselves. They probably also wanted to take part in the political life of Rome and become Roman citizens if they were not so already. In contrast, others were less impatient. They belonged to cities that had had their time of glory and felt no need *a priori* to abandon a status and traditions of which they were proud. Nevertheless the evolution of the whole was taking place, with the result that, in one way or another, consciously or not, under the influence of Hellenistic and Roman models, the various peoples of Italy grew closer to one another and the differences between them became obliterated.

7

THE SOCIAL WAR

There was one moment, however, when history was accelerated and even the most reluctant desired to become incorporated into the community of Roman citizens. It was not that ethnic and cultural disparites had become intolerable; they disappeared. Quite simply, the decisions taken in Rome by those holding power were henceforth so very important in the opinion of local elites that it became essential for them to have some say in what was decided. Roman citizenship was now a necessary condition for the furtherance of their own dominant position. It was refused to them in the name of a difference which, as a result of sharing the same charges and values, was steadily losing its validity. Demands grew, until the day when the break finally happened and what was known as the Social War, because it was the affair of the allies or *socii*, erupted.

The Worsening of Roman Domination

The weight of Roman domination had increased during the second century BC in several ways, both absolute and relative, relatively, for the war effort rendered necessary by conquest fell chiefly on the allies. They supplied many more men than the Romans and continued to finance their soldiers' pay by taxation, whereas since the third Macedonian War Roman citizens had been exempt. It is obvious that such inequality became increasingly intolerable as the memory faded of defeats that in former times had justified these measures.[1]

But it was without doubt the widening scope of the decisions taken by the Roman government that truly altered the situation of the Italian elites. The Roman Senate began to intervene in all important political matters. The very process of the unification of Italy in fact imposed a certain centralization of power. The policies laid down in Rome, above all, had direct consequences on the Italians' living conditions, notably the distribution of lands, which hit their interests hard without their having a means of defence capable of countering the threat.

Some events naturally demanded a single, determined reaction which could come only from Roman magistrates. The slave rebellions, for example, which regularly erupted from the early second century, could not be put down by any other means than the use of troops, often in large numbers, led by Roman commanders who came onto the territory of the allied cities without in any way submitting to their authority. These were matters of war which did not lend themselves to discussion.

The affair known as that of the Bacchanalia was in the same category. In 186 Rome became aware of a network, or several networks, of followers of Dionysus who were organized in bands (*thiasi*) and celebrated a cult whose initiatory nature aroused anxiety. Apparently the whole of Italy, from Lucania to Etruria, was involved. This episode is striking, if only for the fact that it reveals the degree of religious and cultural unification in Italy in the early second century. For the Roman authorities, strong and clandestine solidarities carried the risk of thwarting the exercise of the legitimate powers of the Romans and allies. The repression was savage. The measures taken gave no consideration to the autonomy of cities and peoples except when their authorities collaborated in the inquiry proceedings.[2] In any case they had an interest in the matter, for the setting up of these religious sects certainly threatened the power of local aristocrats as well as that of members of the Roman senatorial order.

At the same time as these urgently required interventions there were others, to which an inscription found at Polla in Lucania bears perfect witness. A consul describes the action he took there: 'I built this road from Reggio to Capua . . . and when I was praetor in Sicily I hunted down fugitive slaves of the Italici, bringing back

917. And I was the first to make the livestock-breeders withdraw from the *ager publicus* in favour of the farmers. I also founded this Forum and had public buldings constructed.'[3] The management of the *ager publicus* and building the road justified this magistrate's measures. It is clear, however, that those whom they harmed or, in contrast, those whom they benefited were far from being all Roman citizens. With the reorganization that had followed the second Punic War, then with the policies of the Gracchi, such interventions had multiplied. They were obviously decided upon in the interests of Rome, but probably also of the Italians, as if the idea of a generalized administration of Italy was starting to appear, leading the Roman authorities to intervene in one way or another in the affairs of allied cities and peoples.

This political and administrative hegemony took yet another form. When two cities or peoples came into conflict, the solution could no longer be found except by the arbitration of the Senate, which delegated the matter to some magistrate or the patrons of the groups concerned. The temptation must have been great for anyone who was sure of benefiting from a certain audience to take his cause to Rome, so that he could win by virtue of the influence he might have there. So all major controversies between cities, and also within cities, however little they concerned Roman citizens, ended by being referred there for settlement. Local authorities thus had their responsibilities removed and, to preserve themselves from unfavourable decisions, had no other recourse than to commit themselves still further to client–patron relationships.

Nevertheless, from a strictly formal viewpoint, the autonomy of city-states continued to be respected. Cases of the legal extension of the competence of Roman tribunals to the allies by a unilateral decision in Rome seem to have been fairly rare. At the most, one can pick out for certain the case of the *lex Sempronia* of 193 which, in order to prevent Roman debtors from being harmed by the transfer of their debt to a non-Roman, allowed them to have Roman law applied.[4] In the normal course of their operations, Roman authorities apparently did not seek to impose their laws systematically on other cities, but some of the latter were nevertheless able to adopt them on their own initiative. There is evidence of this procedure, which was called *fundifactio*.[5] There is no doubt that, in the same way that some cities attributed to their magistrates the titles and functions of those of

Rome, the same ones or others replaced the standards of their public and private legislation with Roman legal arrangements which facilitated their entry to the new social and political ensemble that was being created. The process then differed little from the one described earlier, which led to the Romanization of values and tastes.

Abuses of power committed by Roman magistrates were altogether more serious. They in fact introduced the fear that Italians were no longer protected by their autonomy against improper acts committed by the holders of Roman authority. I have already mentioned the case of the consul of 173 who had demanded from Praeneste lodgings and labour service that it did not owe,[6] and that of the other consul who had a municipal magistrate of Teanum Sidicinum birched.[7] There were obviously other instances, such as the excessive demands made by Scipio's legate, Q. Pleminius, on the Locrians in 205–200,[8] or the theft perpetrated by Q. Fulvius Flaccus, censor in 174, when he took the marble tiles covering the temple of Hera Lacinia at Croton[9] to be used on a building in Rome.

The Italians were not helpless in the face of such practices. The fact that they were denounced and, in the case of Pleminius and Flaccus punished, indicates this. The relationships of patronage very often enabled grievances to be considered by the Senate. In issues of extortion, procedures known as *de repetundis*, which aimed at the restitution of the sums exacted, could be brought into effect. The Italians were not the only ones involved, and provincials, even more than they, were victims of Roman magistrates' pillaging. During the second century legislation was gradually strengthened, so that from 149 a special court of enquiry (*quaestio*) was instituted, its composition and procedures being laid down once and for all in order to tackle such crimes more efficiently. But at all events, whether or not complaints were dealt with satisfactorily, the whole process had only one outcome, placing the fate of Italian communities still further in the hands of Roman aristocrats.

The issue that caused a worsening in cities' dependence and a perceptible change in relations between Romans and the allies was the use of the *ager publicus*. As we know, it was raised by the policies of Tiberius Sempronius Gracchus, tribune of the plebs in 133. As a remedy for the dwindling numbers of men able to be mobilized, he wanted to try to rebuild the peasant classes who, in people's opinion and still largely in fact, formed the recruitment pool for the civic army. His plan was simple. It consisted of restricting ownership of the *ager publicus* to 500 jugera, with the addition of 250 per child, recovering the surplus areas and allocating them individually to colonists, using for their settlement the riches bequeathed to the Roman people by Attalus III, king of Pergamum. A commission of three Roman magistrates would have the task of research, confiscation and distribution.

This kind of project struck directly at the interests of the rich Romans and allies who made up the main body of owners of the *ager publicus*. These lands had been confiscated after the second Punic War from those who had collaborated with Hannibal. Some had been allocated to colonists, others rented by censors to Romans, but the majority had remained in the hands of the erstwhile defeated. At least some, it seems, may have been taken from collective lands, which would to some extent have complemented peasants' individual chances of farming, so that the de facto balance of economic and social life in the communities involved would not have been too much affected.[10] It is even quite probable that in some cases the allies obtained guaranteed use of the *ager publicus* through the treaties that bound them to Roman authority. The allocations envisaged by Tiberius Gracchus were in the main intended for poor Roman citizens, the rural plebs who found themselves placed in a fragile position by the burden of military recruitment they constantly had to bear.[11] They could not help but strip Italian cities, at least in part, of the possessions which certainly no longer belonged to them but which remained the basic means of their own survival. In any case they affected aristocrats more than others, first because if there were local owners of large areas they could not belong in any other category, and then because, if these lands happened to form part of a collective farm, the aristocrats' own status as rulers depended on their ability to preserve the city's heritage and safeguard their fellow-citizens' means of existence.

What action could they take against the plans of Tiberius Gracchus? Once again, they could resort to the influence of patrons, and it is not surprising to find that a Roman senator, in this instance Scipio Aemilianus, acted as spokesman for their opposition.[12] It was undoubtedly effective. They did not manage to stop the adoption of Tiberius Gracchus' agrarian law, but they succeeded in preventing consequences that were too damaging.

Nevertheless, the question had been raised, and every time that rulers in Rome contemplated the promulgation of an agrarian law, the interests of Italian communities were threatened. Now, as a result of the upsurge in popular demands and democratic programmes, projects continued to increase.

The Demand for Roman Citizenship

The question then arose, more keenly than before, of the opportunities that were or were not open to Italian aristocrats to take a hand in Roman political life and to seek to obtain citizenship.

Hitherto, the matter of acquisition had never been settled. When, for example, the Romans wanted to reward the Praenestians who had fought relentlessly against Hannibal at Casilinum, as well as various forms of recompense they offered them the chance to become Roman citizens.[13] The offer was refused; they preferred to retain their own identity. For several decades to come, the issue remained a source of dispute and reluctance.

From reading the sources, in fact, one notices a current of emigration from the Latin cities to Rome, and of other peoples to the Latin cities. By its size and continuity this phenomenon represented a fundamental movement of Italian society. It was probably a response to the transformations affecting the peninsula's economy, and committed certain impoverished or marginalized elements to looking elsewhere for ways of surviving.[14] But at the same time the beneficiaries of Latin rights who settled in Rome also sought to make use of the *ius migrationis* that allowed them to become Roman citizens as soon as they had been included in the census there. In parallel, however, the authorities of the city-states that were being denuded of their population came to the Senate to protest.

In 178,

> the Senate was also impressed by the deputations from allies with Latin rights who, having pestered the censors and preceding consuls, were finally allowed to come before the Senate. Fundamentally, their complaints concerned the fact that their fellow-citizens who were included in the Rome census had mostly

emigrated there; if that state of affairs continued, it would take only a few five-year periods before their abandoned towns, their deserted fields, could no longer supply any soldiers at all. Moreover, the Samnites and Peligni complained that four thousand families had left them to settle in Fregellae, yet both groups were expected to provide just as many soldiers as before.[15]

The matter of contributions in men and money to be supplied to the Roman army was obviously the most important point, and for both parties. There was even a possible clause in treaties between Rome and its allies banning Roman authorities from granting citizenship to any individual without the consent of his native city.[16] There were probably much deeper reasons. With the diminution of the population, the network of dependants of the local aristocrats and the very capacity of the city to develop and spread its influence grew weaker. Ultimately the power and civic pride of the local elites were affected.

In Rome, they were only too happy to hear these grievances. An influx of new citizens disturbed the political and *clientelae* equilibrium. Some patrons, who for one reason or another had the means, won new clients for themselves, so that others relatively lost their influence. On several occasions therefore, in 206, 187, 177, 173 and 126, measures of control and expulsion were taken, which showed themselves to be largely ineffectual as they were regularly renewed.

With the emergence of the agrarian question, the problem became even more acute. The need to be able to take a part in Roman political life became more imperative. At the same time as the cities and people of Italy, at a greater or lesser pace and to a greater or lesser depth but following a process that affected them all, were merging in one and the same Hellenistic and Roman *koine*, allegiances to local civic identity gradually became weaker. Whether in the army, where they shared the same techniques and weapons, or in the provinces where they spoke the same language and had adopted the same customs, Italians were less and less distinguishable from Romans, or from one another. A new identity made its appearance, those who participated in the Empire of Rome but who had no opportunity of deriving all the benefits from it or, above all, of playing a role in its government. Thus demands multiplied and widened, here again at a pace and with a range specific to each people, but irreversibly and with an increasing need to be taken into account.

In Rome, however, it took a long time for the rulers to understand that this was necessary. The initiator of such a policy was the consul M. Fulvius Flaccus, in 125. He was the first, explains Appian, to 'urge the Italians to seek to obtain Roman citizenship and emerge from the condition of subjects to take part in the government of the Empire'.[17] He proposed to grant them citizenship, and although some were against it, to give them the right of *provocatio* which would allow them to appeal to the Roman people against any major judgement by a Roman magistrate. His plan was set aside. Immediately a revolt broke out at Fregellae, one of the cities, as we have seen, where the matter of emigration had manifested itself most forcefully. It was ruthlessly put down and Fregellae was destroyed. This was certainly only a forerunner and an isolated case, but its very violence gave cause for reflection. It was probably at this point, in order to reduce the tension and partly meet the demand for citizenship, that an important measure was introduced which noticeably altered the institutions of cities with Latin rights; those who held magistracies there would henceforth automatically obtain the status of Roman citizen.

From then on the question was constantly posed. With the help of Fulvius Flaccus, in 123 Gaius Gracchus resumed his brother's plans and gave them an even more systematic form, creating colonies in Italy, notably at Scolacium in Bruttium and Tarentum itself. He also planned to recruit Italians for the colony he founded on the site of Carthage. Chiefly, in 122 he introduced in his turn a proposal aiming to grant citizenship to those with Latin rights, and probably award the same Latin rights to all the other allies. The opposition he aroused was certainly one of the causes of his downfall. The Senate, by way of response, issued a senatorial decree obliging all those without the right to vote to depart from Rome; this the consul C. Fannius was able to apply strictly and Gaius Gracchus dared not challenge it.[18]

The failure and death of Gaius Gracchus and Fulvius Flaccus resulted in plans for granting citizenship being shelved for some decades. Several measures also helped to ease the tension. In the application of the agrarian law, account was taken of the rights and interests of the allies by permitting them to preserve their possessions or awarding them others in exchange for what was being taken from them.[19] The door to the status of citizen remained ajar. The laws governing criminal procedures against dishonest magistrates viewed citizenship as a reward granted to an accuser who might get a guilty party sentenced. And when C. Marius obtained the right to found colonies with Roman rights, he also received the right to include a very small number of allied veterans.[20] When one considers the number of beneficiaries, which must have totalled only about a hundred individuals, the effect of these last two measures was hardly other than symbolic. They undoubtedly emphasized that citizenship remained accessible to those who proved themselves virtuous and courageous. Above all, in parallel, the opportunity for magistrates of Latin cities to become citizens continued to work effectively in integrating those who were the most meritorious and Romanized. Furthermore, it was probably not always difficult for anyone who could meet the most expected criteria and possessed a little knowhow, wrongfully to assume a citizenship that could later be recognized on the occasion of a fairly easygoing census.

The Social War

The fundamental reasons that prompted Italians to demand Roman citizenship, like those that enabled them to renounce their own identity, still persisted, however, and an ever-increasing number settled in Rome and aspired to take part in political life.

There are several indications of this. Among the magistrates who busied themselves during the years running up to the Social War, especially among those who supported C. Marius' action, a sizeable proportion of individuals from Italy's city-states had managed to carve a niche for themselves in the Roman political class.[21] This fact is similarly borne out by the increase among the accusers who came before the *quaestiones*, those courts intended to combat abuses by Roman magistrates, in the number of those of municipal origin who made use of their talents in the art of oratory. They tried to get themselves known by the Roman people and if possible to embark upon a political career. Sometimes they were successful and represented a danger to the conservative aristocracy. Indeed, they occasionally succeeded in getting a senator sentenced, but they also helped to strengthen the democratic or Marianist tendencies which were the most likely to take account of their aspirations.[22]

During the nineties two repressive measures were taken and these relaunched the conflict. In 95 the consuls L. Licinius Crassus and Q. Mucius Scaevola resumed the old measure of returning Italians who were not citizens to their cities of origin, and set up an inquiry procedure to prosecute those who had wrongfully assumed citizenship. In 92 the censors Cn. Domitius Ahenobarbus and the same L. Licinius Crassus took the step of banning the teaching of rhetoric in Latin; this was certainly a response to the disquiet aroused by the growing influence of these orators of modest origin who were eluding the control of the aristocracy.

However, it was the vast programme of reforms instituted by the tribune M. Livius Drusus in 91, and chiefly its failure, that lit the powder keg. Like Gaius Gracchus thirty years earlier, trying to resolve one problem with another, Drusus had undertaken to deal at one and the same time with certain political questions that were agitating Rome, the agrarian matter and the demand for citizenship. The latter he proposed to grant to all Italians, probably to reap the benefit of their massive support and defeat his opponents. His failure and assassination provoked an uprising. A fair part of the peninsula took up arms and prepared for war with Rome, a state of which the insurgents felt themselves to be members but which had so far systematically rejected them. The frustration and anger in the face of a scorn manifested so many times resulted in a ferocious war that ravaged central Italy for three years.

Not all reacted in the same way, however. Where some rebelled, others remained loyal. The dividing line split peoples, communities, cities, even families; some took Rome's side, others were against. It would obviously be interesting to know the reasons for their choices. In detail, of course, they remain unknown, but the attitudes that were adopted at that time by large sections of the population nevertheless give us some understanding of the varying degrees of desire for integration.

The Latin colonies did not revolt: the majority of their aristocrats had already received Roman citizenship through the exercise of magistracies. Conversely, other cities continued not to seek it. When, in the first years of the war, it was granted to the allies who stayed loyal, Naples and Heraclea questioned whether there was any need to accept it. These cities were long-time allies of the Roman people, and the treaties that bound them were not very restrictive. They feared they might lose out by changing. But also, perhaps some of their rulers were too proud of the antiquity and prestige of their own cities, which had always been influenced by Hellenism, to contemplate merging into the vague mass of the new Roman-ness.[23]

Elsewhere the difficulties were certainly even more profound. The Etruscans and Umbrians had sent delegations to Rome to protest against Livius Drusus' proposals. They wanted to avoid being once more dispossessed of part of their territory. But neither did they wish to acquire the citizenship that would have allowed them to benefit more widely from the distributions envisaged by Drusus. In any case they engaged belatedly and very marginally in the Social War. People have read various reasons into this,[24] one of which underlines the diversity of situations. Etruscan society included that category of semi-free people who, if they became Roman citizens, would be completely emancipated and become the equals of their former masters.[25] To this deep anxiety about possible social upheavals was probably added a cultural and political conservatism that was also connected with a lesser participation in conquest and exploitation of the eastern world.

In central and southern Italy the reaction was quite different and the rebellion reached an extraordinary volume among the Picentini, Marsi, Peligni, Vestini, Marrucini, Hirpini, Samnites, Apulians, Lucanians and some of the Campanians.

There the consequences of the second Punic War had been most serious, and subjection to Roman power also the most abject. Evidence lies in the very large confiscations of land and the important agrarian allocations carried out by virtue of the Gracchan laws. They had probably involved more frequent and repeated interventions by the Roman authorities than elsewhere, and more difficult ones to endure. Treaties that had been concluded probably also imposed swingeing military contributions. At all events, it is in these regions that the greatest quantity of Roman coins has been discovered. As this money was struck for the purpose of paying soldiers' wages, it is supposed that the men of these regions, whose reputation as fighters was renowned, were mobilized more than others.[26]

Nevertheless, these were the regions that had opened up the most to the Hellenistic world. For if so many soldiers had been recruited there, it meant that they had taken part in campaigns in the East from which they had profited both financially and culturally. Similarly, these same populations had provided a large proportion of the merchants and traders to be found in Greek ports and markets, notably Delos. They had thus grown rich and opened up to the Hellenistic world, even though in an uneven fashion. Certainly Campania, which had experienced the greatest economic boom, by far outdid all the others. But the development of sanctuaries, whose importance we have noted, chiefly at Pietrabbondante, shows that the interior of the peninsula had not stayed on the sidelines.

In these conditions, a century after Hannibal's defeat, the subjection to Rome that the defections of that time had justified became increasingly intolerable. For three generations the aristocratic families of these regions had taken part in Rome's war efforts, had blended with the Romans in the provinces and had adopted in their own lives the new values that had come from Hellenism. Because their civic traditions were not as strong as those of the Etruscans and Greeks, they could easily envisage acquiring a Roman citizenship that would afford them in law the recognition of an equality which they considered they had already gained in fact.

Anyway, one had only to examine the demands of the Italians as quoted by the early writers to understand the reasons for their rebellion. They wanted nothing more than to share in the government of an empire which they had helped to establish.[27] They rejected a domination that had lost its legitimacy. An allusion to a probably genuine oath of loyalty to Livius Drusus, said to have been uttered by those most desperate to obtain citizenship, is a clear enough indication. The concept of Italy as a common fatherland for all its inhabitants had made remarkable progress among the Italic peoples who were at the very core of the rebellion. The gods they invoked were among those they had in common with the Romans,[28] and in their view what justified their being accepted into the new community was that they had a real family relationship with them.

The organization they adopted confirmed that they saw themselves as representatives of an Italy whose government the

Romans had usurped. They formed themselves into a federation of twelve peoples and made their capital Corfinium, of the Paeligni, renaming it Italica. As government they appointed two consuls, twelve praetors and a senate of 500 members; the coins they struck in the name of Italy celebrated their association by the scene of an oath, their liberation by the effigy of *Liber pater* and their will to bring Rome down by the image of a bull trampling a she-wolf. These peoples of central and southern Italy were probably better placed to conceive such a political system since they still hardly knew anything other than organization in *pagi* and *vici*. Sharing little or nothing of the sense of civic identity held by Etruscans, Greeks or Romans, they could easily imagine an Italy united according to the ethnic criteria which were precisely those on which their identity was structured. But it was this difference that helped to make it so difficult for the Romans to incorporate them into their civic community.

The war was long and hard, but here we will not go back over the various operations and campaigns: it lasted until 87. But as early as 90 Rome realized that its refusal to grant citizenship was untenable. Measures were taken. A *lex Calpurnia* permitted military leaders to bestow it as a reward to the allies who fought courageously, and at the end of the year a *lex Iulia* granted it to the Latins and other allies who had stayed loyal. Lastly, in 89, a *lex Plautia Papiria* extended the concession to those who resided in the same cities. In Cisalpine Gaul, however, which had been conquered more recently, the Latin colonies received citizenship and the other allied cities, thanks to a *lex Pompeia*, obtained Latin rights. Those who remained rebellious were incorporated after their *deditio* according to arrangements of which we are ignorant. As for the islands, they did not belong to Italy as it was conceived, and were not involved. But once citizenship was granted, two acute problems presented themselves.

The first was political and internal to the new Roman citizenship. In which tribes were the hundreds of thousands of new citizens going to vote? This was one of the most urgent issues. As we have already noted, it justified the fears that had prompted members of the Roman aristocracy to refuse the Italians' demands. The entire civic balance of the state was called into question. The opportunity of certain Roman aristocratic families to ensure their political future or not hung on the answer that would be given, for those who obtained large numbers of clients would be sure of winning. Our sources do not enable us to reconstruct exactly the procedure that was adopted. To start with, two new tribes were probably created by the *lex Calpurnia*, but that was not enough. There was then an attempt to distribute them in a limited number of tribes, new or, more likely, old ones that were doubled.[29] Crammed as they must have been into a quarter of the new ensemble, the Italians could not do much harm, but neither would they have any power. When they became aware of this, they agitated and protested. At length, to reconcile them, the Marianist tribune of 88, P. Sulpicius Rufus, had a law passed dividing them into the old tribes whose number was thus restored to the traditional 35. Civic organization remained as it was. But it took time for this measure to be accepted and made effective. The principle of an equitable integration was upheld by Sulla after a number of violent episodes when the interests of old and new citizens were in clear opposition. And in actual fact, although the censors of 86 had made a good start on recording the Italians who had received citizenship, the latter had to wait until the census of 70–69 before being completely divided among the various units of the civic community.

The second problem was of a social and legal nature. How could cities whose institutions were so ancient and varied be merged into a single new constitutional whole? The procedure existed, and it was sufficient to enlarge it. This was the *fundifactio*. The cities made a clean sweep of all measures in their law and civic organization that might be contrary to Roman rules, and asked the Roman authorities to appoint the first college of magistrates of the new city, who would give it its constitution.[30]

This was an important stage in the unification of Italy. One after the other, taking advantage of the laws that allowed them to do so, the cities asked to be integrated. The magistracies were reorganized, most frequently following a common model.[31] Colleges of quattuorvirs appeared almost everywhere in the peninsula, replacing the old traditional magistrates. A homogeneous municipal system was being put into place. The Latin and allied cities all became Roman citizens and received like institutions. Then they took the name of *municipium* which had hitherto defined the communities that had formerly been incorporated in the Roman state. Roman colonies whose members already possessed citizenship finally acquired the autonomy they lacked.[32] The other communities of the *ager romanus*, the *fora* and *conciliabula*, together with the prefectures, were at last transformed into true states.

Some differences remained, however, which were still connected with the concern of some to preserve an identity of which they were proud or, conversely, the desire of others to be like Rome. Some cities obtained permission for their magistrates to retain their ancient titles, doubtless on condition that their competence and conditions of recruitment were compatible with Roman laws. Naples, for instance, kept its archons, but adapted them to the collegial system. Reggio did likewise for its *prytanes*. Caere was content to Latinize its *purth* without altering his prerogatives.[33] Others kept strictly to the institutions that were proposed to them as models. So the small town of Bantia adopted a good number of the Roman magistracies and procedures at one fell swoop: censorship, praetorship, quaestorship and tribuneship of the plebs, *manus iniectio* and trials by comitia included. All the same, it published its new constitution in Oscan, because that was the language still understood by its citizens.[34]

Above all, the process of municipalization which had already commenced in the late first century took on a quite different dimension.[35] The Roman model was eventually imposed where it had not yet been so. All communities, if they were not already organized in states, had to start to function as such in order to comply with Roman legal and political requirements. Such a change obviously had profound consequences for all those peoples who were organized in *pagi* and *vici*, notably the Italic populations of the centre of the peninsula. Towns or large villages had to define themselves as capital towns of the new states and regroup the surrounding territories under their authority. The federal sanctuaries that until then had polarized social and political life lost their role. The one at Pietrabbondante ceased to be used and the one of Mefitis at Rossano di Vaglio was henceforth managed by the magistrates of Potentia in whose area of jurisdiction it had fallen.[36]

A state was not composed of institutions alone. It had to affirm its existence by putting into operation urban planning which would show the world that it was the perfect framework for political life and that its members were prosperous, even if, in order to do so, it had to cover itself in buildings of a magnitude entirely out of keeping with the true size of its population. The process of laying out the urban landscape and building civic monuments took on a new impetus once the destruction of the civil and Social War was over. Regions as yet little involved became committed in their turn, natably central Italy and Cisalpine Gaul, where building works were started.[37] Italy was becoming unified in both architecture and town planning.

This movement of municipalization, however, was not a themeless or aimless mechanism. Its participants were either Roman patrons or local aristocrats. The former intervened at every opportunity in the definition of new institutions, the choice of the civic centre when it had not been decided, the construction of buildings to adorn the new city. According to Caesar, that was how Cingulum received its constitution from T. Labienus, one of his lieutenants. He probably had himself appointed as one of its magistrates. He had also built it with his own denarii, if we take that to mean that he had had its principal public buildings constructed at his expense.[38] By acting in this way he had not only made himself the benefactor of the city to which he had given its laws, but had also donned the mantle of a new founder. He organized its operational rules and bestowed upon it all the architectural and urbanistic accoutrements which gave Cingulum the attributes of a real city. So it was then totally part of his clientele, to the point where the inhabitants immediately provided Caesar with the soldiers he needed to fight Pompey.

Local aristocrats certainly did not intend to be left out of things. They took initiatives leading to the establishment of budding constitutions, probably negotiating their terms, and some participated in the foundation procedures. As far as possible they tried to control the important decisions that defined the new civic framework, for their future position would be dependent on them. By acts of public benefaction they contributed to the beauty and prestige of the new cities. At the same time, they were all integrated henceforth in a single social and political ensemble of rich and honourable Roman citizens, having a solid local base, often members of the equestrian order, sometimes capable of entering the Roman senatorial order. They were thus brought to play a major role in Roman political life.

A dual process was in operation. Socially, culturally and politically, Italy was becoming united. As Cicero noted in a famous passage,[39] from now on Italians had two homelands, their native city and Rome. But at the same stroke political stakes shifted. Certainly, important decisions were still taken by the Senate and

Roman magistrates, but the weight of these new citizens, especially when they were rich and influential, was steadily growing. From now on it was they, in competition with the people of Rome, who recognized values and decided careers. From then on, the great leaders whos conflicting claims would lead to confrontation in the civil wars found them a force to be reckoned with.

8

THE CIVIL WARS:
VIOLENCE AND PACIFICATION

With the civil wars the process of integration and unification expanded and accelerated. The principal leaders in conflict for the government of Rome were forced to mobilize all the resources they could lay hands on throughout Italy: money, of course, but also supporters and soldiers who had to be rewarded once victory was won. Proscriptions and confiscations which hit the losers but allowed the victors to be paid resulted in a vast traffic of men and goods from one end of the peninsula to the other. Another result was that the small protected pockets, together with specific ethnic and political characteristics, were finally obliterated.

However, the phenomenon was not confined to those aspects most concerned with conflict in the period. All the instruments of power were concentrated definitively in the hands of a few. Those with the means to mobilize entire armies against their foes were also the ones who had succeeded in amassing considerable fortunes, and had won over crowds of dependants and allies to carry them to the summit of political prestige. Therefore no more than a mere handful of men could really decide the destiny of Rome. Soon, by successive eliminations, they were reduced to two or three, then one alone who became the first monarch of the Empire. Similarly, the whole of Italy became the almost united arena of political life. It was the sphere inside which tensions were exerted and justifications proclaimed. The old ethnic and civic divisions remained, in that they were still the foundation of a great number of identities and solidarities. They lost their effectiveness, however, because they no longer defined the framework of political decisions. The Roman people had expanded to the point of embracing the entire Italian population. In so far as political decisions, in order to be justified, still had to obtain the people's implicit assent, in default of being always approved according to the ritual of the comitia, other forms of political expression made their appearance: they completed the process of integrating the Italians into the Roman political ensemble.

Concentrating the Instruments of Power

In order to dominate society and dictate to their fellow-citizens, the members of the Roman senatorial aristocracy used three main instruments: money, prestige and the support provided by clients and other dependants. The three were connected, for nobody could profit much from one without being soundly assured of the other two. The concentration of these three forms of social and political wealth was a far from insignificant consequence of, first, the wars of conquest and then the civil wars.

We have already noticed the size of the gains that generals and governors could extract from exploiting the provinces. They were also best placed to reap the maximum benefit from Italy's economic transformations. The first two factors alone enable us to understand the extraordinary nature of the wealth of certain persons who completely dominated Roman political life. We must also reckon with the effects of the civil wars. The proscriptions which in 82 struck at the Marianists and, in 43, the supporters of Caesar's murderers, were the opportunity for some to get very rich from purchasing the possessions of the defeated at a low price.

In this way, during the first century, the levels of wealth of certain rulers of the state reached absolutely unheard-of figures. If Cicero's property wealth is estimated at 3.5 million denarii and that of Lucullus at 25 million, Crassus the triumvir's approached 50 million while Pompey's exceeded even that. These figures must be compared with those we know of senators from preceding generations: 280,000 for Aemilius Paulus, and a little under a million for Scipio Aemilianus, though they were top-level people,[1] and with those known for the revenue of the entire Roman state: 50 million denarii per annum before the year 62.

In evaluating the social importance of such fortunes one becomes aware of the level of power and the range of influence to which they gave access. In fact these figures imply ownership of dozens, possibly hundreds of properties scattered throughout Italy, quite apart from places of residence: houses or premises in Rome and other towns, vast areas of grazing land for large flocks or herds, and many estates, since Roscius, an aristocrat of Ameria with an estimated fortune of 1.5 million denarii, already owned thirteen.[2] These personages were therefore directly responsible for thousands of slaves, freedmen and tenant farmers whose labour certainly helped to make them rich but who also, by their sheer numbers, demonstrated the might and standing of their masters. So the most important of them had such social power that, if the need arose, they could avail themselves of formidable private armies.

According to Crassus, one could not claim to be rich unless one could maintain an army with one's own wealth.[3] In Picenum, which was populated by his father's clients, Pompey had mobilized the troops which enabled him to oppose the Marianists.[4] L. Domitius Ahenobarbus recruited between 10,000 and 13,000 men to fight Caesar, promising them lands that he would take from his own estates.[5]

As is indicated by this concentration of wealth during the second and first centuries BC, the Roman senatorial aristocracy was being defined according to a new qualitative criterion. The phenomenon appears even more clearly in the way they dealt with the charisma imparted by victory. The great leaders rivalled one another in their efforts to inscribe the memory of their exploits and the visible sign of their pre-eminence in the urban landscape. In the first century the size and quality of buildings exceeded everything that had been done before. The chief ambition of the great *imperatores* was no longer merely to embellish the city by the construction of a few buildings that would be added to others. They actually restructured the political area so as to impose references to their own victories as the only ones worthy of being seen by the people and serving as a setting for civic rituals. Gradually, therefore, pretensions to monarchic domination made their appearance in the urban landscape.

The first to take this route was Sulla. He had tried to impart a certain coherence to the forum area by entrusting one of his partisans, Q. Lutatius Catulus, with the task of reconstructing Jupiter's temple, which dominated it, and building the *tabularium* which united it to the Capitol. In his wake, Pompey could scarcely use the area which was already covered with buildings, and turned his efforts to the Campus Martius. There he had a grandiose monumental group built, composed of a theatre whose *cavea* was surmounted by a temple to Venus, his protectress, and extended by a quadriportico which in size outstripped anything that Rome had known before. Overall, it was certainly intended for the beautification of the town and the people's pleasures, but it was also used for the functioning of institutions, as the Senate sometimes met in its curia.

Not to be left out, Caesar had the *saepta* built, the meeting-place of the *comitia centuriata*, and undertook to have his own forum created, on the Capitol's flank, inaugurating it when he had become sole ruler after Pompey's death. After him, Augustus, finding himself in the same situation, proceeded in an identical fashion. He completely restructured the old forum and had another built which extended beyond Caesar's. In every case the principle governing the lay-out of these squares was the same. They were enclosed, bordered or surrounded by porticoes and dominated by temples, to Venus Genitrix, the deified Caesar or Mars the Avenger. In one way or another, these monuments proclaimed the glory of the founder and the legitimacy of his authority. All the ceremonies of public life that could be were transferred to areas that were specially constructed and the best adapted to symbolic control. Situated in the midst of an architectural ensemble whose setting remained politically unambiguous, the actors on the scene seemed to have placed themselves under the emperor's protection and to be intervening only by virtue of his authority.[6]

The concentration of clienteles and other forms of dependence actively instituted networks of relationships that completed the unification of Italy. The mechanism worked in two main ways. The first was the expression of the traditional pattern of patron–client bond. The second corresponded to the development of recruitment to the army: soldiers depended increasingly on the military leaders who henceforth became their natural protectors. In both instances, the violence of the civil wars played an important part in the establishment and especially the development of these relationships.

Generally speaking, the networks of clients tended to concentrate themselves in the hands of the most powerful men. Some measures that followed the Social War had in fact modified the former equilibrium. The submission of the conquered regions had earned the victorious generals considerable gains. Certainly Pompeius Strabo had in this way built up vast clienteles in Picenum from which his son was able to profit. But account must also be taken of the results of conceding rights of citizenship to the great masses of Italians: the same Pompeius Strabo, who enabled the inhabitants of Transpadana to obtain Latin rights, was able to add them to the already considerable number of those who were loyal to him. When Caesar had occasion to grant them Roman rights, he in turn won them to his side.

But if power was becoming concentrated, clienteles followed the same path. Clients obviously went to whoever was capable of defending and protecting them, and it is hard to imagine that they would have contented themselves with personages or families who had become secondary. Thus we note that Cicero, about whom we are best informed, had succeeded in obtaining the backing of entire regions such as Sicily and a large part of Bruttium and Lucania, or cities like Atella, Cales, Capua, Rieti, Volterra and of course Arpinum. He had intervened to defend the interests of a whole community or he had protected some powerful aristocrat who had brought all his company with him.[7]

At the summit of Roman society, above all, things were changing. The most powerful managed to subdue those who had not quite achieved their level of authority. For example, Cicero had been forced by Pompey to defend some of his worst enemies and, by doing so, publicly to go back on his word and virtually dishonour himself. It had even been one of the aims of the first triumvirate to mobilize the influential resources of the three parties in order to make the other members of the aristocracy knuckle under. What occurred then was the arrangement of a hierarchy of powers within the Roman aristocracy. The real princes of the state had entourages which brought together to their advantage the power of each of their members. They then enjoyed the increased range of influence afforded them by dominating such imposing associations, and through their agency managed the network of clients bound to them by ties of patronage.

All in all, the new structure of Roman political power was eventually transformed into a pyramid, where a few dynasts dominated the state and increasingly controlled broad sections of Italian society to their own advantage. Relations with the army, in so far as the civil wars turned it into one of the main participants in the political and social life of Italy in the first century, also introduced other imbalances in the state's political life. These upset the social equilibrium of the peninsula to the point where the results of the spread in violence completed its unification.

The Army of the Civil Wars and Italy

The development of the army, its recruitment and relations with political government, is one of the important subjects in the history of Rome in the second and first centuries BC. It was in fact marked by two general trends which made it the instrument of the wars between the principal leaders of the state at the end of the Republic.

The first concerns the lowering of the property-rating conditions governing recruitment. In the third-century civic army, soldiers had to provide their own equipment. So, in the hierarchic system of the *centuriae* many more comfortably-off citizens were recruited than poor ones, for the former had the means to make up the phalanx of suitably cuirassed infantry.

With the second Punic War this situation began to change under pressure of the enormous requirements in men. The levels of wealth that distinguished the various classes were lowered, directly by diminishing their nominal value and indirectly by the devaluation of the bronze coins in which they were expressed. Later, perhaps under the Gracchi, the total of the minimum rating from which men were recruited was again reduced. Lastly, in 107, by a decision that remains famous, Marius, who had to face up to war with Jugurtha, enrolled all who presented themselves to the *dilectus* without bothering about how much money they had. At the same time, the state was obliged to take responsibility for equipping and paying soldiers. Arms were already supplied in the period of the Punic Wars. The remainder was provided under the Gracchi. As for pay, it rose from 90 denarii annually to about 225 in Caesar's time.[8] Thus the proletarian army (in the Roman sense of the term) came into being, sometimes and rather hastily considered responsible for all the evils of the civil wars.

It is nevertheless true that this army tended to stand apart from the rest of the civic body. Certainly, the basic values that gave it legitimacy were still those of the state. Conscription rules remained the same in theory and in fact, even when massive recruitment became necessary under the Triumvirate. But two factors weighed heavily and led, if not to professionalization in the full sense of the word, at least to the constitution of a particular identity associated with specific forms of behaviour.

Periods of service had lengthened. Although very variable, it could not be ruled out that soldiers might be mobilized for years on end, as we have already noticed. Above all, campaigns of conquest taking armies far afield prevented men for long periods from returning to Italy. Being uprooted in this way certainly hampered their chances of being reabsorbed.

Furthermore, the relations that leaders had with their men took on a much more personal character. Campaigns lasted longer and the same magistrates kept their command for several years running. We have only to think of the campaigns of Sulla and Pompey in the East, from 87 to 84 for the former and 67 to 61 for the second, or the one that kept Caesar in Gaul from 58 to 51. Moreover, these same leaders had a tendency to invest themselves with the virtues of the Hellenistic sovereigns and from their victories extracted a charisma which redounded on their men. Even for a simple legionary it was not a matter of indifference to have been among those led by Pompey or Caesar to the farthest corners of the known world. In any case, it was a commander's duty to know his men and take care of each of them, which enabled personal ties, or at least the illusion of them, to be created.

This kind of relationship would have been of little consequence if it had not found a very concrete recompense in the distribution of money and lands which henceforth followed conquests.

The first were traditional, and extended the sharing of booty. They simply tended to follow the inflation of wealth. At the end of his campaigns Lucullus allotted 950 denarii to each of his men. Pompey gave them 1,500. With the civil wars the stakes mounted still higher: at the time of his triumph, in 46, Caesar distributed

5,000 or 6,000 per head. These were still actual distributions; promises could be even more generous.[9]

In contrast, the second gained real importance only during the first century. After the second Punic War, the veterans of Scipio Africanus had received plots of land with an area in proportion to the number of their years of service. But the real demands began with the bills of the tribune Appuleius Saturninus who, in 103 then in 100, proposed agrarian laws to reward Marius' veterans. The plots to be allocated were of 100 jugera (25 hectares), an area consistent with that in general use. But these concessions apparently applied to the foundation of colonies in the provinces, especially Africa and Corsica, where the interests of no Italians could be harmed.

The project met with only partial success, but despite that it was a sign of a perceptible development. As Velleius Paterculus, a first-century AD writer, noted, the only colonies created then were to reward veterans.[10] For the most part, the soldiers who made up the Roman army were of rural origin, coming mainly from the regions of central Italy which were perhaps the most affected by Italy's economic transformation and where the uprooting of populations was also hardest. This recruitment meant either that conscription helped to break down the social fabric, or that the rural exodus freed men for the army. However, to some extent these soldiers remained peasants. For them the award of a plot of land was no empty recompense, but certainly represented both the hope of a decent life and recognition of status.

So, until the time of Augustus, military leaders sought to meet this expectation by promising lands to those they mobilized and trying to obtain them for those who had survived campaigns. Although to the advantage of their own soldiers, they were thus resuming the agrarian policy of the Gracchi and their successors by combining in the same concern rewards for their men and the restoration of an Italian peasantry. The difficulty lay in the fact that the *ager publicus* was eventually exhausted. Lands had been granted in a regular fashion. Owners had obtained confirmation of their rights. It was therefore necessary to consider buying lands to complement what could be taken from the public domain, even, in especially urgent situations and civil wars, deciding to dispossess the legitimate owners.

On several occasions these great operations of land distribution took place, completing the unification of the social, ethnic and cultural landscape of Italy: in 82, on Sulla's victory over his Marianist adversaries; in 59 when, thanks to the first triumvirate, Pompey succeeded in obtaining recompense for his men; from 47 to 44, after Caesar vanquished him; in 41, 36, and 30, when the combatants in the last civil wars had to be discharged. Each time, there were thousands of men to be settled: 80,000 in 82; 50,000 in 59; between 130,000 and 150,000 between 47 and 14; that is, a total of between 260,000 and 280,000 individuals[11] with the families they had sometimes had the time to establish. If the number of free inhabitants in the peninsula in that period could reach from 4 to 5 million people, a very large proportion of the population, at least 10 per cent and possibly more, was gathered together, uprooted and transplanted.

The demobilized men were not divided evenly throughout the whole of Italy. The lands they desired and sometimes demanded to be allocated had to form holdings from which they could make a living, situated in fertile zones, provided with farm buildings and the necessary labour. Under normal circumstances, it took time to meet these desires. The magistrates in charge of the operation had to decide, state by state, on the parts of the territory that would be affected by purchases or confiscations, and the land-surveyors had to get on with the work of measuring and setting boundaries.[12] That is why the settlement of Caesar's veterans, which was started in 47, was still not completed on his death in 44.[13] When the urgency of war ruled and it was necessary to accede immediately to the demands of soldiers who had the means of making themselves heard, notably during the period of the triumvirate, estates had to be taken from their owners just as they were. Thus in 43, to mobilize their troops, the triumvirs announced in advance which towns would be affected by the rewards to be granted to them. Eighteen were chosen, among the most important and prosperous in Italy: Capua, Reggio, Venusia, Beneventum, Nuceria, Rimini and Vibo Valentia, for example, each of which in 41 had to receive between several hundred and 3,000 or 4,000 men, to the point where, if there was a shortage of land, confiscations were extended to the neighbouring states.[14]

It is true that some beneficiaries of these concessions did not succeed in truly putting down roots. Cicero said so, for instance, about those who had been settled by Sulla in the territory of

Praeneste. Despite a ban on the resale of plots, he explained, a small number of owners had concentrated lands in their hands.[15] He also claimed that among Catiline's partisans some of the veterans had ended in debt.[16] Some of these settlements must have been fairly frail, and many events could occur that might jeopardize them. But in Pompeii, for example, which had been the site of a large colonization by Sulla and of which one can trace the development with some precision, the veterans succeeded in settling down, even dominating local political life for a while and not tolerating a return to power of the former dominant families until several decades had elapsed.[17] Looked at as a whole, by its very size this process necessarily resulted in extremely large transfers of population.

The settlements had many consequences. First, ethnic and cultural ones: the regions affected by these measures were chiefly those whose lands were devoted to intensive farming, where the density of population was relatively heavy. They experienced great changes in the composition of their population. Some completed their Romanization, for instance, Etruria and Cisalpine Gaul. Others went further ahead in the process which until then had only partly touched them: this was the case for Corsica, which received its first Roman colony from Marius; and Sicily and Sardinia, where some of Augustus' colonies were installed: Catana, Palermo, Syracuse, Taormina, Thermae and Tyndaris in the first instance, Porto Torres in the second.

The immediate social consequences were just as heavy. Within the states concerned there were what seem to have been important transfers of property. At Volterra, when the triumviral allocations were made, veterans received plots of 25, 35, 50 or 60 jugera, between 6.5 and 15 hectares, depending on the rank they had held.[18] They were only small holdings, but the number of recipients created truly traumatic conditions. Not all were equally hit, however. In 41, Roman senators and the families of soldiers were spared, so that the main burden of confiscations fell on the owners, large or small, in the municipia. When the latter were dispossessed, they had no other recourse than to leave or become the sharecropper (*colonus*) of the soldiers who received their estate. In Venusia, for example, this befell the Ofellus whose estate was passed over to a certain Umbrenus, and whose stoic frugality was described by Horace, a native of the same city.[19]

This process of brutal confiscation, as I have said, cropped up only in the context of the civil wars, in 82 or after 43. In the first case, the violent situation and the political conditions made these transfers of property understandable. The lands of states which had resisted the victor could be confiscated without anyone having much to say about it. In this way the territories of Volterra and Praeneste, which had opposed Sulla, were confiscated and turned into *ager publicus* as if they had behaved like Rome's enemies. Praeneste's land was shared out and allocated, Volterra's was left as it was. Although the results were not of the same magnitude, in both cases they profoundly affected the two communities.

In 41 the situation had worsened. Needs were such that Caesar Octavianus, who presided over the operation, had to impose his choices on populations who had not necessarily sided with his father's murderers. Serious troubles ensued. He had to fight L. Antonius, the triumvir's brother, who had assumed leadership of the opposition, and defeat him by laying siege to Perusia where he had gone to ground. Skirmishes broke out here and there between the wronged peasants and the newcomers.[20] Agricultural production was affected and food shortages threatened Rome.[21] It was because the demands of soldiers outweighed all other considerations that the future Augustus behaved in this manner. Later, when conditions had become calmer, he tried to moderate the effects of his allocations, as Pompey and Caesar had done before him, the former by buying land when there was not enough, and the latter by installing part of his veterans in colonies founded in the provinces or dispersing them in smaller groups.[22]

Only the relations that these leaders maintained with their men justified the application of such measures. By settling them and giving them a livelihood they were keeping the promises they had made and earning their loyalty. The colonies thus created became so many states which entered their clientele and offered them a network of supporters on whom they judged that they could rely. Such a process reinforced the phenomenon of the concentration of power. The relationship that was established was not always immediate, however. Often the leader himself did not found the colony; he left this task to some of his relatives or trusted followers, who carried out all the rites, set up the institutions and appointed the first magistrates. Sulla's nephew, for example, founded the one installed in the town of Pompeii. The hierarchies of relationships of patronage also worked in this way and helped to set up a new system of government. Though the essential part of authority remained well and truly in the hands of the monarch who ruled the empire, he delegated it to a few powerful aristocrats who derived their own influence from him and remained his subordinates.

Violence and Pacification

The civil wars were not confined to this single aspect of confiscations carried out to the advantage of the soldiers engaged in the service of the main adversaries. They also touched a large section of the Italian population either directly or indirectly.

Proscriptions played an important part. They affected the members of the senatorial or equestrian aristocracy who had declared themselves adversaries of the victors: they were pursued because, having some weight in the state, they had been able to play a large part in the conflict.[23] We have already noticed the importance of the transfers of wealth and power to which these procedures gave rise, but the effects of this repression did not stop there. A fairly large number of these personages originated from various municipia of Italy. With them, others who belonged to municipal aristocracies had been drawn into the upheaval and had perished. We have only to think of the thousands of Samnite prisoners massacred by Sulla after the capture of Rome. Wars, mobilizations and losses of men were equally factors which brought their train of upheaval into the life of the states, although it is not easy to make precise estimates. Locally, social and political balances shifted with each episode of these repeated conflicts.

A first strictly social occurrence was taking shape, and there have been some attempts to evaluate it. It was a matter of the elevation of people who had become powerful through acquiring wealth and authority. For example, the C. Quinctius Valgus of whom Cicero said, probably without much exaggeration, that thanks to Sulla he owned the whole territory of the Hirpini,[24] concurrently held the offices of quinquennial duumvir in a neighbouring municipium of Abellinum and of duumvir then quinquennial duumvir at Pompeii. He was sufficiently rich and

influential to have been the patron of Aeclanum and especially to
have participated in the construction of a large number of public
buildings in all these cities. At Pompeii he helped to finance the
erection of a second theatre and the amphitheatre.[25] He thus
fitted in perfectly with the group of local potentates although his
status was of recent date: he owed it to the civil wars.

The social equilibrium of the states was sometimes profoundly
affected, and in some cases the entire state felt the effects. At
Praeneste, for instance, the whole of the population was massacred on Sulla's orders.[26] On those of Caesar Octavianus, so were
the members of Perusia's senate.[27] These were extreme cases. In
other places, where circumstances had not brought about such
dramatic results, some families surmounted the ordeal. The
Caecinae, Cilnii, Maecenates and Volumnii of Volterra, Arezzo
and Perusia managed to live through the Sullan period and hold
their position at the head of large states, despite the heavy colonization that had impinged on Etruria.[28]

Everything in fact depended on the intensity with which the
process of confiscation and allocation of lands was carried out
locally. At Brindisi, which was not affected, out of twenty-eight
family names, generally landed property owners, which are
attested in the second century, thirteen kept their position beyond
the reign of Augustus. In contrast, at Venusia, Horace's homeland, out of the four known names of magistrates prior to the
triumviral colonization only one still remained under the Empire,
whereas out of the thirty-five others about a score persisted.[29]
Compare this with the situation at Picenum: out of the forty-odd
families of senators or knights to be found in the first century,
sixteen are no longer attested after the wars of the triumvirate and
twelve appear later, whereas the others survived from one period
to the other.[30]

The whole of Italy was subjected to the pressure of confiscations and allocations. Large groups of individuals were
dispossessed, and replaced by others. Among the latter, some did
not succeed in settling and soon left again. All travelled around
at the whim of the conflicts and rallying that took place under one
leader or another. All this created conditions of mobility, itself the
source of political instability and insecurity. So rebellions and
conspiracies such as those of Aemilius Lepidus in 78–77 and
Catiline in 63 found support in these uprooted and marginalized
populations.[31] This is also why, in some instances, the civil wars

were stoked by one or other of the protagonists being joined by the fleeing victims of his adversaries.

Similarly, in the states affected by these changes there was nothing idyllic in the relations between the original inhabitants and the newcomers. Conflicts rose to the surface, passing on and heightening the sufferings and bitterness due to the other effects of the civil wars. Some echoes remained in literature, especially in some defence speeches. In the *Pro Roscio Amerino* Cicero defended the son of a proscribed man accused of having killed his father. In the *Pro Caecina*, it was a certain aristocrat of Volterra at loggerheads with some neighbours, newcomers to the region.[32] Horace too, originally from Venusia, referred with a mixture of sourness and humour to the presence of the rich centurions who had installed themselves in his town. Virgil and Propertius both took up the same doleful theme.[33]

Communities came into opposition, corresponding to the various waves of settlement. Sometimes they had different names. At Arezzo, for example, there were the *Arretini veteres*, *fidentiores* and *iulienses*. The first were obviously the original inhabitants, the last Caesar's colonists or their descendants, and the second probably Sulla's. At Chiusi too, there were the *veteres* and the *novi*. Sometimes the memory of their legionary solidarity united veterans, like the old soldiers of the eleventh legion who at Bovianum continued to call themselves the *Undecumani*. In this way, such epithets marked the differences between categories determined to preserve their identity. From this point of view, it may be supposed that they were likely to be used for a long time, even when relations became more peaceable.

Bu the names were not reduced merely to that role. The slightly earlier example of Agrigentum makes this understandable. In respect of the local senate the *Agrigentini veteres* in fact had the advantage of such a proportion that they were assured of a majority in relation to the *coloni novi*.[34] In other states dispositions of the same kind must have worked, but to the advantage of the veterans. They protected them from the hostility of local aristocrats and enabled the higher ranks among them to achieve and maintain the position of notables that they had sometimes been promised. Oppositions inevitably made their appearance and could occasionally become structured institutional and political conflicts. In Pompeii, Cicero explained in the course of a defence speech he made for P. Cornelius Sulla, the dictator's nephew, who had participated in the foundation of the colony and became its patron, the colonists and Pompeians had seriously clashed over questions which, as far as we know, involved the exercise of voting rights. And in fact, during the years following the foundation, the old families lost their supremacy to the advantage of the newcomers who had been imposed upon them.[35] This was a grave matter which needed to be treated seriously. The city's patrons were apprised of the matter and resolved it by arbitrating between the interests of both sides.[36]

This episode is intriguing because it reveals that client–patron relations could also be used to control and regulate tensions. It suggests chiefly that throughout all these years the members of the Roman senatorial aristocracy intervened on various occasions in the administration and political life of the Italian states. Each time, in effect, that colonists or other groups of individuals were installed, the institutions of the community in which they were placed probably had to be remodelled to take account of the new conditions which had thus been created.

The outcome was that during the whole of the first century the states of Italy underwent intense constitutional activity. The first stage was the integration of the allied states into Roman citizenship. Hard on its heels came Sullan colonization. Sulla himself modified the institutions of certain states, either by punishing them, like Volterra, or giving them greater autonomy, like Pozzuoli. Caesar's agrarian legislation in 59 soon made the reorganization of some communities necessary.[37] The wars that followed his victory over Pompey, then his assassination, further accentuated the process, since between 47 and 14 no fewer than fifty Italian towns out of around 400 were settled as colonies or received that status.[38]

In these conditions the principles were laid down that were to complete the definition of the ideal state, simultaneously Italian and Roman. The experience that was gradually accumulated ultimately produced results,[39] first on the legislative level. An important text, already referred to, bears witness to this: the inscription discovered at Heraclea in Lucania. It records a series of arrangements with a bearing on procedures to be observed in the matter of tax-rating, town planning and public building, as well as the recruitment of magistrates and senators.[40] The collection of these standards, which no one will date precisely, was the fruit of a continual accumulation of institutional decisions. These had been taken throughout the period and preserved a unity proper to rules which must in any case have been close to those of Rome and at the very least compatible with them. The same tendency is revealed on the level of town planning. At the end of the period the architect Vitruvius gave a serious explanation of the principles to be followed when creating a town, the site to be chosen, the placing of the walls, squares and main buildings. These remarks were certainly a response to the building and rebuilding that had been going on during the same period.[40]

In other respects, the intervention of members of the Roman aristocracy continued to increase. Henceforth the great leaders were able to decide the essentials of political life. Those close to them strove to influence their decisions in order to protect a state belonging to their clients. Their friends and dependants received from them the task of founding a city or resolving specific problems. Patron–client relations grew deeper and intensified at this time, a phenomenon that started in the aftermath of the Social War. The states, becoming incorporated into the Roman civic entity, strengthened their ties with the aristocrats: their protection was all the more necessary as the threats were greater.

Besides, the continuous process of municipalization allowed the politicians who had a hand in it to secure for themselves the loyalty of the cities they were helping to found. When there was a modification of Arpinum's constitution, for example, Cicero saw to it that his son and nephew were elected magistrates there in order to get their share of the benefits of prestige attached to these offices.[42] Matters like this were certainly not the smallest stakes in the war that set the Marianist leaders against Sulla. The former had probably profited from the years 87 to 83 to win for themselves the first states, notably Campanian, Etruscan and Umbrian, to have been incorporated into the Roman community.[43] As for Sulla, he had won them back and, quite apart from proscriptions, the repression inflicted on municipal politicians had probably played a no less important role in the concentration of clienteles than in that of fortunes.[44]

This is why members of the Roman aristocracy in the first century developed a taste for holding municipal offices. In fact some, and by no means the most modest, like L. Calpurnius Piso Caesoninus, L. Cassius Longinus, T. Annius Milo or Caesar, had themselves elected to the head of cities like Capua, Lavinium, Bovianu, Saticula, Alba Fucens or Vibo Valentia.[45] Even if, in some instances, they were their native cities, they probably recognized in them the opportunity of intervening in local political life and entrenching more solidly than ever the ties they had been able to create.

The position of these Roman aristocrats in the political life of Italian states then tended to assume hitherto unheard-of forms. In 36, for instance, certain cities decided to place Caesar Octavianus among the civic deities.[46] It was a first step leading to the imperial cult. Others bestowed honours upon him which, without reaching this extreme, seem to have come close to it. In fact, here and there certain monuments can be identified which really liken the figure of a patron to that of a hero, the founder or saviour of the state. Thus at Alba Fucens, or Herdonia, vast wrestling-schools (*palaestrae*) built on the model of Greek gymnasia were dominated by some building or exedra which, in the form of a *heroon*, contained the statue of the city's great personage and left the visual memory of his presence and generosity.[47] With this unprecedented degree of celebration, the patron–client relationship acquired a liveliness and acuteness it had not reached before. During the civil wars, the intensity of feelings was obviously in keeping with the violence of events.

At the same time, the conflicts and tensions of Roman political life had spread to all Italy. The process which had been at work since the second century culminated in the civic integration that followed the Social War and the upheavals of the civil wars. The modification of political personnel and the role of Italian public opinion bear witness.

The unification of Italy into a single civil whole in fact enabled an even greater number of municipal aristocrats to make a career in Rome.[48] In the main, the succession of conflicts, from battles to proscriptions, reduced the number of senatorial families. And as soon as each of the successive victors had made sure he was really in power, he rewarded those of his partisans who came from towns in the peninsula by seeing that they gained admission to the Senate and held prestigious magistracies. To take only a few examples, Pompey's Picentini: L. Afranius, T. Labienus or M. Lollius Palicanus; or among the very first partisans of Caesar Octavianus, an Apulian named Domitius, Caesennius Lento of Tarquinia, M. Insteius of Pesaro, T. Munatius Plancus Bursa of Tibur; and of far greater calibre, M. Vipsanius Agrippa and Q. Salvidienus Rufus from the Vestine area.[49] Some promotions created a scandal, like those received by some of Sulla's centurions who became senators, or even worse, some Gauls, Cisalpine or Narbonensian, honoured in this way by Caesar.[50]

Roman politicians were thus broadly replenished. There was hardly a region of Italy that, at the end of the first century, had not provided some senatorial family. Another outstanding fact is that even the descendants of those who had fought Rome in the Social War found themselves carried to the summit of the civic hierarchy. C. Asinius Pollio, the grandson of Herius Asinius, leader of the Marrucini, was consul in 40. P. Ventidius Bassus who, it was said, had as a child been one of the Picentine prisoners forced to march in Pompeius Strabo's triumphal parade, was suffect consul in 43 and held a triumph in his turn.

Similarly, Italian public opinion had become a stake in Roman politics. This also meant that it had become united. Roman politicians tried to mobilize it to their own advantage. Cicero's brother, in his campaign advice for the consulship, emphasized this point: one had to win over the most important personages in the municipia.[51] In Rome, conditions of civic life had deteriorated. Violence had invaded assemblies and the votes of the comitia had lost their validity, all the more because the new citizens who peopled Italy took hardly any part. The decisions taken in the states of Italy, especially the decrees passed by local senates, assumed an increased importance: they represented the opinion of worthy citizens.[52] Cicero stressed the fact that they were the ones who had persistently demanded his return from exile and helped him to obtain it.[53]

All these events obviously reached their climax in the effort made by Octavian to gather around him all the political forces of the peninsula on the eve of his combat with Antony. He made all the states swear an oath of loyalty, with the exception of Bologna, which belonged to his foe's clientele. At that moment Italy appeared as a single body united against the danger of eastern monarchy lurking behind Antony and Cleopatra. What a distance had been travelled in half a century. Indeed in 91, when the Italians had committed themselves by oath to the side of Livius Drusus, it had been a criminal step, for the allies were not citizens and were threatening Rome. Henceforward they were, and this same gesture gave the future Augustus his legitimacy.[54]

Thus the political and ideological unification of Italy was completed. Of course the civic procedures had yet to be set up which, in the rediscovered peace of the early Empire, would permit the management of this unprecedented organism of a state expanded to the dimensions of such a vast territory.

The Transpadane cities, which had received Latin rights only after the Social War, had been incorporated into the community of Roman citizens by Caesar, probably in 49. Augustus joined them with some of the Alpine populations who had hitherto remained autonomous.[55] Political Italy had thus reached its natural frontier. The islands began to follow suit. There Augustus granted Roman rights to some cities which thus became municipia similar to those of the peninsula, and he confirmed the concession of Latin rights which Caesar had granted to Sicily as a whole.[56] Little by little, the process that would lead the states of the Empire to form a single political whole pursued its course.

The unification of Italy that had taken place no longer allowed any backward step in the organization of relations between Rome and the rest of the peninsula. In his attempt to restore – on the face of it – the ideal state, Augustus kept this in mind.

He completed the policy of colonization that he had begun during the triumvirate, but respecting ownerships and buying land instead of confiscating it. He had roads repaired and set up the first stages of an administration entrusted, out of respect for tradition, to members of the senatorial aristocracy. He created an initial communications system by couriers, which later became the imperial postal service.[57] Everywhere, he encouraged the construction of monuments and public buildings, contributing from his personal fortune to the embellishment of Italian cities, or urging his relatives and close friends to do likewise.[58] Having become the protector of the whole peninsula by the oath of 32, he was also its first benefactor, so that in every town could be found the setting that encompassed the definition of the ideal city in the expression of his renown.

He also tried to organize new forms of institutional life; the opinion of Italian aristocracies might have been considered. Local senates were invited to recommend worthy persons who might possibly become Roman knights.[59] Moreover, he set up a system of voting by correspondence which allowed decurions of the peninsula states to take part in the selection, henceforward strictly controlled, of Rome's magistrates. He also pursued a process of extending political life to the aristocratic strata of Italy,[60] while at the same time continuing the one leading to the removal of the *populares* circles in Rome. So the Italy of the notables tended eventually to form a unified sphere of political life.

Perhaps, however, the measures that best signify symbolically the achievement of Italy's unification and Romanization were quite simply those made necessary by the administrative management of this new Roman people. The old framework of thirty-five tribes had now lost its relevance. Another was required to collect the tax-rating information issuing from the states. It was quite naturally geographical, and thus ceased to be political. The peninsula was divided into eleven regions that roughly corresponded to the former great ethnic groups, with which states were classified topographically.[61] Order was no longer concerned with status, since only that of Roman citizen was left, or with the length or quality of relations with Rome, since all, whether they had been municipia or colonies, had been more or less radically refounded. Having become a united territory, peninsular Italy retained from its former heterogeneity only local identities that were surely still piously preserved but slowly melted away beneath the feeling, henceforth totally shared, of belonging to the community of the masters of the Empire.

CONCLUSION

In AD 14 Augustus died at Nola in Campania, 'at thirty-five days short of seventy-six years. The decurions of the municipia and colonies transported his body from Nola as far as Bovillae, by night because of the heat, and by day he was placed in the basilica of each town or its largest temple. At Bovillae he was handed over to the knights, who carried him to Rome and placed him in the vestibule of his house.'[1]

In 205 BC, the Locrians who had suffered the exactions of one of Scipio's legates, Q. Pleminius, sent ambassadors to Rome: 'Ten ambassadors of the Locrians, dirty and in rags, proffering suppliants' bandeaux and olive branches, as is the Greek custom, to the consuls sitting in the *comitium*, prostrated themselves on the ground before their tribunal uttering pitiful cries.'[2]

Although the situations relating to these episodes were not alike, the attitudes adopted reveal profound analogies. In both cases, in fact, it was a matter of communities showing their cohesion in the relationship they had with the Roman government. Between one and the other, however, definitions had changed. In 204, on the evidence, Rome and Locris were two states that were alien to each other. In contrast, in 14, although a frontier was still marked at Bovillae, at the boundary of the old territory of Rome, it was no longer anything more than symbolic. Between the two events, the real political area had been completely unified.

The cultural zone had followed the same path. In 204 the

Locrians had adopted the appearance that was familiar to them when they left in an embassy to seek the benevolence of a superior power. The way in which they behaved was customary for the Greeks, but remarkable enough in Roman eyes for the memory of it to have been passed down as far as Livy. In AD 14 there was no longer any difference to distinguish the senators of Campania's towns from the knights of Rome, or even among themselves. Everywhere, decurions of Roman states, clad – one may suppose – in similar attire, went to the boundary of their municipium, received the corpse of Augustus from their neighbours, carried it to their temples or basilicas, built according to identical designs, then the next day resumed the chain leading to Rome.

The precise unity of the ritual implied shared feelings. A single mourning gathered all the states of Italy in equal sorrow. Even more, it brought together a new people. Linked to one another by the pious handing on of the Emperor's remains, by their fervour local aristocracies testified to their adherence to the same civic entity. Received and then handed over, this dead body transformed into a symbol was the possession of all while belonging to none. By a sort of sharing similar to that which Romulus' body was said to have received on the part of senators, it had become the heroic relic which, in a succession of resting-places, revealed the new community by the juxtaposition of civic identities and the quality of devotions. That Roman power which the Locrians had formerly entreated in the person of the consuls, was henceforth the common possession of all Italians.

It had taken two centuries and a great deal of violence. First, the violence of the wars, Punic, Social and then civil, which had depopulated Italy, allowed confiscations of land and compelled the displacement of populations. No zone of the peninsula had remained untouched by these upheavals. Almost all had had to submit, willingly or by force, to the injunctions of the magistrates and the evaluations of the surveyors. But there was also the gentler though no less effective violence of the long-term trends in trade expansion. Where land had been confiscated, where conditions were favourable to the development of speculative agriculture whose produce would spread to Mediterranean markets, Roman and Italian masters had imposed the presence of their large farms on enfeebled traditional societies, imported their slaves, sometimes expanded their estates at locals' expense and given a spur to the exodus that affected the most vulnerable groups. In this respect, even if in various degrees and at various paces, all the peoples of the peninsula and the islands had eventually opened up to external influences and mingled, so that only residual forms remained of the differences of the late third century.

Forms of expression, from the most concrete to the most symbolic, had become common. In fact, in the whole area only two or three types of amphora were made for the transport and sale of wine. Markets and trade became unified since the same measures were accepted. Similarly, the use of the denarius as a monetary unit meant that, at this elementary level of communication at least, unity had been achieved.

This was so in the use of languages too. Late in the first century, Latin was not the only language in Italy, but certainly everyone understood it and, apart from Greek, no other could have been used as a common vehicle of speech. It was the language of trade, social life, law, literature and politics. It structured communication and was thus the basis of the unity of the Italian world.

Other codes, symbolic and plastic, were certainly used less than language. They had been established in the meeting of Roman, Italic and, above all, Hellenistic traditions. But they were sufficiently widespread: everywhere the same architectural styles defined temples, public buildings and houses. Architecture and town planning formed an art, unified by teaching and manuals, which imparted a homogeneous appearance to the towns of Italy. In the same way, public behaviour and attitudes, by which citizens were recognized, had merged into a single whole under the pressure of Roman standards and models, notably those of rhetoric. Everywhere the same topics justified attitudes and rules governing the use of words, speeches and gestures, thus creating the conditions for a common political language.

These standards were far from being evenly mastered: not all houses had an atrium or mosaic decorations, and not all citizens were capable of uttering authoritative opinions on the future of their community. For the most part they allowed aristocrats to establish themselves as such. They would henceforth help to enhance and develop those models formerly set up in the Hellenistic world. By sharing them with all those of the same rank they included themselves in a culture which by its age and extent seemed universal, thus deriving from it some of their legitimacy.

By keeping its use reserved to themselves locally, they set themselves apart from the ordinary people who had access to it in only a minor way, and so acquired the means of governing.

The new political sphere being formed was that of a Roman people enlarged and replenished by the incorporation of the *domi nobiles* of the peninsula. Since all the Italians had entered the community of citizens, the city-state had ceased to preserve its former definition. It could no longer be contained in the former organization of a town and its surrounding territory. It assumed an ideal dimension, an identity which, across the diversities, had preserved the essence of what made the *bonus vir*: worthiness and the means of upholding it, at the same time enhanced by the new characteristics borrowed from the Hellenistic world. Old political procedures had lost their efficacy and even their relevance when it came to administering the whole of the Empire overall. But they remained in theory and in the reality of the intense civic life that animated colonies and municipia.

The feeling of belonging to the single identity of a conquering people supported the solidity and cohesion of the whole. Repeated at every moment of public life, it compelled unity and reverence for the Emperor who was its guarantor. In the management of affairs, when important decisions had to be taken, it was to him that the questions were directed. Of course, the old mechanisms of patronage and the representation of interests continued to function, but in a social environment that was more homogeneous. A city's natural defenders were often those of its members who belonged to the ruling circles of the Empire. Unification in this sense was complete, for the diversity of civic allegiances had been obliterated in favour of alliances and clienteles. Italy had become a single body politic which, at the end of the first century, was distinct from the rest of the world.

The latter, however, became Romanized in its turn. States, sometimes entire provinces, began to receive Latin rights. Roman rights would follow. Italy nevertheless preserved its precedence. An 'Italic' privilege (*jus italicum*) remained, drawing its origins from the time when Roman citizens, enriched by conquest, had stopped paying direct tax. The men and wealth of the peninsula remained exempt. Those of the provinces, with a few rare exceptions, were subject to it. There was thus a profound difference separating them. The civic community that had been formed in the first century rested on deep affinities, some original and others acquired, and it was not thought that they could be shared with other peoples in a relationship of equal intensity.

Thus for a few centuries yet an astonishing relationship was maintained, one that had passed from the domination of one state over the others to the constitution of a social and political unity that was relatively stable and homogeneous, in which the sharing of a common collective personality had caused the obliteration of ancient differences. There was in fact one moment, which varied from people to people, when the affirmation of a former identity ceased to have any meaning, so greatly had it been effaced by new values and the intensity of trade. There was another when the majority of Romans realized that, if domination was to be justified and maintained, it would have to be shared. From those two moments was born a new Roman-ness and a new citizenship. The former, freeing itself from its original framework, was enabled to expand and stamp its mark on the world. The second, ceasing to be actual, became ideal and thus universal; and we are its heirs.

ABBREVIATIONS

ANRW: Temporini, H. ed., *Aufstieg und Niedergang der römischen Welt*, Berlin and New York, 1972–.

BCH: *Bulletin de correspondance hellénique*, Paris.

CAH: Walbank, F. W. et al. eds, *The Cambridge Ancient History*, 2nd edn, Cambridge, 1984–.

CIL: *Corpus Inscriptionum Latinarum*, Berlin, 1863–.

CRAI: *Comptes rendus de l'Académie des Inscriptions et Belles-Lettres*, Paris.

DA: *Dialoghi di Archeologia*, Rome.

FIRA: Riccobono, S., et al. eds, *Fontes Iuris Romani Antejustiniani*, Florence, 1941.

ILLRP: Degrassi, A., ed., *Inscriptiones latinae liberae rei publicae*, 2nd edn, Florence, 1965.

ILS: Dessau, H. ed., *Inscriptiones latinae selectae*, Berlin, 1892.

JRS: *Journal of Roman Studies*, London.

MEFRA: *Mélanges de l'Ecole française de Rome, Antiquité,* Rome.

MDAI(R): *Mitteilung des deutschen archäologischen Instituts (Rom. Abt.)*, Mainz.

PBSR: *Papers of the British School at Rome*, London.

RBPh: *Revue belge de Philologie et d'Histoire*, Mechelen.

RD: *Revue historique de droit français et étranger*, Paris.

REA: *Revue des études anciennes*, Talence.

REL: *Revue des études latines*, Paris.

RSI: *Rivista Storica Italiana*, Naples.

SCO: *Studi Classici ed Orientali*, Pisa.

TAPhA: *Transactions and Proceedings of the American Philological Association*, Cleveland.

NOTES

Introduction

1 Polybius, VI, 17 2; Cato, Orig., fgt. 85 P.
2 Varro, *Res Rust.*, I, 2, 1; see T. Hölscher, MDAI(R), 85, 1978, pp. 344ff.
3 I am indebted to the generosity of Mireille Cébeillac-Gervasoni who allowed me access to the manuscript of the proceedings of the symposium on *Les Elites municipales italiennes de l'Italie péninsulaire des Gracques à Néron*, when it was still with the printers. I am chiefly indebted to the critical talents of Anne -Marie Adam and Xavier Lafon who agreed to reread the pages of this book when it was nearly complete. I offer them my thanks here, assuring the reader that any errors or inexactitudes encountered are my responsibility alone.

Chapter 1   The Peoples of Italy

1 E. Sereni, *Comunità rurali, passim.*
2 C. Peyre, *La Cisalpine*, pp. 26ff.
3 Polybius II, 17, 5; C. Peyre, *La Cisalpine*, pp. 31–2.
4 G. Fogolari, in M. Pallottino, ed., *Popoli e Civiltà*, IV, pp. 105ff.; A. M. Chieco Bianchi, in A. M. Chieco Bianchi et al., *Italia omnium terrarum alumna*, pp. 90ff.
5 See C. Peyre, *La Cisalpine*, pp. 37–8.
6 A. M. Chieco Bianchi, in D. Vitali, ed., *Celti ed Etruschi*, pp. 191ff.
7 V. Kruta, in A. M. Chieco Bianchi et al., *Italia omnium terrarum*

alumna, pp. 292ff.; M. Torelli, in D. Vitali, ed., *Celti ed Etruschi*, pp. 1ff.; D. Vitali, ibid., pp. 309ff.

8 C. Peyre, *La Cisalpine*, pp. 15ff.

9 II, 2, 17, transl. D. Roussel.

10 Livy, X, 26, 11; XXIII, 24, 11–12.

11 C. Peyre, *La Cisalpine*, pp. 54ff.

12 Livy, XXXII, 30, 6.

13 C. Peyre, *La Cisalpine*, pp. 56ff.

14 V. Kruta, in A. M. Chieco Bianchi et al., *Italia omnium terrarum alumna*, pp. 290ff.

15 V. Kruta, ibid., pp. 306ff.

16 M. Torelli, *Storia*, pp. 218ff.; M. Cristofani in M. Pallottino et al., *Rasenna*, p. 146; see also V. Jolivet, MEFRA, 92, 1980, pp. 681–724.

17 W. V. Harris, *Rome in Etruria*, pp. 114ff.

18 M. Torelli, *Storia*, pp. 234ff.; see also A. Restelli in M. Sordi, ed., *Conoscenze etniche*, pp. 150ff.

19 M. Torelli, *Storia*, pp. 223ff.; see also R. Lambrechts, *Essai sur les magistratures, passim*.

20 M. Torelli, *Storia*, pp. 240ff.

21 M. Torelli, *Elogia Tarquinensia*, Florence, 1975.

22 F. Coarelli, DA, III, 1, 1983, pp. 43ff.

23 G. Colonna in M. Pallottino et al., *Rasenna*, p. 72.

24 M. Torelli, *Storia*, pp. 251ff.; W. V. Harris, *Rome in Etruria*, pp. 147ff.

25 M. Humbert, *Municipium*, pp. 403ff.

26 M. Torelli in M. Pallottino et al., *Rasenna*, p. 72.

27 Livy, X, 3, 2.

28 Zonaras, 8, 7; Florus, I, 16. See W. V. Harris, *Rome in Etruria.*, pp. 114ff.

29 G. Devoto, *Italici, passim*.

30 A. L. Prosdocimi, in *La Cultura italica*, pp. 29–74.

31 See especially A. La Regina, DA, IV–V, 1970–1, pp. 443ff.; idem, in J. Mertens and R. Lambrechts, *Comunità indigene*, pp. 147ff.; C. Letta, ibid., pp. 157ff.

32 Strabo, V, 4, 12.

33 See A. Restelli in M. Sordi ed., *Conoscenze etniche*, pp. 150ff.

34 F. Roncalli in A. M. Chieco Bianchi et al., *Italia omnium terrarum alumna*, pp. 400ff.; P. Fontaine, RBPh, LXIX, 1991, pp. 156ff.

35 W. V. Harris, *Rome in Etruria*, p. 152, adds that of the Roman citizens of Aesis, the foundation of which in 247 is uncertain.

36 Strabo, V, 4, 2; Pliny, *Nat. Hist.* III, 13, 110–11.

37 M. Landolfi in A. M. Chieco Bianchi et al., *Italia omnium terrarum alumna*, p. 321.

38 E. T. Salmon, *Making*, pp. 21ff.

39 E. T. Salmon, *Making*, pp. 7ff.
40 M. Torelli, DA, V, 1987, pp. 43ff.
41 E. T. Salmon, *Samnium*, pp. 77ff.; *Making*, pp. 13ff.; A. La Regina, in *Sannio*, pp. 11ff.; M. Gaggiotti, in *La Romanisation du Samnium*, pp. 35ff.
42 E. T. Salmon, *Samnium*, pp. 289ff.
43 F. Sartori, *Problemi di storia costituzionale*, pp. 42ff.
44 M. Frederiksen, *Campania*, especially pp. 134ff.; J. Heurgon, *Capoue* pp. 59ff.; F. Sartori, *Problemi di storia costituzionale*, pp. 17ff.
45 J. Heurgon, *Capoue*, pp. 157ff.
46 G. Pugliese-Carratelli, ed., *Magna Grecia, Lo sviluppo*, pp. 285ff.; A. Bottini, ibid., pp. 269ff.; idem in G. Pugliese-Carratelli, ed., *Magna Grecia, Vita religiosa*, pp. 70ff.; A. Marinetti and A. L. Prosdocimi, ibid., pp. 30ff.; B. D'Agostino in C. Ampolo et al., *Italia omnium terrarum parens*, pp. 233ff.; M. Lombardo, ibid., pp. 286ff.; M. Lejeune, *Mefitis, passim*.
47 B. M. Scarfi, in *Studi sulla città antica*, pp. 285ff.
48 E. M. De Juliis in A. M. Chieco Bianchi et al., *Italia omnium terrarum alumna*, pp. 617ff.; F. D'Andria, ibid., pp. 686ff.; see also B. D'Agostino in M. Pallottino ed., *Popoli e Civiltà*, II, pp. 227ff.; E. T. Salmon, *Making*, pp. 19ff.; M. Mazzei in J. Mertens and R. Lambrechts, eds, *Comunità indigene*, pp. 109ff.
49 E. M. De Juliis in A. M. Chieco Bianchi et al., *Italia omnium terrarum alumna*, pp. 619ff.
50 F. D'Andria, ibid., p. 712.
51 P. Wuilleumier, *Tarente*, pp. 43ff.; F. Sartori, *Problemi di storia costituzionale*, pp. 84ff.
52 P. Wuilleumier, *Tarente*, p. 183.
53 P. Wuilleumier, *Tarente, passim*; G. Gualandi, in M. Pallottino et al., *Popoli e Civiltà*, VII, pp. 304ff.
54 See J. Carcopino, *La Loi de Hiéron*, pp. 45ff.
55 V. Tusa in M. Pallottino et al., *Popoli e Civiltà*, III, pp. 45ff.
56 La Rosa, in C. Ampolo et al., *Italia omnium terrarum parens*, pp. 70ff.; F. Coarelli in E. Gabba and G. Vallet, eds, *La Sicilia*, pp. 371ff.
57 F. Barreca in E. Atzeni, *Ichnussa*, pp. 379ff.

Chapter 2   Rome, Italy and Hellenism

1   See C. Nicolet, *Les structures*, pp. 77ff.
2   A. N. Sherwin-White, *Roman Citizenship*, pp. 38ff.; M. Humbert, *Municipium*, pp. 3ff.; H. Galsterer, *Herrschaft und Verwaltung*, pp. 70ff.
3   A. N. Sherwin-White, *Roman Citizenship*, pp. 73ff.
4   M. Humbert, *Municipium*, pp. 335ff.; H. Galsterer, *Herrschaft und Verwaltung*, pp. 64ff.
5   Livy, IX, 20, 5–6.
6   Polybius, I, 6–7; Valerius Maximus, II, 7, 15.
7   Livy, XXIII, 2, 6–7; see J. Heurgon, *Capoue*, pp. 155ff.; M. Frederiksen, *Campania*, pp. 221ff.
8   See generally, E. T. Salmon, *Roman Colonization*.
9   H. Galsterer, *Herrschaft und Verwaltung*, pp. 41ff.
10 A. N. Sherwin-White, *Roman Citizenship*, pp. 80ff.; H. Galsterer, *Herrschaft und Verwaltung*, pp. 84ff.
11 R. Meiggs, *Roman Ostia*, pp. 20ff.; C. Pavolini, DA, VI, 1988, pp. 117ff.
12 M. Humbert, *Municipium*, pp. 85ff.
13 *De Leg. agr.*, II, 73.
14 See F. E. Brown, *Cosa*; M. Torelli, DA, VI, 1988, pp. 65ff.; J. Mertens, ibid., pp. 87ff.; and on the ideological and religious foundation of Paestum as it has been possible to deduce it from the monumental environment of the new city, see M. Torelli, in *Poseidonia–Paestum*, pp. 33ff.
15 F. Cassolà, DA, VI, 1988, pp. 5ff.
16 H. Galsterer, *Herrschaft und Verwaltung*, pp. 61ff.
17 J.-P. Morel, DA. VI, 1988, pp. 49ff; idem in J. Mertens and R. Lambrechts, eds, *Comunità indigene*, pp. 125ff.
18 M. Humbert, *Municipium*, pp. 186ff.
19 C. Nicolet, PBSR, XXXIII, 1978, pp. 1ff.
20 P. A. Brunt, *Italian Manpower*, p. 384.
21 J.-P. Morel in A. Momigliano and A. Schiavone, eds, *Storia di Roma*, II, 1, pp. 143ff; id, CAH VIII, 479
22 J.-P. Morel, MEFRA, 91, 1969, p. 59ff; id, CAH VIII, 480, C. G. Starr, *The Beginnings of Imperial Rome*, p. 33f.
23 F. Coarelli and J.-P. Morel in *Roma medio repubblicana*, pp. 57ff.; D. Ricciotti, ibid., pp. 72ff; CAH VIII 480, C. G. Starr, *The Beginnings of Imperial Rome*, p. 33f.
24 M. H. Crawford, *Coinage and Money*, pp. 28ff.; cf. H. Zehnacker, *Moneta*, Rome, 1973, pp. 197ff.
25 Pliny, *Nat. Hist.*, XXXIV, 26; on the date, see F. Coarelli, *Il Foro romano*, II, Rome, 1985, pp. 119ff.

26   T. Hölscher, *Akt. XIII. int. Kong. kl. Arch*, pp. 73ff.
27   M. Torelli, P. Pensabene, F. Coarelli and D. Ricciotti in *Roma medio repubblicana*, pp. 138ff.
28   P. Grimal, *Le Siècle des Scipions*, pp. 49ff.
29   K. J. Hölkeskamp, *Die Entstehung der Nobilität*, pp. 204ff.
30   J.-P. Morel, CAH, VIII, pp. 486ff.; A. Hesnard et al., in *Amphores romaines et histoire économique*, pp. 21ff., see A. Tchernia, *Le Vin*, pp. 42ff.
31   F. Coarelli, in *Roma medio repubblicana*, pp. 200ff.
32   F. Zevi, ibid., pp. 234ff.
33   See especially T. Hölscher, MDAI(R), 85, 1978, pp. 315ff.; *Akt. XIII. int. Kong. kl. Arch.*, pp. 73ff.
34   F. De Martino, *Storia della Costituzione romana*, II, pp. 151ff.
35   C. Nicolet, *Les Structures*, p. 343; and the remarks of L. Ross Taylor, *Voting Districts*, pp. 303ff.; E. S. Staveley, CAH, VII, p. 440.

Chapter 3   Hannibal in Italy

1   Polybius, III, 2, 40; Livy, XXI, 25–6, 2.
2   Polybius, III, 69, 2.
3   Polybius, III, 77; cf. III, 67; 85; Livy, XXI, 48, 10; XXII, 58, 2ff.; XXIII, 15, 4.
4   Livy, XXII, 61, 11–12; cf. Polybius, III, 118.
5   Livy, XXVII, 1 (in 210); XXIV, 20 (in 214).
6   Livy, XXIII, 7, 1–2; cf. Polybius, V, 25.
7   XXVI, 6, 16; cf. XXIII, 6, 6–8; 7, 1–2.
8   Livy, XXIV, 1, 1; cf. 3, 12.
9   XXIII, 14, 7; XXIV, 2, 8.
10   J. Von Ungern-Sternberg, *Capua*, pp. 63ff.
11   Appian, *Hann.*, 45–7; see Livy, XXVI, 38, 6ff. with some differences.
12   P. A. Brunt, *Italian Manpower*, pp. 62ff.; C. Nicolet, *Les Structures*, p. 86.
13   P. A. Brunt, *Italian Manpower*, pp. 66, 417ff.
14   C. Nicolet, *Les Structures*, pp. 243ff.; M. H. Crawford, *Coinage and Money*, pp. 60ff.
15   Livy, XXIV, 18; cf. XXVII, 11, 8, 12–16.
16   See J. Bleicken, *Das Volkstribunat der klassischen Republik*, Munich, 1955, especially pp. 46ff.
17   W. V. Harris, *Rome in Etruria*, pp. 134ff.
18   Livy, XXVII, 24; cf. 21, 7–8; 35, 11.
19   Livy, XXVII, 9, 13–14; 10, 10.
20   Livy, XXIX, 15, 6–10.
21   Livy, XXVI, 16, 6–11; cf. Cicero, *De leg, agr.*, I, 19; II, 88–9.

22　J. Von Ungern-Sternberg, *Capua*, pp. 77ff.

23　See Livy, XXVI, 34, on the fate reserved for the various categories of the population, with a few differences however from XXVI, 16, 6–11.

24　H. Galsterer, *Herrschaft und Verwaltung*, pp. 77–8; C. Nicolet, *Les Structures*, pp. 283ff.

25　Livy, XXVIII, 10, 4; XXIX, 36, 10–12; XXX, 26, 12; W. V. Harris, *Rome in Etruria*, pp. 135ff.

26　Livy, XXX, 24.

27　Festus, p. 28 L.; Aulus Gellius, 10, 3, 19; Strabo, V, 4, 13.

28　A. J. Toynbee, *Hannibal's Legacy*, II, pp. 26ff.

29　Livy, XLII, 1, 7–12.

30　Aulus Gellius, X, 3, 3.

31　A. J. Toynbee, *Hannibal's Legacy*, II, pp. 26ff.

32　E. Gabba, *Ktèma*, II, 1977, pp. 269ff.

33　See C. Nicolet, *Les Structures*, pp. 124ff.

34　P. Guzzo, in J. Mertens and R. Lambrechts, eds, *Comunità indigene*, pp. 77ff.; M. Mazzei, ibid., pp. 109ff.

35　C. Nicolet, *Les Structures*, pp. 120ff.

36　Idem, p. 86.

37　Livy, XXIV, 20.

38　Livy, XXVI, 40.

39　Livy, XLI, 28.

40　See A. J. Toynbee, *Hannibal's Legacy*, II, pp. 654ff.

41　T. P. Wiseman, PBSR, XXXVIII, 1970, pp. 122ff.

42　C. Nicolet, *Les Structures*, p. 125.

43　See H. Galsterer, *Herrschaft und Verwaltung*, p. 46ff.

44　See the example of Modena; M. Pasquinucci, *Athenaeum*, 64, 1986, pp. 55ff.

45　See the remarks of G. Bandelli, *Ricerche*, pp. 35ff.

46　E. Gabba, *Athenaeum*, 63, 1985, pp. 265ff.

47　E. T. Salmon, *Roman Colonization*, pp. 95ff.

48　Livy, XL, 43, 1; before regretting it, see Livy, XLV, 13, 10.

49　Livy, XXIII, 49, 1–5; XXV, 3–4.

50　E. Badian, *Publicans and Sinners*, pp. 16ff.; C. Nicolet, *Les Structures*, pp. 261ff.

51　Livy, XXVIII, 45, 13.

52　XXVI, 40, 15; XXVII, 8, 18; XXIX, 36, 1–2.

53　A. J. Toynbee, *Hannibal's Legacy*, pp. 210ff.; G. Clemente, Κωκαλοζ XXVI–XXVII, 1980–1, pp. 192ff.

54　Livy, XXIV, 7, 10.

55　M. Frederiksen, *Puteoli*, 4–5, 1980–1, pp. 5ff.

Chapter 4 Transformations in the Italian Economy

1 Livy, XXXIX, 7, 1–3; 5.
2 T. Frank, ed., *An Economic Survey*, I, pp. 126ff.; C. Nicolet, *Les Structures*, pp. 257ff.
3 C. Nicolet, *Les Structures*, pp. 255ff.
4 XLII, 32, 6.
5 Cicero, 1 *Verr.*, 56; 2 *Verr.*, I, 27; cf. *Div. Caec.*, 19.
6 Cicero, *Pro Rab. Post.*, 4, trans. A. Boulanger; cf. 22.
7 C. Nicolet, *Les Structures*, p. 269.
8 M. H. Crawford, *Econ. Hist. Review*, 30, 1977, pp. 42ff.; see also K. Hopkins, JRS, 70, 1980, pp. 101ff.
9 A. J. Toynbee, *Hannibal's Legacy*, II, pp. 45ff.; P. A. Brunt, *Italian Manpower*, pp. 422ff.
10 See K. Hopkin's remarks, *Conquerors and Slaves*, p. 25ff.
11 A. J. Toynbee, *Hannibal's Legacy*, II, p. 75.
12 P. A. Brunt, *Italian Manpower*, pp. 400ff.
13 Ibid., pp. 214ff.
14 Nevertheless, see the remarks of K. Hopkins (*Conquerors and Slaves*, pp. 64ff.) which, based on very hypothetical figures, tend to dramatize the process.
15 Valerius Maximus, IX, 2, *ext*. 3; Plutarch, *Sulla*, 24; see P. A. Brunt, *Italian Manpower*, pp. 224ff.
16 P. A. Brunt, *Italian Manpower*, pp. 227ff.; C. Nicolet, *Les Structures*, pp. 87ff.
17 J. Hatzfeld, BCH, 36, 1912, pp. 5ff.; A. J. N. Wilson, *Emigration*, pp. 105ff.
18 J. Hatzfeld, *Les Trafiquants*, pp. 228ff.; M. Torelli in J. H. D'Arms and E. C. Kopff, eds, *The Seaborne Commerce*, pp. 313ff.
19 See J. Andreau in J. Andreau and H. Bruhns, eds, *Parenté et stratégies familiales*, pp. 501ff.
20 J. Hatzfeld, *Les Trafiquants*, pp. 243ff.
21 E. Campanile, in *La cultura italica*, pp. 103ff.
22 J. Hatzfeld, *Les trafiquants*, pp. 257ff.
23 Strabo, XIV, 5, 2; C. Nicolet, *Les Structures*, pp. 212ff.
24 P. A. Brunt, *Italian Manpower*, pp. 121ff.; C. Nicolet, *Les Structures*, pp. 83ff., 209ff.; K. Hopkins, *Conquerors and Slaves*, pp. 99ff.
25 See especially J.-C. Dumont, *Servus*, pp. 57ff.
26 P. Gros, *Architecture et société*, pp. 14ff.
27 C. Pavolini in A. Giardina and A. Schiavone, *Società romana*, II, pp. 139ff.
28 J. P. Morel in A. Giardina and A. Schiavone, *Società romana*, II, pp. 81ff.; C. Delplace, *Ktèma*, 3, 1978, pp. 55ff.
29 Cicero, *De orat.*, II, 284.

30 *Res Rust. II, praef.*, 6.
31 Ibid., II, 9, 6.
32 A. Giardina in A. Giardina and A. Schiavone, *Società romana*, I, pp. 84ff.
33 A. Tchernia, *Le Vin*, pp. 56ff.
34 S. Panciera in J. H. D'Arms and E. C. Kopff, eds, *The Seaborne Commerce*, pp. 125ff.; E. Lyding Will, in *Amphores romaines et historie économique*, pp. 297ff.
36 A. Fraschetti in A. Giardina and A. Schiavone, *Società romana*, I, pp. 53ff.
37 D. Manacorda in A. Giardina and A. Schiavone, ibid., I, pp. 3ff.
38 Cato, *De Agricult.*, 10–11; Varro, *Res Rust.*, I, 18–19.
39 A. Carandini in J. H. D'Arms and E. C. Kopff, eds, *The Seaborne Commerce*, pp. 2ff.
40 E. Gabba and M. Pasquinucci, *Strutture agrarie*, pp. 21ff.
41 E. Gabba, *Ktèma*, 2, 1977, pp. 269ff.
42 P. De Neeve, *Peasants in Peril*.
43 See J. D. Jones, PBSR, XXX, 1962, pp. 116ff.; XXXI, 1963, pp. 100ff.; A. Kahane, L. Murray Threipland and J. Ward-Perkins, PBSR, XXXVI, 1968; A. Carandini, ed., *La romanizzazione dell'Etruria*, pp. 80ff.
44 See P. W. De Neeve, *Colonus, passim*.
45 See F. Coarelli, in *La Romanisation du Samnium*, pp. 177ff.
46 C. Nicolet, *Les Structures*, p. 87; K. Hopkins, *Conquerors and Slaves*, pp. 96ff.
47 M. H. Crawford, *Coinage and Money*, pp. 103, 115, 143ff.

Chapter 5   Italian Municipal Aristocracies

1 A. N. Sherwin-White, *The Roman Citizenship*, pp. 80ff., 117ff.; H. Galsterer, *Herrschaft und Verwaltung*, pp. 120ff. The attendants and symbols of distinction are attested in the first century, but there is no reason to think they were a recent invention.
2 J.-M. Flambard, in *Les "Bourgeoisies" municipales*, pp. 75ff.
3 Vetter, No. 1, quoted by H. Galsterer, *Herrschaft und Verwaltung*, p. 125.
4 U. Laffi in *Les "Bourgeoisies" municipales*, pp. 59ff.
5 P. Castrén, *Ordo populusque*, pp. 41ff.
6 Cicero, *De leg.*, III, 35ff. See C. Nicolet, REL, 45, 1967, pp. 276ff.
7 P. Castrén, *Ordo populusque*, pp. 269ff.
8 G. Bandelli, in *Les "Bourgeoisies" municipales*, pp. 175ff.
9 M. Cébeillac-Gervasoni, *Mélanges P. Lévêque*, 3, pp. 67ff.

10   F. H. Massa-Pairault in J. Andreau and H. Bruhns, eds, *Parenté et stratégies familiales*, pp. 333ff.
11   P. Moreau, in *Les "Bourgeoisies" municipales*, pp. 99ff.
12   FIRA, I, No. 18, (= M. H. Crawford, *Roman Statutes* no. 15, line 28).
13   FIRA, I, No. 21, (= M. H. Crawford, *Roman Statutes* no. 25, Ch. 91).
14   M. Cébeillac-Gervasoni, MEFRA, 102, 1990, p. 699ff.
15   M. Gaggiotti, in *La Romanisation du Samnium*, pp. 35ff.
16   P. Castrén, *Ordo populusque*, pp. 40ff.
17   F. Coarelli in M. Cébeillac-Gervasoni, ed., *Les Elites municipales*.
18   G. Camodeca, *Puteoli*, 2, 1979, pp.17ff.
19   F. Coarelli in M. Cébeillac-Gervasoni, ed., *Les Elites municipales*.
20   Cicero, *De offic.*, I. 151 (trans. M. Testard).
21   FIRA, I, No. 13, (= M. H. Crawford, *Roman Statutes* no. 24, line 108).
22   See especially Cicero, *Pro Mur.*, 19ff.
23   Cicero, *De leg.*, III, 36.
24   R. Lambrechts, *Essai sur les magistratures*, pp. 121ff.
25   C. Letta, *I Marsi*, pp. 91ff.
26   Cicero, *Brutus*, 169–70.
27   Plutarch, *Cato maj.*, 22, 2.
28   The first known is L. Papirius of Fregellae, whose speech to the Senate is dated to 177 (Cicero, *Brutus*, 170), but the happening seems to have acquired importance only afterwards.
29   *De Benef.*, VI, 34, 1–2.
30   See W. Johannowsky in P. Zanker, ed., *Hellenismus in Mittelitalien*, pp. 387ff.
31   D. Pandermalis in P. Zanker, ed., *Hellenismus in Mittelitalien*, pp. 267ff.
32   J. R. Clarke, *The Houses of Roman Italy*, pp. 81ff.
33   F. Coarelli in *La Romanisation du Samnium*, pp. 177ff.
34   P. Zanker in *Les "Bourgeoisies" municipales*, pp. 251ff.
35   P. Zanker in idem ed., *Hellenisums in Mittelitalien*, pp. 581ff.
36   See M. Cébeillac-Gervasoni, MEFRA, 102, 1990, pp. 699ff.; idem, *Cahiers du centre Glotz*, II, Paris, 1991, pp. 189ff.
37   CIL, I, 2nd edn, 1529 = ILS, 5348 = ILLRP, 528.
38   F. Zevi in P. Zanker, ed., *Hellenismus in Mittelitalien*, pp. 84ff.
39   F. Coarelli, *I santuari del Lazio*, pp. 35ff.
40   P. Gros, *Architecture et Société*, pp. 41ff.
41   See C. Letta, *I Marsi*, pp. 52ff.; T. P. Wiseman in *Les "Bourgeoisies" municipales*, pp. 299ff.
42   H. Jouffroy, *La Construction publique en Italie*, pp. 15ff.
43   F. Coarelli in E. Gabba and G. Vallet, eds, *La Sicilia antica*, II, 2, pp. 371ff.
44   M. Verzar Brass in *Les "Bourgeoisies" municipales*, pp. 205ff.
45   M. Torelli in P. Zanker, ed., *Hellenismus in Mittelitalien*, pp. 97ff.

46 M. H. Crawford in *La Romanisation du Samnium*, pp. 135ff.

Chapter 6   The Mechanisms of Unification

1 See F. Coarelli, PBSR, XLV, 1977, pp. 1ff.; P. Gros, *Architecture et société*, pp. 11ff., 35ff.
2 F. Coarelli in P. Zanker, ed., *Hellenismus in Mittelitalien.*, pp. 21ff.
3 The attribution is disputed; see M. R. Wojcik, *La villa dei papiri ad Ercolano*, Rome, 1986; M. Gigante, *La Bibliothèque de Philodème et l'épicurisme romain*, Paris, 1987.
4 See E. Rawson, *Intellectual Life*, pp. 81ff.; J. L. Ferrary, *Philhellénisme et impérialisme*, Rome, 1988, pp. 589ff.
5 See, for example, ILS, 6093. E. Badian, *Foreign Clientalae*, pp. 154ff.
6 See F. Landucci Gattinoni, *Aevum*, 63, 1989, pp. 30ff.; M. J. Strazzulla Rusconi and M. P. Rossignani in *La città nell'Italia settentrionale*, pp. 279ff.
7 Livy, XLV, 13, 10. Among the members of the commission one notes the presence of Q. Fabius Buteo who, in 180, had participated in the founding of Luna, and of C. Appuleius Saturninus, possibly connected with L. Appuleius Saturninus who, in 183, had contributed to an allocation of lands *viritim* in Liguria.
8 FIRA, III, No. 163.
9 J. Andreau in *Les "Bourgeoisies" municipales*, pp. 9ff.
10 See, for example, Plutarch, *Marius*, 3, 2–5.
11 Livy, XLI, 13, 6–8.
12 M. Torelli, *Poseidonia-Paestum*, pp. 100ff.
13 H. Galsterer, *Herrschaft und Verwaltung*, pp. 145ff.
14 See M. Cébeillac-Gervasoni, MEFRA, 102, 1990, pp. 699ff.
15 See T. P. Wiseman, *New Men*, pp. 13ff.; M. Cébeillac-Gervasoni, *Ktèma*, 3, 1978, pp. 277ff.
16 Plutarch, *Marius*, 8, 6–9, 1 (trans. R. Flacelière and E. Chambry).
17 See for example Cicero, *Att.*, II, 14, 2; 13, 2; V, 2, 2.
18 These figures are taken from indications provided by the authors of the contributions published in *Epigrafia e Ordine senatorio, II, Tituli 5*, Rome, 1982.
19 E. Peruzzi, *I Romani di Pesaro, passim*.
20 Catullus, *Carm.*, 84 (trans. G. Lafaye); see Cicero, *Brutus*, 242–3.
21 Cicero, *De orat.*, III, 42; see J. M. David in *Les "Bourgeoisies" municipales*, pp. 309ff.
22 See W. V. Harris, *Rome in Etruria*, pp. 169ff.; J. Kaimio in P. Bruun, *Studies*, pp. 85ff.
23 M. Lejeune, *Mefitis*, pp. 25ff.
24 F. Costabile, *Municipium Locrensium*, pp. 66ff.

25 M. Lejeune, *Ateste*, pp. 117ff.
26 Livy, XL, 43, 1. This episode probably had more to do with public law than with linguistic Romanization.
27 G. Devoto, *Cahiers d'histoire mondiale*, 3, 1, 1956, p. 443ff.
28 H. Galsterer, *Herrschaft und Verwaltung*, pp. 120ff.

Chapter 7   The Social War

1   C. Nicolet, *Les Structures*, pp. 284ff.
2   J. M. Pailler, *Bacchanalia*, pp. 247ff.
3   ILS, 23. There is much argument over the identity of this person, but the date of the inscription must be set in the third quarter of the second century.
4   W. V. Harris, *Historia*, 21, 1972, pp. 639ff.
5   B. Albanese, *Studi in Memoria di G. Donatuti*, Milan, 1973, pp. 1ff.; W. Seston, CRAI, 1978, pp. 259ff.
6   Livy, XLII, 1, 7–12.
7   Aulus Gellius, X, 3, 3.
8   Livy, XXIX, 8, 6–9; 16, 4–22.
9   Livy, XLII, 3.
10 E. Gabba and M. Pasquinucci, *Strutture agrarie*, pp. 38ff.
11 See lastly on this point, J. Bleicken, 'Tiberius Gracchus und die italischen Bundesgenossen', *Festschrift C. J. Classen*, Stuttgart, 1990. pp. 101ff. and D. A. Kukofka, 'Waren die Bundesgenossen an den Landesverteilungen des Tiberius Gracchus beteiligt', *Tychè*, 5, 1990, pp. 45ff.
12 Appian, *Civil Wars*, I, 19.
13 Livy, XXIII, 17, 7–20, 2.
14 See especially F. Coarelli in *La Romanisation du Samnium*, pp. 177ff.
15 Livy, XLI, 8, 6–8.
16 Cicero, *Pro Balb.*, 32.
17 Appian, *Civil Wars*, I, 34; see 21; Valerius Maximus, IX, 5, 1.
18 Appian, *Civil Wars*, I, 23; Plutarch, *C. Gracch.*, 5, 2; 8, 3; 12.
19 *Lex agraria*, FIRA, I, No. 8, in particular l. 21–3.
20 Cicero, *Pro Balb.*, 48: the text gives the figure three. It is so low that an amendment of 300 has been suggested.
21 Emphasized first by E. Badian, *Foreign Clientelae*, pp. 192ff.
22 J. M. David, MEFRA, 91, 1979, pp. 135ff.
23 Cicero, *Pro Balb.*, 21.
24 Appian, *Civil Wars*, I, 36; W. V. Harris, *Rome in Etruria*, p. 202.
25 E. Gabba, in particular in *Esercito e Società*, pp. 193ff.
26 M. H. Crawford in *La Romanisation du Samnium*, pp. 135ff.

27 Appian, *Civil Wars*, I, 39; *Velleius Paterculus*, II, 15.
28 Diodorus, XXXVII, 11; see A. Bancalari Molina, SCO, XXXVII, 1987, pp. 407ff.
29 C. Nicolet, *The World of the Citizen in Republican Rome*, pp. 233ff.
30 FIRA, I, No. 13, (= M.H. Crawford, *Roman Statutes* no. 24); F. Costabile, *Istituzioni e forme costituzionali*, pp. 109ff.
31 See U. Laffi, *Vestigia*, 17, 1973, pp. 37ff.; H. Galsterer, RD, 65, 1987, pp. 181ff.
32 See, for example, D. Pulice, *Puteoli*, 1, 1977, pp. 27ff.
33 H. Galsterer, *Herrschaft und Verwaltung*, pp. 122ff.; F. Costabile, *Istituzioni e forme costituzionalie*, pp. 109ff.
34 See H. Galsterer, 'Die lex Osca Tabulae Bantinae, Eine Bestandsaufnahme', *Chiron*, I, pp. 191ff.; M. H. Crawford (ed), *Roman Statutes* I, pp. 271ff. Although disputed, the attribution to the Oscan law of Bantia of a date subsequent to the Social War is the most likely.
35 E. Gabba, SCO, XXI, 1972, pp. 73ff.
36 M. Lejeune, *Mefitis*, pp. 36ff.
37 See M. P. Rossignani in *La città nell'Italia settentrionale*, pp. 305ff.
38 *Civil Wars*, I, 15, 2.
39 Cicero, *De leg.*, II, 5.

Chapter 8   The Civil Wars

1 I. Shatzmann, *Senatorial Wealth*, pp. 243, 248, 375, 378, 403.
2 Cicero, *Pro Rosc. Amer.*, 6; 20.
3 Plutarch, *Crassus*, 2, 9.
4 Plutarch, *Pompey*, 6.
5 P. A. Brunt, *Latomus*, 39, 1975, pp. 619ff.
6 See P. Zanker, *Forum Augustum*, Tübingen, n.d.; *Forum romanum*, Tübingen, 1972; P. Gros, *Architecture et société*, pp. 59ff.
7 See L. Harmand, *Le Patronat*, pp. 15, 132ff., 138.
8 See E. Gabba, *Republican Rome. The Army and the Allies*, pp. 1ff.; P. A. Brunt, *The Fall of the Roman Republic*, pp. 240ff.; C. Nicolet, *Le Métier du citoyen*, pp. 122ff.
9 P. A. Brunt, *The Fall of the Roman Republic*, pp. 264ff.; J. Harmand, *L'Armée et le Soldat à Rome de 107 à 50 avant notre ère*, Paris, 1967, pp. 468ff.
10 I, 15, 5.
11 P. A. Brunt, *Italian Manpower*, p. 300ff.; L. Keppie, *Colonisation*, p. 127.
12 See E. Gabba, *Athenaeum*, 63, 1985, pp. 265ff.
13 L. Keppie, *Colonisation*, pp. 49ff.

14 *Appian*, Civil Wars, IV, 3; L. Keppie, *Colonisation*, pp. 58ff.
15 Cicero, *De leg. agr.*, II, 78.
16 Cicero, *Pro Mur.*, 49; *Catilin.*, II. 20.
17 P. Castrén, *Ordo populusque*, pp. 52, 92; J. Andreau, REA, 82, 1980, pp. 183ff.; H. Mouritsen, *Elections*, pp. 86ff.
18 L. Keppie, *Colonisation*, pp. 87ff.
19 *Sat.*, II, 2.
20 Cassius Dio, XLVIII, 9; Appian, *Civil Wars*, IV, 85.
21 See E. Gabba in A. Momigliano and A. Schiavone, *Storia di Roma*, II, 1, p. 803.
22 L. Keppie, *Colonisation*, pp. 49ff.
23 F. Hinard, *Les Proscriptions*, in particular, pp. 59ff.
24 Cicero, *De leg. agr.*, III, 8. He was probably the father-in-law of P. Servilius Rullus, tribune in 63.
25 ILLRP, II, 523, 598, 645, 646; see P. Castrén, *Ordo populusque*, pp. 89ff.
26 Appian, *Civil Wars*, I, 94.
27 Appian, *Civil Wars*, V, 48.
28 W. V. Harris, *Rome in Etruria*, p. 266.
29 M. Silvestrini in M. Cébeillac-Gervasoni, ed., *Les Elites municipales*.
30 C. Delplace, ibid.
31 W. V. Harris, *Rome in Etruria*, pp. 271ff.
32 See B. W. Frier, *The Rise of the Roman Jurists*, Princeton, 1985, pp. 3ff.
33 Horace, *Sat.*, I, 6, 72ff.; Virgil, *Bucol.*, I, IX; Propertius, *Eleg.*, IV, 1, 126ff.
34 Cicero, 2 *Verr.*, II, 123ff.; see L. Keppie, *Colonisation*, pp. 101ff.
35 See no. 17.
36 Cicero, *Pro Sulla*, 60–2.
37 L. Ross Taylor, in P. R. Coleman Norton ed., *Studies in Honor of A. C. Johnson*, pp. 68ff.
38 L. Keppie, *Colonisation*, p. 14.
39 See H. Galsterer, RD, 65, 1987, pp. 181ff.
40 FIRA, I, No. 13 = Crawford (ed) *Roman Statutes* no. 24.
41 Vitruvius, I, IV–VII; see P. Gros in A. Momigliano and A. Schiavone, eds, *Storia di Roma*, II, 1, pp. 831ff.
42 Cicero, *Ad Fam.*, XIII, 11, 3.
43 The events reported by Appian (*Civil Wars*, I, 65, 67, 76) lead to this supposition.
44 See Cicero, *Pro Cluent.*, 25.
45 R. Scuderi, *Athenaeum*, 67, 1989, pp. 117ff.
46 Appian, *Civil Wars*, V, 132.
47 M. Torelli in J. Mertens and R. Lambrechts, eds, *Comunità indigene*, pp. 39ff.

48 The figures for new men in the Senate given by T. P. Wiseman (*New Men*, p. 182ff.) are as follows: 74 before 90, 130 from 89 to 70, 105 from 69 to 50, 133 from 49 to 29, then 94 during the 42 years of Augustus' reign. However, not all were of municipal origin.

49 R. Syme, *The Roman Revolution*.

50 R. Syme, PBSR, XIV, 1938, pp. 1ff.

51 Quintus Cicero, *Comment. Petit.*, 24.

52 E. Gabba, RSI, 98, 1986, pp. 653ff.

53 See in particular Cicero, *De dom.*, 75.

54 R. Syme, *The Roman Revolution*.

55 G. Luraschi, *Foedus, Ius Latii, Civitas*, pp. 188ff.

56 G. Manganaro, ANRW, II, 11, pp. 11ff.

57 See W. Eck, *Die staatliche Organisation*, pp. 25ff.

58 See H. Jouffroy, *La Construction*, pp. 105ff.

59 C. Nicolet, MEFR, 79, 1967, pp. 29ff.

60 C. Nicolet, *L'Inventaire du monde*, pp. 216ff.

61 C. Nicolet, *Cahiers due centre Glotz*, II, 1991, pp. 73ff.

Conclusion

1 Suetonius, *Aug.*, 100, 2–3.

2 Livy, XXIX, 16, 6.

GLOSSARY

ager publicus   'Public land', i.e. land belonging to the Roman people, mostly acquired by conquest and annexation, which could be leased for cultivation or pasturage by Roman citizens in exchange for a rent paid to the state, but which could be reclaimed by the state at any time for the foundation of a *colony or for *viritim distribution.

ager Romanus   Roman territory, under the direct jurisdiction of the Roman state. It comprised both *ager publicus and ager privatus, land held in private ownership by Roman citizens.

amphora (pl. **amphorae**)   A large pottery container with a narrow neck and two handles, used for the transport and storage of liquids, particularly wine and olive oil.

atrium (pl. **atria**)   The central room of a Roman house.

Capitol   One of the seven hills of Rome, the site of the temple of Jupiter, Juno and Minerva. This feature, the religious and symbolic centre of ancient Rome, was reproduced in Roman colonies, each of which had a 'Capitol' with a temple to the three divinities, usually situated on a raised platform at one end of the forum.

cardo (pl. **cardines**)   An axial line, usually running north–south, in a *centuriation grid. See also *decumanus.

castrum   A fortified settlement.

censor   One of two Roman *magistrates, elected every five years for a term of eighteen months, whose principal task was to draw up a register (*census*) of all Roman citizens, graded according to wealth and status. Similar officials, known as *quinquennales*, existed in colonies and *municipia*.

centuriation A Roman method of dividing land into sections on a grid pattern.

century (*centuria*) (1) A military unit of 100 men.

(2) A voting unit in the *comitia centuriata*. Roman citizens were assigned to their centuries by the *censors on the basis of their age, wealth and status, in such a way that the older, richer citizens had the greatest influence on the vote.

(3) The area of land within one of the squares of a *centuriation grid, measuring 200 *iugera* (i.e. 100 standard plots of 2 *iugera*).

citizenship without suffrage (*civitas sine suffragio*) A form of Roman citizenship granted to communities (such as Capua in 338 BC) whose inhabitants were liable for tax and military service, but who did not possess the right to vote in Roman assemblies or to hold political office at Rome.

clientela (1) A body of clients, a clientele.

(2) In an abstract sense, the relationship of dependence based on the unequal exchange of benefits and services between patrons and clients.

clients (*clientes*) Persons of inferior status who were attached to powerful patrons by ties of obligation based on *fides*; they were required to show them deference and respect, and to give them political and material support.

collegium (pl. *collegia*) (1) A board or 'college' of *magistrates of equal rank.

(2) A private club, society or association.

colony (*colonia*) A self-governing community founded by the Roman state on conquered territory. The formal act of foundation took place after a *deductio*, a procession in which the colonists were led to the site in military formation, symbolizing the colony's function as a strategic outpost in hostile territory. The land was divided by *centuriation and allocated in allotments to the colonists. The earliest colonies were autonomous communities whose inhabitants possessed *Latin Rights, but colonies founded after the 180s BC possessed full Roman citizenship.

comitia (sing. *comitium*) The formal designation of a Roman political assembly, in which voting took place by groups (an 'electoral college' system, whereby the majority of those voting in a group determined the vote of the group). There were different types of assembly with different functions, according to whether the voting groups were the local *tribes (the *comitia tributa*) or *centuries (the *comitia centuriata*).

comitium A place of assembly. In Rome the Comitium was a circular area in the north-west corner of the Forum. Excavations at Paestum and elsewhere suggest that Roman colonies and *municipia* also had designated assembly places in imitation of Rome.

commercium See *Latin Rights.

conciliabulum An assembly place and administrative centre for Roman citizens living in rural areas of the *ager Romanus*.

conubium See *Latin Rights.

curia A meeting-place for an association, corporation or council and, in particular, the Senate House in Rome. In colonies and *municipia*, *curia* became the standard term for the local senate, whose members were known as *curiales*.

decumanus A boundary line drawn across a piece of centuriated land, usually in an east–west direction, at right angles to the *cardines*. See *centuriation; *cardo*.

deditio A formal act of surrender, by which a community entrusted itself to the *fides* of the Roman People.

deductio See *colony.

denarius (pl. *denarii*) A Roman silver coin worth 10 bronze *asses* (*denarius* means literally 'a tenner'), but revalued before 100 BC at 16 *asses*.

dilectus The military levy, an annual process whereby Roman soldiers were recruited for the legions.

Equites (sing. *Eques*) 'Knights', a term originally used to designate the cavalry, but later to define an élite class of Roman citizens of free birth and ancestry whose property was valued by the *censors at more than 400,000 sesterces (= 100,000 *denarii*).

ergastulum (pl. *ergastula*) A slave prison.

fabula A theatrical performance, a play.

fabula praetexta A play with a historical theme.

fides 'Trust' or 'good faith'.

foedus (pl. *foedera*) A treaty of alliance, usually requiring military assistance. The word is the origin of such modern terms as federation, confederacy, etc.

formula togatorum 'The list of those who wear the toga'. Although the evidence is poor, the *formula togatorum* seems to have been a document or charter that set out the (maximum?) numbers of troops the *socii* were obliged to contribute to the Roman army under the terms of their treaties.

forum (1) The civic and political centre of Rome and, by extension, of every Roman town.

(2) An officially designated place for assizes and other public meetings for Roman citizens living in rural areas. Often established along the major roads, the *fora* in some cases developed into substantial towns, e.g. Forum Livii (modern Forli).

fundifactio A legal term signifying the formal approval by a community of the basis for a major change in its status, notably acceptance of the Roman citizenship.

gens A clan or lineage; a Roman kinship group whose members shared a common name (e.g. Julius, Cornelius) and claimed agnatic descent from a common ancestor.

heroon A Greek term for a hero shrine.

hospitium publicum 'Public hospitality', an arrangement between communities whereby the citizens of one could visit the other and there enjoy all the private rights and privileges of its citizenship, but be free from its obligations and burdens.

imperium The supreme power conferred on the senior Roman magistrates, the consuls and praetors. The holder of *imperium* had absolute authority over the soldiers under his command, and had the right of jurisdiction over civilians, including the infliction of the death penalty (but see *provocatio). See also *provincia.

isopoliteia See *Latin Rights.

Italiotes The Greeks of southern Italy.

iugerum (pl. *iugera*) A Roman measurement of land area, equivalent to 0.25 hectares (= 0.633 acres).

iuniores Roman citizens of military age, i.e. aged between 17 and 45.

ius migrationis See *Latin Rights.

koine A linguistic term signifying a dialect which has spread to become the common language of a wider area; often used metaphorically by archaeologists and historians to describe a common culture embracing several political units and ethnic groups.

Latin League An association of communities in Latium which in archaic times (down to 338 BC) were united in a military alliance and shared certain reciprocal rights (see *Latin Rights).

Latin Rights The rights of Latins in relation to Rome. These included the rights of *conubium* (the capacity to contract a legitimate marriage with a Roman citizen), *commercium* (the right to trade with Roman citizens under Roman law), and the so-called *ius migrationis* (the right to obtain Roman citizenship by taking up residence in the *ager Romanus). These rights were reciprocal, in the sense that Roman citizens could obtain similar privileges in the territory of Latin communities. Greek sources define this reciprocity of rights as 'isopolity' (isopoliteia).

lex (pl. **leges**) A law or statute passed by a vote of the *comitia. Individual statutes were identified by the name of the magistrate or *tribune of the people who promoted it, hence lex Ogulnia, lex Publicia, etc.

magistrates (from Latin magistratus) A generic term for the holders of political offices in republican city-states. In addition to jurisdiction, they exercised a wide range of civic, political, religious and military functions. Magistrates were usually elected, held office for one year, and were members of boards or colleges of two or more. In Rome the annual magistrates were, in descending order of seniority, consuls, praetors, aediles and quaestors. Equivalent bodies of magistrates existed in colonies and municipia, known as duoviri, quattuorviri or octoviri (boards of two, four and eight respectively), assisted by aediles, quaestors, etc. Other Italian communities retained their native, pre-Roman magistrates – among the Etruscans zilath, purth; in Umbria marones; in Oscan-speaking communities *meddix, and in the Greek cities demarchoi, prytaneis, etc.

manus iniectio 'Laying on of a hand', forcible seizure, arrest.

meddix The title of a magistrate in Oscan. The meddix tuticus (equivalent to Latin magister populi, and meaning something like 'leader of the people') was a single supreme magistrate and unusual in not being one of a college of equal magistrates.

municipium A self-governing community of Roman citizens. A municipium was created when an existing non-Roman community, after military defeat or voluntary surrender, was incorporated into the Roman state and its inhabitants made Roman citizens.

negotiatores Businessmen, traders.

nobles (Lat. **nobiles**) A general term for Romans of aristocratic status – that is, persons born into the Roman political élite, and in particular the descendants of consuls. Often contrasted with 'new men' (i.e. political parvenus). Members of local élites in colonies and municipia were sometimes sneeringly called domi nobiles ('home-town nobles').

oppidum (pl. **oppida**) (1) A hill fort.

(2) A nucleated settlement, a town.

pagus (pl. **pagi**) A rural district. The countryside around a Roman town was divided into pagi, which had some basic administrative functions. Non-urbanized communities in Italy consisted entirely of *pagi* and **vici*.

palaestra A place ued by aristocratic young men for naked exercise, especially wrestling. It was normally a courtyard surrounded by colonnades and rooms for undressing and washing.

patronage See **clientela*.

poculum (pl. **pocula**) A pottery drinking cup.

pomoerium The sacred boundary of a city, marked by an open space on either side of the wall, and symbolizing the division between the urban area and the surrounding country.

praefectura A community in the **ager Romanus* without self-governing status, administered by a prefect (*praefectus*) sent from Rome.

praefectus fabrum A senior army officer.

Praetor See **magistrates*.

provincia A 'province' – originally a special task or function assigned to a senior magistrate with **imperium*, often a military command in a given geographical area; hence, by extension, a dependent territory outside Italy, governed by a magistrate with *imperium* (a 'provincial governor').

provocatio An appeal to the people against a capital penalty imposed by a magistrate with **imperium*. The right of appeal (*ius provocationis*) was one of the most valued attributes of Roman citizenship.

prytaneis The title of **magistrate in some Greek cities.

publicani Roman entrepreneurs who contracted to provide public services (such as military supplies, construction and repair of public buildings, and collection of taxes) on behalf of the State.

purth The title of an Etruscan **magistrate*.

quaestio A tribunal of inquiry with judicial and penal powers, set up by statute to investigate particular scandals and cases of wrongdoing. In the late Republic, permanent tribunals (*quaestiones perpetuae*) were set up to try persistent public crimes, such as extortion by magistrates (the *quaestio de repetundis*), and became part of the regular system of criminal justice.

quaestio de repetundis See **quaestio*.

saepta Enclosures for the voting groups in the **comitia*.

seniores Roman citizens aged 46 and over, who were no longer eligible for the regular **dilectus*.

Social War See *socii*.

socii 'Allies'. The *socii* were inhabitants of Italian communities allied to Rome by treaty (see **foedus*). The 'Social War' was therefore the war between Rome and the *socii* (91–89 BC).

suffetes Carthaginian magistrates.

Tabularium The Roman Record Office, from 78 BC housed in a purpose-built structure on the Capitol, overlooking the Forum.

tirocinium The initial period of military service for a new recruit (Latin, *tiro*).

touto The Oscan term for 'people' (equivalent to Latin *populus*).

tribes (*tribus*) Divisions of the Roman people based on locality (and therefore also local divisions of the **ager Romanus*). There were 35 tribes in all, 4 based in the city of Rome (the 'urban' tribes) and 31 embracing the rest of Rome's territory (the 'rustic' tribes). The tribes were the constituent voting units of the **comitia tributa*.

tribune of the people (*tribunus plebis*) One of a board of ten annual officers of the Roman people, equivalent to *magistrates, whose function was (in theory) to protect and promote the interests of the people.

vicus (pl. *vici*) In rural areas, a small settlement or village. Towns (including Rome) were also subdivided into *vici* (wards) for the purposes of local administration.

viritim ('man by man') A term used to describe a distribution (especially of land) to individuals, as envisaged for example in Tiberius Gracchus' agrarian law.

SUGGESTIONS FOR FURTHER READING (IN ENGLISH)

General

Detailed discussion of most of the topics covered in this book can be found in the revised edition of the *Cambridge Ancient History* (henceforth *CAH²*), volumes IV, VII.2, VIII, IX, and X (Cambridge University Press, 1988–96). The *CAH²* is authoritative and up-to-date, and has extensive classified bibliographies.

The most recent general book on Roman Italy is E.T. Salmon, *The Making of Roman Italy*, London, Thames and Hudson 1983; among older works, J. Whatmough, *The Foundations of Roman Italy*, London: Methuen 1937, is still worth consulting. Selected sources and documents in translation can be found in H.K. Lomas, *Roman Italy, 338 BC–AD 200: a Sourcebook*, London: UCL Press 1996.

The archaeological picture of ancient Italy is constantly changing and is often inaccessible. For a useful guide see T.W. Potter, *Roman Italy*, London: British Museum 1987. Surveys of recent work include M.H. Crawford, 'Italy and Rome', *JRS* 71 (1981), 153–60; E. Curti, E. Dench, J.R. Patterson, 'The Archaeology of Central and Southern Italy: Recent Trends and Approaches', *JRS* 86 (1996, forthcoming). For an example of how archaeological survey techniques have transformed our knowledge of the landscape see T.W. Potter, *The Changing Landscape of South Etruria*, London: Elek 1979.

Regional studies include E.T. Salmon, *Samnium and the Samnites*, Cambridge: Cambridge University Press 1967; W.V. Harris, *Rome in Etruria and Umbria*, Oxford: Clarendon Press 1971; M.W. Frederiksen, *Campania*, London: British School at Rome 1984; H.K. Lomas, *Rome and the Western Greeks 350 BC–AD 200*, London: Routledge 1993. E. Dench, *From Barbarians to New Men: Greek, Roman, and Modern Perceptions of Peoples from the Central Apennines*, Oxford: Clarendon Press 1995, is a fascinating study of regional identities and attitudes.

Chapter 1: The Peoples of Italy
The pre-Roman background is surveyed in M. Pallottino, *A History of Earliest Italy*, London: Routledge 1991; see also E.T. Salmon, 'The Iron Age: the Peoples of Italy', *CAH²* IV (1988), 676–719; D. and F.R. Ridgway (eds), *Italy before the Romans*, Edinburgh: Academic Press 1979, deals with archaeological evidence. On the languages of pre-roman Italy, see E. Pulgram, *The Tongues of Italy*, Cambridge, Mass.: Harvard University Press 1958; J.H.W. Penney, 'The Languages of Italy', *CAH²* IV (1988), 720–38. For the Roman conquest of Italy see T.J. Cornell, *The Beginnings of Rome: Italy and Rome from the Bronze Age to the Punic Wars*, London: Routledge 1995.

Chapter 2: Rome Italy and Hellenism
Important studies of the organization and methods of Roman rule include E. Badian, *Foreign Clientelae, 264–70 BC*, Oxford: Clarendon Press 1958; A.J. Toynbee, *Hannibal's Legacy: the Hannibalic War's Effects on Roman Life*, London: Oxford University Press 1965, volume I; E.T. Salmon, *Roman Colonization under the Republic*, London: Thames and Hudson 1969; A.N. Sherwin White, *The Roman Citizenship*, second edition, Oxford: Clarendon Press 1973. On Rome in the third century, C.G. Starr, *The Beginnings of Imperial Rome*, Ann Arbor: Michigan University Press 1980; T.J. Cornell, 'Rome in the Age of the Italian Wars', *CAH²* VII.2 (1989), 391–419; J.-P. Morel, 'The Transformation of Italy, 300–133 BC; the Evidence of Archaeology', *CAH²* VIII (1989), 477–516.

Chapter 3: Hannibal in Italy
The best recent account of the war is J.F. Lazenby, *Hannibal's War: a Military History of the Second Punic War*, Warminster: Aris & Phillips 1978; see also J. Briscoe, 'The Second Punic War', *CAH²* VIII (1989), 44–80; T.J. Cornell, N.B. Rankov, P.A.G. Sabin, *The Second Punic War: a Reappraisal*, London: Institute of Classical Studies 1996. On the effects of the war see above all A.J. Toynbee, *Hannibal's Legacy* (cit.), volume II.

Chapter 4: The Transformation of the Italian Economy
In general see E. Gabba, 'Rome and Italy in the Second Century BC', *CAH²* VIII (1989), 197–243. On the influx of wealth, K. Hopkins, *Conquerors and Slaves*, Cambridge: Cambridge University Press 1978. On the management of public finances, E. Badian, *Publicans and Sinners*, Oxford: Blackwell 1972. On population changes A.J.N. Wilson,

Emigration from Italy in the Republican Age of Rome, Manchester: Manchester University Press 1966; above all P.A. Brunt, *Italian Manpower, 225 BC–AD 14*, Oxford: Clarendon Press 1971 (the standard work on Italian demography, but ranging further than its title suggests). Of the vast literature on Roman agriculture, notice especially K.D. White, *Roman Farming*, London: Thames and Hudson 1970; A.E. Astin, *Cato the Censor*, Oxford: Clarendon Press 1978; D.W. Rathbone, 'The Development of Agriculture in the *Ager Cosanus* during the Roman Republic', *JRS* 71 (1981), 10–23; P.W. de Neeve, *Peasants in Peril: Location and Economy in Italy in the Second Century BC*, Amsterdam: J.C. Gieben 1984. On amphorae and the wine trade: D. Manacorda, 'The Ager Cosanus and the Production of the Amphorae of Sestius', *JRS* 68 (1978), 122–131; J. Paterson, 'Salvation from the Sea: Amphorae and Trade in the Roman West', *JRS* 72 (1982), 146–57; N. Purcell, 'Wine and Wealth in Ancient Italy', *JRS* (1985), 1–19; important papers on this topic can be found in J.H. D'Arms and E. Kopff (eds), *The Seaborne Commerce of Ancient Rome*, Rome: American Academy in Rome 1980; and in P. Garnsey, K. Hopkins and C.R. Whittaker (eds), *Trade in the Ancient Economy*, London: Chatto and Windus 1983. See also W. Jongman, *The Economy and Society of Pompeii*, Amsterdam: J.C. Gieben 1988.

Chapter 5: Italian Municipal Aristocracies
On municipal politics and local elites see P. Castren, *Ordo Populusque Pompeianus*, Rome: Bardi 1975; H. Mouritsen, *Elections, Magistrates and Muncipal Elite: Studies in Pompeian Epigraphy*, Rome: 'L'Erma' di Bretschneider 1988. On the 'Hellenization of taste' see J.H. D'Arms, *Romans on the Bay of Naples: A Social and Cultural Study of the Villas and their Owners from 150 BC to AD 400*, Cambridge, Mass.: Harvard University Press 1970; A. Wallace-Hadrill, *Houses and Society in Pompeii and Herculaneum*, Princeton, N.J.: Princeton University Press 1994; T.J. Gornell and H.K. Lomas (eds), *Urban Society in Roman Italy*, London: UCL Press 1995. On public benefaction and 'euergetism' see P. Veyne, *Bread and Circuses*, London: Allen Lane the Penguin Press 1990 (French original 1976).

Chapter 6: The Mechanisms of Unification
On the Roman aristocracy and its values see M. Gelzer, *The Roman Nobility*, Oxford: Blackwell 1969 (German original 1912); D.C. Earl, *The Moral and Political Tradition of Rome*, London: Thames and Hudson 1967; T.P. Wiseman, *New Men in the Roman Senate, 139 BC–14 AD*, Oxford: 1971; T.P. Wiseman, '*Domi nobiles* and the Roman Cultural Elite', in *Les bourgeoisies municipales italiennes aux IIe et Ier siècles av. J.-C.*, Paris–Naples: CNRS 1983, 299–307. On Patronage, R. Saller, *Personal Patronage under the Early Empire*, Cambridge: Cambridge

University Press 1982; A. Wallace-Hadrill (ed.), *Patronage in Ancient Society*, London: Routledge 1989. On the spread of Latin see J. Kaimio, 'The Ousting of Etruscan by Latin in Etruria', in P. Bruun (ed.), *Studies in the Romanisation of Etruria*, Rome: Bardi 1974, 85–245.

Chapter 7: The Social War

E. Gabba, 'The Origins of the Social War and Roman Politics after 89 BC', in *Republican Rome, the Army and the Allies*, Oxford: Blackwell 1976 (Italian original 1954); E. Badian, 'Roman Politics and the Italians (133–91 BC)', *Dialoghi di Archeologia* 4–5 (1970–71), 373–409; A. Keaveney, *Rome and the Unification of Italy*, London: Croom Helm 1987; P.A. Brunt, 'Italian Aims at the Time of the Social War', in *The Fall of the Roman Republic and Related Essays*, Oxford: Clarendon Press 1988, 93–143; E. Gabba, 'Rome and Italy: the Social War', *CAH²* IX (1994), 104–28.

Chapter 8: The Civil Wars

On the civil wars see R. Syme, *The Roman Revolution*, Oxford: Clarendon Press 1939; P.A. Brunt, *The Fall of the Roman Republic and Related Essays*, Oxford: Clarendon Press 1988, 1–92 ('The Fall of the Roman Republic'); 240–280 ('The Army and the Land in the Roman revolution'). On military aspects see also E. Gabba, 'The Roman Professional Army from Marius to Augustus', in *Republican Rome: the Army and the Allies*, Oxford: Blackwell 1976, 20–69 (Italian original 1951); R.E. Smith, *Service in the Post-Marian Roman Army*, Manchester: Manchester University Press 1958; L. Keppie, *Colonisation and Veteran Settlement in Italy*, 47–14 BC, London: British School at Rome 1983. On the final unification of Italy see M.H. Crawford, 'Italy and Rome from Sulla to Augustus', *CAH²* X (1996), 414–33. On the eleven Augustan Regions, R. Thomsen, *The Italic Regions*, Copenhagen: Glydendal 1940.

T.J. Cornell

SELECTED BIBLIOGRAPHY

Amphores romaines et histoire économique, dix ans de recherche. 1989. Rome.

Ampolo, C., Briquel, D., et al. 1989: *Italia omnium terrarum parens*. (In series *Antica madre*, ed. G. Pugliese Carratelli.) Milan.

Andreau, J. 1987: *La vie finàncière dans le monde romain*. Rome.

Andreau, J. and Bruhns, H. (eds) 1990: *Parenté et stratégies familiales dans l'Antiquité romaine*. Rome.

Arthur, P. 1991: Romans in northern Campania. *Arch. Mon. British School in Rome*, no. 1.

Atzeni, E., Barreca, F., et al. 1981: *Ichnussa: La Sardegna dalle origini all'età classica*. (In series *Antica madre*, ed. G. Pugliese Carratelli.) Milan.

Badian, E. 1958: *Foreign Clientalae*. Oxford.

—— *Publicans and Sinners: Private enterprise in the service of the Roman Republic*. Oxford.

Bancalari Molina, A. 1987: Gli interventi degli Italici nella lotta politica romana durante il tribunato di Livio Druso (91 a. C.) *SCO*, 37, 407.

Bandelli, G. 1988: *Ricerchi sulla colonizzazione romana della Gallia Cisalpina*. Rome.

Les "Bourgeoisies" municipales italiennes aux IIe et Ier siècles avant J.-C. Naples.

Bradley, K. R. 1989: *Slavery and Rebellion in the Roman World (140 B.C.–70 B.C.)*. London.

Brown, F. E. 1980: *Cosa: The making of a Roman town*. Ann Arbor.

Brunt, P. A. 1971: *Italian Manpower, 225 B.C.–A.D.14*. Oxford.

—— 1975: Two great Roman landowners. *Latomus*, no. 39, 619ff.

—— 1988: *The Fall of the Roman Republic*. Oxford.

Bruun, P. 1975: *Studies in the Romanization of Etruria*. Rome.

Camodeca, G. 1979: La gens Annia puteolana in età giulio-claudia. *Puteoli*, no. 2, 17ff.

Campanile, E. and Letta, C. 1979: *Studi sulle magistrature indigene e municipali in area italica*. Pisa.

Carandini, A. (ed.) 1985: *La romanizzazione dell'Etruria: il territorio di Vulci*. Milan.

Carandini, A. and Ricci, A. 1988: *Settefinestri: una villa schiavistica nell'Etruria romana*. Modena.

Carcopino, J. 1914: *La Loi de Hiéron et les Romains*. Paris.

Castrén, P. 1975: *Ordo populusque pomepianus: Policy and society in Roman Pompeii*. Rome.

Cébeillac-Gervasoni, M. 1978: Problématique de la promotion politique des magistrats de Latium. *Ktéma*, no. 3, 227ff.

—— 1989: Le mariage dans l'aristocratie dirigeante des cités du Latium et de la Campanie à la fin de la République et sous Auguste. *Mélanges P. Lévêque* (Besançon), 3, 67ff.

—— 1990: L'évergétisme des magistrats du Latium et de la Campanie des Grecques à Auguste à travers les témoignages épigraphiques. *MEFRA*, no. 102, 699ff.

—— 1991: Les travaux publics à la fin de la République, dans le Latium et la Campanie du Nord: la place de la classe dirigeante et des familles de notables. *Cahiers du centre Glotz* (Paris), II, 189ff.

Cébeillac-Gervasoni, M. (ed.) (forthcoming): *Les Elites municipales de l'Italie péninsulaires des Grecques à Néron*. Naples.

Chevallier, R. 1983: *La Romanisation de la Celtique du Pô*. Rome.

Chieco Bianchi, A. M., Colonna, G., et al. 1988: *Italia omnium terrarum alumna*. (In series *Antica madre*, ed. G. Pugliese Carratelli.) Milan.

Chouquer, G., Clavel-Lévêque, M., Favory, F. and Vallat, J.-P. 1987: *Structures agraires en Italie centro-méridionale, cadastres et paysages ruraux*. Rome.

La città nell'Italia settentrionale in età romana. 1990. Trieste and Rome.

Clarke, J. R. 1991: *The Houses of Roman Italy, 100 B.C.–A.D. 250: Ritual, space and decoration*. Berkeley, CA.

Clemente, G. 1980–1: Considerazioni sulla Sicilia nell'impero romano (III. sec. a.C.-V sec. d.C.). Κῶκαλοζ XXXVI–XXXVII, 192ff.

Coarelli, F. 1977: Public building in Rome between the second Punic War and Sulla. *PBSR*, XLV, 1ff.

—— 1987: *I santuari del Lazio in età repubblicana*. Rome.

—— 1988: La colonizzazione romana tra la guerra latina e la guerra annibalica. *DA*, VI.

Compatengelo, R. 1989: *Un Cadastre de pierre: le Salento romain*. Paris.

Costabile, F. 1976: *Municipium Locrensium: Istituzioni ed organiz-*

zazione sociale di Locri romana. Naples.

—— 1984: *Istituzioni e forme costituzionali nelle città del Bruzio in età romana*. Naples.

Crawford, M. H. 1977: Rome and the Greek world: economic relationships. *Economic History Review*, 30, 42ff.

—— 1985: *Coinage and Money under the Roman Republic: Italy and the Mediterranean economy*. London.

Crawford, M. H. (ed) 1996: *Roman Statutes*. London.

La Cultura italica: Atti del Convegno della Società di Glottologia, Pisa, 1977. Pisa.

D'Arms, J. H. 1970: *Romans on the Bay of Naples*. Cambridge, MA.

D'Arms, J. H. and Kopff, E. C. (eds) 1980: The seaborne commerce of Ancient Rome. *MAAR*, 36.

David, J.-M. 1979: Promotion civique et droit à la parole: L. Licinius Crassus, les accusateurs et les rhéteurs latins. *MEFRA*, no. 91, 135ff.

—— 1992: *Le Patronat judiciaire au dernier siècle de la République romaine*. Rome.

De Martino, F. 1964–7: *Storia della costituzione romana*. Naples.

De Neeve, P. W. 1984: *Colonus: Private farm tenancy in Roman Italy during the Republic and the early Principate*. Amsterdam.

—— *Peasants in Peril: Location and economy in Italy in the second century B.C.* Amsterdam.

Deniaux, E. 1981: Civitate donati: Naples Héraclée, Côme. *Ktéma*, no. 6, 133ff.

—— 1991: Les recommendations de Cicéron et la colonisation césarienne: les terres de Volterra. *Cahiers du centre Glotz* (Paris), II, 215ff.

Devoto, G. 1951: *Gli antichi Italici*. Florence.

—— 1956: La romanisation de l'Italie médiane. *Cahiers d'Histoire mondiale*, 3, 443ff.

Dumont, J. C. 1987: *Servus: Rome et l'esclavage sous la République*. Rome.

Eck, W. 1979: *Die staatliche Organisation Italiens in der hohen Kaiserzeit*. Munich.

Fabre, G. 1981: *Libertus: Recherches sur les rapports patron-affranchi à la fin de la République romaine*. Rome.

Felletti Maj. B. M. 1977: *La Tradizione italica nell'arte romana*. Rome.

Frank, T. (ed.) 1933: *An Economic Survey of Ancient Rome*. Volume I. *Rome and Italy of the Republic*. Baltimore, MD.

Frederiksen, M. 1980–1: Puteoli e il commercio del grano in epoca romana. *Puteoli*, no. 4–5, 5ff.

—— 1984: *Campania*. Rome.

Frézouls, E. (ed.) 1992: *La Mobilité sociale dans le monde romain*. Strasbourg.

Gabba, E. 1972: Urbanizzazione e rinnovamenti urbanistici nell'Italia centro-meridionale del I. sec. a.C. *SCO*, no. 21, 73ff.

—— 1973: *Esercito e società nella tarda repubblica romana*. Florence.

—— 1977: Considerazioni sulla decadenza della piccola proprietà contadina nell'Italia centro-meridionale del II sec. a.C. *Ktéma*, no. 2, 269ff.

—— 1985: Per un'interpretazione storica della centuriazione romana. *Athenaeum*, no. 63, 265ff.

—— 1986: Le città italiche del I sec. a.C. e la politica. *RSI*, no. 98, 653ff.

Gabba, E. 1976: *Republican Rome: the Army and the Allies*. Oxford.

Gabba, E. and Pasquinacci, M. 1979: *Strutture agrarie e allevamento transumante nell'Italia romana (III–I sec. a.C.)*. Pisa.

Gabbe, E. and Vallet, G. 1980: *La Sicilia antica*. II.2. *La Sicilia romana*. Naples.

Galsterer, H. 1976: *Herrschaft und Verwaltung im republikanischen Italien, die Beziehungen Roms zu den italischen Gemeinden vom Latinerfrieden 338v. Chr. bis zum Bundesgenossenkrieg 91 v. Chr.* Munich.

—— 1987: La loi municipale des Romains: chimère où réalité. *RD*, no. 65, 181ff.

Gelzer, M. 1912: *Die Nobilität der römishcen Republik*. Leipzig and Berlin.

Giardina, A. and Schiavone, A. 1981: *Società romana e produzione schiavistica*. Rome and Bari.

Grimal, P. 1975: *Le Siècle des Scipions: Rome et l'hellénisme au temps des guerres puniques*. 2nd edn. Paris. (First published in 1953).

Gros, P. 1978: *Architecture et société à Rome et en Italie centro-méridionale aux deux derniers siècles de la République*. Brussels.

Gros, P. and Torelli, M. 1989: *Storia dell'urbanistica: il mondo romano*. Rome and Bari.

Harmand, L. 1957: *Le Patronat sur les collectivités publiques des origines au Bas-Empire*. Paris.

Harris, W. V. 1971: *Rome in Etruria and Umbria*. Oxford.

—— 1972: Was Roman law imposed on the Italian allies? *Historia*, 21, 639ff.

Hatzfeld, J. 1912: Les Italiens résidents à Délos mentionnés dans les inscriptions de l'île. *BCH*, no. 36, 5ff.

—— 1919: *Les Trafiquants italiens dans l'Orient hellénique*. Paris.

Heurgeon, J. 1942: *Recherches sur l'histoire, la religion et la civilisation de Capoure préromaine des origines à la deuxième guerre puniques*. Paris.

Hinard, F. 1985: *Les Proscriptions de la Rome républicaine*. Rome.

Hölkeskamp, K. J. 1987: *Die Entstehung der Nobilität: Studien zur sozialen und politischen Geschichte der römishcen Republik im 4. Jhdt. v. Chr.* Stuttgart.

Hölscher, T. 1978: Die Anfänge römischer Repräsentationskunst. *MDAI(R)*, no. 85, 315ff.

—— 1990: Römische Nobiles und Hellenistiche Herrscher. *Akten des XIII. internationalen Kongresses für klassische Archeologie, Berlin, 1988*, 73ff. Mainz.

Hopkins, K. 1978: *Conquerors and Slaves*. Cambridge.

—— 1980: Taxes and trade in the Roman Empire. *JRS*, no. 70, 101ff.

Humbert, M. 1978: *Municipium et Civitas sine suffragio: l'organisation de la conquête jusqu'à la guerre sociale*. Rome.

Hus, A. 1980: *Les Etrusques et leur destin*. Paris.

Ilari, V. 1974: *Gli Italici nelle strutture militari romane*. Naples.

Jouffroy, H. 1988: *La Construction publique en Italie et dans l'Afrique romaine*. Strasbourg.

Keaveney, A. 1982: Sulla and Italy. *Critica Storica*, no. 19, 499ff.

—— *Rome and the Unification of Italy*. Totowa, NJ.

Keppie, L. 1983: *Colonisation and Veteran Settlement in Italy, 47–14B.C.*. Rome.

Laffi, U. 1973: Sull'organizzazione amministrativa dell'Italia dopo la guerra sociale. In Akten des VI. internationalen Kongresses für Griechische und Lateinische Epigraphie. *Vestigia* (Munich), no. 17, 37ff.

Lambrechts, R. 1959: *Essai sur les magistratures des républiques étrusques*. Brussels and Rome.

Landucci Gattinoni, F. 1989: Il tempio repubblicano de Brescia e l'integrazione dei Cenomani nel mondo romano. *Aevum*, no. 63, 30ff.

Lejeune, M. 1976: *L'Anthroponymie osque*. Paris.

—— 1979: *Ateste à l'heure de la romanisation*. Florence.

—— 1990: *Mefitis d'après des dédicaces lucaniennes de Rossano di Vaglio*. Louvain-la-Neuve.

Letta, C. 1972: *I Marsi e il Fucino nell'Antichità*. Milan.

Liverani, P. 1984: L'Ager Veientanus in età repubblicana. *PBSR*, LII, 36ff.

Luraschi, G. 1979: *Foedus, Ius Latii, Civitas: Aspetti costituzionali della romanizzazione in Transpadana*. Padua.

La Magna Grecia nell'età romana: Atti del XV Convegno di Studi sulla Magna Grecia. 1975. Taranto.

Marangio, C. (ed.) 1988: *La Puglia in età repubblicana*. Mesagne.

Meiggs, R. 1973: *Roman Ostia*. 2nd end. Oxford.

Meloni, P. 1975: *La Sardegna romana*. Sassari.

Mertens, J. and Lambrechts, R (eds) 1991: *Comunità indigene e problemi della romanizzazione nell'Italia centro-meridionale (IVo–IIIo sec. av. C.)*. Brussles.

Momigliano, A. and Schiavone, A. (eds) 1988: *Storia di Roma*. Turin.

Mouritsen, H. 1988: *Elections, Magistrates and Municipal Elite: Studies in Pompeian epigraphy*. Rome.

Nicolet, C. 1967: Arpinum, Aemilius Scaurus et les Tullii Cicerones. *REL*, no. 45, 276ff.

—— 1976: *Le Métier de citoyen dans la Rome républicaine*. Paris.

—— 1977: *Rome et la conquête du monde méditerranéen*. 1. *Les Structures de l'Italie romaine*. Paris.

—— 1978: Le *stipendium* des alliés italiens avant la guerre sociale. *PBSR*, XLVI, 1ff.

—— *The World of the Citizen in Republican Rome*. London.

—— 1988: *L'Inventaire du monde*. Paris.

—— 1991: L'origine des *regiones Italiae* augustéennes. *Cahiers du centre Glotz* (Paris), II, 73ff.

Pailler, J. M. 1988: *Bacchanalia: La répression de 186 av. J.-C. à Rome et en Italie: vestiges, images, tradition*. Rome.

Pallottino, M. 1981: *Genti e culture dell'Italia preromana*. Rome.

—— 1985: *Storia della prima Italia*. 3rd edn. Milan.

Pallottino, M. et al. (eds) 1974–8: *Popoli e civiltà dell'Italia antica*. II–VII. Rome.

Pallottino. M., Torelli, M., et al. 1988: *Rasenna: Storia e civiltà degli Etruschi*. (In series *Antica madre*, ed. G. Pugliese-Carratelli.) Milan.

Peruzzi, E. 1990: *I. Romani di Pesaro e i Sabini di Roma*. Florence.

Peyre, C. 1979: *La Cisalpine gauloise du IIIe au Ier siècle av. J.-C*. Paris.

Pugliese-Carratelli, G. (ed.) 1987: *Magna Grecia: Lo sviluppo politico, sociale e economico*. Milan.

—— 1988: *Magna Grecia: Vita religiosa e cultura letteraria, filosofia e scientfica*. Milan.

Pulice, D. 1977: Sviluppo costituzionale della colonia Puteoli in età repubblicana. *Puteoli*, no. 1, 27ff.

Rathbone, D. W. 1981: The development of agriculture in the Ager Cosanus: problems of evidence and interpretations. *JRS*, no. 71, 10ff.

—— 1983: The slave mode of production in Italy. *JRS*, no. 73, 160ff.

Rawson, E. 1985: *Intellectual Life in the Late Roman Republic*. London.

Rome e l'Italia fra i Gracchi e Silla. 1970–1: *DA*, IV–V.

Roma medio repubblicana: Aspetti culturali di Roma e del Lazio nei secoli IVo–IIIo a.C. 1973. Rome.

La Romanisation du Samnium aux IIe et Ier siècles av. J.-C. 1991. Naples.

Salmon, E. T. 1958: Notes on the Social War. *TAPhA*, no. 89, 159ff.

—— 1962: The causes of the Social War. *Phoenix*, no. 16, 107ff.

—— 1967: *Samnium and the Samnites*. Cambridge.

—— 1969: *Roman Colonisation under the Republic*. London.

—— 1982: *The Making of Roman Italy*. London.

Sannio, Pentri e Frentani dal VI al I secolo a.C. 1981. Naples.

Sartori, F. 1953: *Problemi di storia costituzionala italiota*. Rome.

Scuderi, R. 1989: Significatio politico delle magistrature nelle città italiche del I sec. a.C. *Athenaeum*, no. 67, 117ff.

Sereni, E. 1955: *Comunità rurali nell'Italia antica*. Rome.

Seston, W. 1978: La Lex Iulia de 90 av. J.-C. et l'intégration des Italiens dans la citoyenneté romaine. *CRAI*, 529ff.

Shatzmann, I. 1975: *Senatorial Wealth and Roman Politics*. Brussels.

Sherwin-White, A. N. 1973: *The Roman Citizenship*. Oxford.

Sordi, M. (ed.) 1979: *Conoscenze etniche e rapporti di convivenza nell'antichità*. Milan.

Starr, C. G. 1980: *The Beginnings of Imperial Rome*. Michigan.

Studi sulla città antica: Atti del convegno sulla città etrusca e italica preromana. 1970. Bologna.

Syme, r. 1938: Caesar, the Senate and Italy. *PBSR*, XIV, 1ff.

—— 1960: *The Roman Revolution*. Oxford.

—— 1967: *La Révolution romaine*. Paris.

Taylor, L. Ross. 1951: Caesar's agrarian legislation and his municipal policy. In P. R. Coleman Norton (ed.), *Studies in Roman Economy and Social History in Honor of A. C. Johnson*, pp. 68ff. Princeton.

—— 1960: *The Voting Districts of the Roman Republic*. Rome.

—— 1977: *La Politique et les partis à Rome au temps de César*. Paris.

Tchernia, A. 1986: *Le Vin de l'Italie romaine*. Rome.

Torelli, M. 1981: *Storia degli Etruschi*. Rome and Bari.

—— 1988: Paestum romana. In *Poseidonia-Paestum: Atti del XXVIIo Convegno di Studi sulla Magna Grecia*, pp. 33ff. Taranto.

Toynbee, A. J., 1965: *Hannibal's Legacy*. London.

Treggiari, S. 1969: *Roman Freedmen during the Late Republic*. Oxford.

Ungern-Sternberg, J. von. 1975: *Capue im zweiten punischen Krieg*. Munich.

Vitali, D. (ed.) 1987: *Celti ed Etruschi nell'Italia centro-settentrionale dal V secolo a.C. alla romanizzazione*. Imola.

Volpe, G. 1990: *La Daunia nell'età della romanizzazione*. Bari.

Wallace-Hadrill, A. 1988: The social structure of the Roman house. *PBSR*, LXVI, 43ff.

Wilson, A. J. N. 1966: *Emigration from Italy in the Republican Age of Rome*. Manchester.

Wiseman, T. P. 1970: Roman republican road building. *PBSR*. XXXVIII, 122ff.

—— 1971: *New Men in the Roman Senate, 139B.C.–14A.D.* Oxford.

Wuilleumier, P. 1939: *Tarente des origines à la conquête romaine*. Paris.

Zanker, P. 1988: *Pompeji*. Mainz.

Zanker, P. (ed.), 1974: *Hellenismus in Mittelitalien*. Göttingen.

INDEX